CULTURAL MAPPING
AND THE DIGITAL SPHERE

CULTURAL MAPPING AND THE DIGITAL SPHERE

Place and Space

Ruth Panofsky & Kathleen Kellett, Editors

The University of Alberta Press

MAP-LC
AZ
105
.C84
2015

Published by
The University of Alberta Press
Ring House 2
Edmonton, Alberta, Canada T6G 2E1
www.uap.ualberta.ca

Copyright © 2015 The University of Alberta Press

Library and Archives Canada Cataloguing in Publication

Cultural mapping and the digital sphere : place and space / Ruth Panofsky and Kathleen Kellett, editors.

Includes bibliographical references and index.
Issued in print and electronic formats.
Essays chiefly in English; some essays in French.
ISBN 978-1-77212-049-3 (paperback).—ISBN 978-1-77212-056-1 (epub).—
ISBN 978-1-77212-057-8 (kindle).—ISBN 978-1-77212-058-5 (pdf)

1. Humanities—Canada—Data processing. 2. Humanities—Research—Canada—
Data processing. 3. Canadian literature—History and criticism. 4. Canada—Civilization. I. Panofsky, Ruth, author, editor II. Kellett, Kathleen, 1959-, author, editor

AZ105.C84 2015   001.30285   C2015-904252-6

C2015-904253-4

Index available in print and PDF editions.

First edition, first printing, 2015.
Printed and bound in Canada by Houghton Boston Printers, Saskatoon, Saskatchewan.
Copyediting and proofreading by Joanne Muzak and Anna Olivier.
Indexing by Judy Dunlop and François Trahan.

The University of Alberta Press is committed to protecting our natural environment. As part of our efforts, this book is printed on Enviro Paper: it contains 100% post-consumer recycled fibres and is acid- and chlorine-free.

The University of Alberta Press gratefully acknowledges the support received for its publishing program from the Government of Canada, the Canada Council for the Arts, and the Government of Alberta through the Alberta Media Fund.

This book has been published with the help of a grant from the Canadian Federation for the Humanities and Social Sciences, through the Awards to Scholarly Publications Program, using funds provided by the Social Sciences and Humanities Research Council of Canada.

Government of Canada | Gouvernement du Canada   Canada Council for the Arts | Conseil des Arts du Canada   Alberta Government

Contents

VII   *Foreword*
Susan Brown & Mary-Jo Romaniuk

XI   *Preface*
Ruth Panofsky & Kathleen Kellett

PART I   PLACE AND THE DIGITAL FRONTIER

3   1   **MAPPING TAGS AND TAGGING MAPS**
Leveraging Spatial Markup for Literary History
Susan Brown, Isobel Grundy, Mariana Paredes-Olea, Jeffery Antoniuk,
& Breanna Mroczek

25   2   **MODELLING COLLABORATION IN DIGITAL
HUMANITIES SCHOLARSHIP**
Foundational Concepts of an EMiC UA Project Charter
Paul Hjartarson, Harvey Quamen, Andrea Hasenbank,
Vanessa Lent, & EMiC UA

51   3   **AN INTERACTIVE, MATERIALIST-SEMIOTIC ARCHIVE**
*Visualizing the Canadian Theatrical Canon in the
Simulated Environment for Theatre*
Sasha Kovacs and Jennifer Roberts-Smith, Teresa M. Dobson,
Sandra Gabriele, Omar Rodriguez-Arenas, Stan Ruecker,
Stéfan Sinclair, Shawn DeSouza-Coelho

89   4   **"TALK TO THE WORK"**
*Applying ISTC Identifiers to the Digital Edition of the
Canadian Bookman (1909–1941)*
Ravit H. David

107   5   **HOW TO PLAY WITH MAPS**
Bethany Nowviskie

129   **6**   **EDMONTON PIPELINES**
Living and Playing in the Digital City
Heather Zwicker

141   **7**   **REPRESENTING CANADIAN QUEER AUTHORSHIP**
Making the Internet a Women's Place
Michelle Schwartz & Constance Crompton

PART II WRITERS AND READERS: MAPPING TEXTUAL SPACE

159   **8**   **SALOMANIA**
Maud Allan, Postcards, and Early Twentieth-Century "Viral" Circulation
Cecily Devereux

181   **9**   **TORONTO THE GOOD IN THE FICTION AND LIFE OF GRACE IRWIN**
Patricia Demers

197   **10**   **« WHERE ARE YOU FROM? »**
La ville et l'écriture migrante dans l'autofiction de
Marguerite Andersen
Kathleen Kellett

215   **11**   **LANGUAGES AS SPACES, TRANSLATION AS PLAY**
Moving (through) Languages
Lori Saint-Martin

231   **12**   **L'ESPACE ENSORCELÉ**
Les enfants du sabbat d'Anne Hébert
Stéphanie Walsh Matthews

249   **13**   **LIEU HUMAIN / LIEU PERSONNE CHEZ DEUX ÉCRIVAINES
CANADO-VIETNAMIENNES, THUONG VUONG-RIDDICK ET KIM THÚY**
Mireille Mai Truong

263   **14**   **STANDING ON A RAINBOW**
Reading in Place, Position, and Time
Margaret Mackey

279   Contributors / Collaborateurs

289   Index

Foreword

The Canadian Writing Research Collaboratory
Le Collaboratoire scientifique des écrits du Canada

Literary knowledge and scholarship in Canada is on the move. New paths
of inquiry, new connections, and new insights, as this collection richly
illustrates, are emerging as literary research embarks on major new discoveries enabled by new methods of inquiry.

Cultural Mapping and the Digital Sphere: Place and Space emerged
from the second conference of the Canadian Writing Research
Collaboratory, hosted by the Department of English at Ryerson University
in October 2011. The Collaboratory (or cwRC, pronounced "quirk") is a
path-breaking experiment in devising new ways of undertaking scholarship in a digital environment.

In our research, virtually all of us write digitally: we use email,
Internet resources, and word processing software as key tools in our
scholarly work. But email connects us fleetingly, Internet resources often
resemble individual silos, and our research remains in word processing
files on our hard drives until it emerges, in print or digital form, to be
read or studied—but not used interactively or reused in a digital environment. cwRC aims to create a new forum for literary research in and about

Canada. The forum will make it easier for scholars to work together and share the raw materials of their research (such as bibliographies, annotations, timelines, or digitized primary texts) with each other and the wider scholarly community. It also will offer an innovative, non-traditional online venue for publishing and connecting research results. CWRC particularly aims to support the work of junior scholars by mentoring, providing mechanisms for tracking and reporting collaborative contributions, and offering a welcoming space where users may explore the potential of digital research tools.

The Collaboratory is an infrastructure project, not a research project. Funded by the Canada Foundation for Innovation, CWRC intends to create a research environment that will demonstrate the potential of online tools to support literary inquiry and foster practices that contribute to the interoperability and longevity of digital knowledge. It will combine a repository of primary and secondary materials with an array of tools, some for creating or placing materials in the repository and others for gathering, analyzing, visualizing, and mapping materials from within and beyond the repository collections.

At the heart of the Canadian Writing Research Collaboratory, as its name suggests, are participation, partnership, and collaboration—all forms of connection that have been important in scholarship, especially scholarship that has focused historically on women's writing, but that take new prominence and embody new possibilities in the digital era. The scholars whose work is represented in this volume represent a fraction of those affiliated with CWRC. This participation—by scholars who wish to carry forward individual projects into a collaborative environment, by colleagues who focus on technical aspects of the Collaboratory, by extensive team projects such as the Canadian Women's Writing Project or Editing Modernism in Canada—is essential to building CWRC into an environment that will meet scholars' wide-ranging needs.

The diverse investigations that characterize the various projects reported in this volume are representative of ways that digital scholarship can allow us to collaborate outside of a centralized model of large-scale research. So long as we provide the basis for making computer-friendly connections among digital scholarly materials, the wealth of materials produced—bio-critical profiles of writers, bibliographies, readerly or critical responses, analysis patterns in publishing or poetics—will be used within the CWRC environment to facilitate the emergence of as yet unforeseen connections, including to place and space. In this respect, the Collaboratory emerges from the Orlando Project housed at the University of Alberta—upon whose systems CWRC builds—and its vision of the potential for computers to serve feminist literary studies. Canada needs better online representation of the strength of its women's writing and fuller and more inclusive scholarly accounts: this volume highlights the potential for both to enrich our understanding of Canada's cultural wealth.

The digital turn is so thoroughly transforming research as to remake our institutions. Research libraries have a long-established tradition of collecting and preserving scholarly works, albeit in the analog formats in which they were created. As research and scholarship evolve, so must the roles and practices of libraries in this new digital era. The University of Alberta Libraries are national leaders in rethinking the relationship of the library to digital research.

The Education and Research Archive (ERA), which has its genesis and home in the University of Alberta Libraries, is more than a repository for research and scholarly output. ERA embodies a technological and philosophical framework that not only supports collaboration but invites experimentation and fosters a robust relationship with researchers and new ways of undertaking research. The capacity and future potential of ERA has propelled the University of Alberta Libraries to be a more frequent and more active partner in research ventures. The Libraries are partnering with CWRC not only to enhance the repository but also to ensure that CWRC materials are produced and curated in such a way that they are accessible, available for future research, and amenable to preservation.

The mode of publication of this book itself, the result of a four-way collaboration among the University of Alberta Libraries, the University of Alberta Press, CWRC, and SSHRC, signals in important ways the changing roles and relationships of university libraries and academic presses in relation to the dissemination of scholarship. This scholarly work takes advantage of traditional analog publication while simultaneously existing in an enhanced digital environment that contemplates, without presuming the specifics, the future research potential and needs of the scholarly community. This is not simply a monograph with a digital surrogate, but rather something that lives with untapped future potential in its evolving digital representation. Collectively, we are excited by this exemplar of print publishing combined with the power of a repository enabling digital dissemination, access, and preservation, not only as a vehicle for scholarly output but as an impetus for future research and continuing scholarship.

Susan Brown & Mary-Jo Romaniuk

Preface

As lead developers Susan Brown and Mary-Jo Romaniuk outline in their Foreword to this volume, the Canadian Writing Research Collaboratory (CWRC) is an innovative undertaking—a catalyst for progressive research on Canadian literature and culture; a virtual hub for wide-ranging digital activities, most scholarly, others creative, all exploratory; and a repository for projects that either rely on or incorporate digital components. The inventive spirit evoked and fostered by CWRC is evident across this collection of essays, which emerged from the Collaboratory's second annual conference held at Ryerson University in late October 2011. Ryerson University's urban setting in the heart of downtown Toronto gave rise to the conference's triadic theme of "Space / Place / Play." Given the suggestive topic, it is not surprising that the original call for papers generated vigorous response from scholars and practitioners across North America.

The arrangement of this volume highlights the exciting research possibilities in the eclectic and versatile field of digital humanities. Part I of the collection, "Place and the Digital Frontier," opens with essays that limn the discourse of digital projects and digital collaboration, including that endorsed by CWRC. It continues with essays charting the terrain of projects that apply digital practice and methodologies to archival artifacts and the act of storytelling. Part II, "Writers and Readers: Mapping Textual Space," includes essays that emphasize a dynamic engagement with literary texts at the level of writerly and readerly play. Notwithstanding their differing approaches—digital, archival, historical, iterative, critical, creative, reflective—the essays gathered here articulate new ways of seeing, investigating, and apprehending literature and culture.

The essays in Part I showcase evolving digital projects that are intended to push the boundaries of the developing field of digital humanities. The first two essays set out some of the current and potential uses of digital technologies and consider appropriate guidelines for collaborative work in the field. Under the aegis of CWRC, "Mapping Tags and Tagging Maps" sets out the challenges faced by Susan Brown and her colleagues who aim to identify and map the wide range of activities undertaken historically by literary women in Canada. Since the parameters of such a vast project are still unfolding, the attempt to match semantic tags to anticipated mapping requirements is especially challenging. In "Modelling Collaboration," Paul Hjartarson and colleagues initiate a project charter of "trust cluster" principles to guide collaborative editorial work on three projects undertaken under the aegis of Editing Modernism in Canada, a partner project of CWRC funded by a SSHRC Strategic Knowledge Cluster grant. That charter—which elaborates principles of collaboration, credit, documentation, and communication—is shaped as much by the distinctive digital nature of each editorial project as the desire to assign scholarly credit equitably for individual and collaborative contributions.

Emphasizing the hands-on nature of digital humanities research, the next group of essays presents innovative applications of digital technology in literary and archival research. Sasha Kovacs and her colleagues demonstrate the use of their "interactive, materialist-semiotic archive," the Simulated Environment for Theatre, in a comparative analysis of stage performances of Judith Thompson's classic Canadian play *White*

Biting Dog, first at the Tarragon Theatre in 1984 and, more recently, as a Soulpepper production at the Young Centre for the Performing Arts in 2011. This promising archival tool may be used not only to store records of past performances but also to simulate hypothetical ones. Focusing on the *Canadian Bookman*, a periodical that spanned 1900 to 1941, Ravit H. David seeks to digitize a complete run of the periodical and analyze the advertisements, which appeared alongside literary material, as optical codes to reading. In this endeavour, she reveals the usefulness of International Standard Text Code (ISTC), which allows scholars to catalogue literary content, while taking into account the various forms—both existing and future editions—it may take in the digital age.

Other projects focus specifically on storytelling and the creation of narrative in the digital age. In "How to Play with Maps," Bethany Nowviskie highlights undertakings in digital research intended to facilitate storytelling at the Scholars' Lab at the University of Virginia Library, in particular the Neatline project. She demonstrates the ludic possibilities of mapmaking in her study of an illustrated map, created in 1823 by a fourteen-year-old student at the Troy Female Seminary and marked by a distinctively personal interpretation of national geography. As part of the Canadian Institute for Research Computing in Arts' Digital Urbanism Collaboratory, Heather Zwicker and other researchers have created a series of projects known as Edmonton Pipelines to uncover the hidden stories of the "undernarrated" city of Edmonton. In particular, Zwicker shows the usefulness of digital technology to go beyond the linearity of text to recreate and preserve the history of Rossdale Flats from a pre–Treaty 6 Aboriginal settlement to its present-day role as part of Edmonton's Ribbon of Green, created through the expropriation of homes. Finally, Michelle Schwartz and Constance Crompton also are concerned with preserving stories from an undernarrated past—in this case, the history of the lesbian and gay liberation movement in Canada and, in particular, the dearth of materials recognizing women's activism. Beyond a simple digitization of archival materials, Schwartz and Crompton intend to show the benefits of the Text Encoding Initiative to establish personographic records, offering a more nuanced alternative to the "Internet behemoths" Google and *Wikipedia* that currently filter our access to culture in the online universe.

Part II of this collection includes essays that explore the interpretative power of spatio-temporal analysis in the context of writerly and readerly play. Cecily Devereux presents Maud Allan, a Toronto-born dancer whose Salome dance, performed throughout Europe and North America at the turn of the twentieth century, is an early instance of performance "going viral," the dance being described by the media as a veritable form of contagion. This influential representation of mobile "white femininity" owed much of its impact to the newly developed communication technology of the postcard, whose images have been conserved in archives and disseminated through digital media. Celebrating both literal and literary cartographies, essays by Patricia Demers and Kathleen Kellett examine the subjective construction of space in literary representations of the city. Demers guides the contemporary reader through the cartographic imagination of Grace Irwin, whose novels and autobiography capture Toronto the Good as it was before its more bucolic spaces were transformed into city streets. As a textual creation, the city appears as palimpsest; the excitement of seeing the "new" Eaton's store on College Street feels as distant and foreign now as the anguished struggles over faith experienced by the minister who is Irwin's main protagonist. Kellett's analysis of *autofiction* by Marguerite Andersen shows how this author represents Toronto not only as a major centre of Franco-Ontarian culture but also as an urban space implicated in her own family romance, as she draws parallels between the literary institutions of francophone Toronto and those of Berlin, where her father also wrote and fought for authors' rights.

The remaining essays offer serious study of the ludic possibilities of literary space through perspective shifting, translation, and code switching. These essays focus on the creative possibilities of "languages in play." As a scholar, creative writer, and literary translator, Lori Saint-Martin reveals an intimate perspective on her relationship with language(s), beginning with her own personal trajectory from the predominantly unilingual Kitchener, Ontario, to Montreal, an eminently bilingual city. Her essay probes the art of translation—from the technology of simultaneous translation to the intricacies of literary translation and, in particular, self-translation and the ludic opportunities for transgression. Stéphanie Walsh Matthews initiates the reader into the "enchanted space" of Quebec seen through the lens of magic realism in Anne Hébert's 1975 novel *Les enfants du sabbat*. Writing in the wake of the tumultuous Quiet Revolution of the 1960s, with ambiguously dark humour, Hébert takes her place alongside Gabriel García Márquez in celebrating the potentially subversive spirit of the human imagination. Mireille Mai Truong also explores the intertwining of personal journeys and language in her study of two Vietnamese-Canadian writers, Thuong Vuong-Riddick and Kim Thúy. She examines the textual relationship among the cultural nuances of the Vietnamese language and the postcolonial languages of the English memoirs of Vuong-Riddick and the French *autofiction* of Thúy.

In the final essay of the collection, bridging the space between traditional and digital humanities, Margaret Mackey makes the case for literary mapping that captures and contextualizes the role of the reader. Working from her own "tiny case study" of what she remembers of her mother's and her own response to her mother's favourite book, *Stand on a Rainbow* by Toronto author Mary Quayle Innis, she speculates on the possibilities proffered by digital technology to compile meaningful data not only on sales and borrowing figures but also on the responses of multiple readers at different points in time.

The coupling of nuanced critical thought and careful application of theoretical and digital practice that characterizes this volume testifies to the scholarly enterprise of CWRC and the original efforts of the scholars affiliated with the Collaboratory. But this collection of essays, which pulses with the same energy that drove the landmark conference that gave it first life, is also celebratory. Its emphasis on place and space is suggestive of the principle of joyful investigation that shapes the projects described herein, and the deep scholarly satisfaction that comes from successfully applying innovative practice to materials and subject matter that one appreciates deeply—and seeks to bring to a wider community of scholars, critics, and readers.

We acknowledge the generous support of SSHRC in the form of an Aid to Research Workshops and Conferences in Canada grant, additional funding support from Ryerson University, and the research assistance of Emma Renda.

Ruth Panofsky & Kathleen Kellett

PART I

PLACE AND THE DIGITAL FRONTIER

MAPPING TAGS AND TAGGING MAPS

Leveraging Spatial Markup for Literary History

Susan Brown, Isobel Grundy, Mariana Paredes-Olea,
Jeffery Antoniuk, & Breanna Mroczek

Introduction

The "spatial turn" is making itself felt throughout literary studies, as it is
in other areas of the humanities and social sciences. As Barney Warf and
Santa Arias argue,

> Recent works in the fields of literary and cultural studies, sociology, political
> science, anthropology, history, and art history have become increasingly spatial
> in their orientation. From various perspectives, they assert that space is a social
> construction relevant to the understanding of the different histories of human
> subjects and to the production of cultural phenomena....In other ways, how-
> ever, the spatial turn is much more substantive, involving a reworking of the
> very notion and significance of spatiality to offer a perspective in which space is
> every bit as important as time in the unfolding of human affairs, a view in which
> geography is not relegated to an afterthought of social relations, but is intimately
> involved in their construction. Geography matters, not for the simplistic and

overly used reason that everything happens in space, but because where things happen is critical to knowing how and why they happen. (1)

There are always complex reasons for an intensifying interest in space as a topic or analytical category, but there is no question that the current interest is fuelled by the greater accessibility of spatial technologies such as plotting tools and geographic information systems (GIS), made possible by the World Wide Web, that put a dazzling array of maps at our fingertips. These maps allow us to explore digital representations of space by interactively zooming in and out, experimenting with various layers of information, and gathering granular analysis of a vast range of materials. The application of computational spatial analysis in literary studies is relatively new, but the results are already evident in a number of impressive projects. These projects include an overview of the development of printing technologies (Prickman); an analysis of the impact of railway development (Thomas, Healey, and Cottingham); and a study of the circulation of letters in early modern Europe (Coleman, Edelstein, and Findlen).

Given that the Canadian Writing Research Collaboratory (CWRC) is dedicated to creating an online environment for research on writing and seeks to offer traditional scholars a wider array of computational tools than those they typically incorporate into their research, it is hardly surprising that the literary researchers involved in CWRC's development have consistently identified the mapping of literary data as a highly desirable feature of a shared digital tool set. The precise nature of the mapping required for most CWRC projects has yet to be established, but there is definite interest in how the spatial and temporal aspects of literary research intersect. Historical maps are also desirable for their representation of literary materials or activities from the past, as are maps that might represent slices of time or change over time. As Peter K. Bol argues, "if we fail to see that change over time unfolds differently across space, we substitute a single history for the reality of multiple histories" (297). While the study of writing has attended to the impact of place in myriad ways, newly accessible visual representations are fast becoming an effective means of tracking changing spatial and temporal relationships.

All of the research projects affiliated with CWRC have a spatial component. Some are concerned with regional writing. A number of theatre projects seek to spatially track productions and networks of professionals. The Editing Modernism in Canada project at the University of Alberta has developed a smart phone app called "WatsonWalk" based on walks taken by Sheila Watson while she and her husband Wilfred Watson lived in Paris from 1955 to 1956, as documented in her journals. Kristine Moruzi's project "From Colonial to Modern: Transnational Girlhood in Australian, New Zealand, and Canadian Print Cultures (1840–1940)" aims to map the relationship between places of production, places of publication, and places of dissemination. The most ambitious of CWRC's pilot projects is "Magazines, Travel, and Middlebrow Culture in Canada 1925–1960," led by Faye Hammill of the University of Strathclyde. This project investigates geographical mobility as a form of upward mobility, and is designed to distinguish leisure travel from the enforced movement of migration and diaspora. The project uses middlebrow magazines to map shifts in travel patterns. If one takes seriously the claim that space "is not simply a passive reflection of social and cultural trends, but an active participant, i.e., geography is constitutive as well as representative" (Warf and Arias 10), then to make available a dynamic mapping environment that visualizes spatial relations is to give scholars a potentially transformative tool for investigating those constitutive relations. Yet, given the wide range of CWRC projects, the task of devising even a basic generalized system of mapping is a considerable challenge, as the project's core development team learned in its initial experiments with spatial data contained in its largest seed project, the Orlando Project, housed at the University of Alberta.

Orlando is the founding project behind CWRC. Initiated in the mid-1990s by a small team of literary researchers, Susan Brown, Patricia Clements, and Isobel Grundy, just as graphical browser environments were exponentially expanding the usage of the World Wide Web, this research project sought to produce, from scratch, a history of women's writing in the British Isles using computers (Brown and Clements et al.). Rather than digitizing existing texts—the focus of many digital literary projects then and now—Orlando sought to produce born-digital scholarship in a form intended from the outset to take advantage of the digital medium. That meant trying to imagine how the scholarly text that one is researching and creating might take advantage of the yet emerging possibilities of a web publication environment. Hence, on the advice of our digital humanities co-investigator Susan Hockey, the project adopted Standard Generalized Markup Language (the precursor to Extensible Markup Language or XML) as a means of encoding the text in a form that would make it amenable to reuse in applications that could not be developed during the initial stages of the Orlando Project.

Members of Orlando were keen to map its contents. From the start, they assiduously tagged locations throughout the text base using nested tags, based on those developed by the Text Encoding Initiative (TEI), to label places mentioned in many different contexts so that it would be possible to search and eventually map the materials that were being written. Thus, spatial information in Orlando was tagged with labels that specify that the text enveloped in the tag is a reference to a place, with sub-tags or nested tags demarcating the subcomponents of the spatial information. For example, the markup for the city of London is

```
<PLACE><SETTLEMENT>London</SETTLEMENT><REGION REG=Middlesex>
</REGION><GEOG REG=England></GEOG></PLACE>
```

Such tagging distinguishes this particular reference to London from the more than two dozen other settlements around the world (including London, Ontario) that take their name from the English city, from building names such as London House, and from proper names such as Jack London.

The Orlando text base comprises several types of materials in which such spatial information occurs: bibliographical entries that identify locations of publishing activities; events that usually (though not always) specify the places where those events occurred; and detailed bio-critical entries on particular writers that contain information about locations related to their subjects' lives and writing careers, as well as the places involved in the poems, plays, novels, travel writings, or other texts they produced. Orlando's bio-critical entries on writers thus contain rich spatial information, as do the bibliographical and contextual event material. Among Orlando's more than eight million words of born-digital scholarship, there are (at the time of writing) a total of 65,488 place tags and a total of 10,657 unique place names. On the basis of this extensive set of materials, the Orlando and CWRC teams have conducted experimental geographical visualizations as a means of exploring how best to implement mapping functionality within the Collaboratory platform. We have begun with information related to writers' places of residence, travel, migration, and social networks, and how this biographical data may relate to facets of their writing careers, such as places of production or reception, literary settings, and topographical descriptions. Here, we report the results of this first foray into the complex interrelationship of data, tools, and graphical interfaces.

Because the range of available spatial information varies considerably, the digital mapping of place and space contained in a literary history such as Orlando demands a flexible system that combines spatial identification with contextual information. Places may be real or fictional, domiciles or travel destinations, sites of political activity, publication, or reception of texts, and all of these place types are included in the spatial information encoded in Orlando's text base. A map that represented all such information without distinction would be difficult to read. Moreover, the project's historical sweep soon made it evident that many places require definition in time as well as space in order to be represented meaningfully, particularly since place names and boundaries have changed over the course of British (and international) history. Location is similarly pertinent to matters of biography and literary reception. Visualizations may be space-dominant or time-dominant, and one of our challenges is to better integrate spatial and temporal dimensions in the production of geographical representations of literary history, as Ian Gregory advocates in "Exploiting Time and Space: A Challenge for GIS in the Digital Humanities."

Orlando's texts use tags based on TEI for entities such as place, but they also use a custom tag set designed specifically by the research team for the production of a digital literary history. This tag set demarcates spans of text according to several contexts, such as discussions of writers'

residences, travels, or migrations; fictional settings or non-fictional topographical descriptions; sites of theatrical productions; or where a writer
engaged in political activism. Thus, the tagging of a sentence such as
"Frances Brooke sailed from England to join her husband in Québec"
under a "location" tag allows place as a destination of travel to be distinguished from a sentence such as "This novel is best known for its picture
of settler or habitant life in Lower Canada, which Frances Brooke drew
from her own years there" (Brown, Clements, and Grundy). Places often
mentioned under the "politics" tag, for instance, include Hyde Park and
Trafalgar Square in London, the nuclear research station at Aldermaston
in Berkshire as the site of demonstrations, and Holloway Prison as the
place where London suffragettes were incarcerated. These references to
London as a place are all distinguishable from London as a place of birth,
death, or publication, even within the current published interface of
Orlando, which is entirely textual.

As a result of having implemented such semantic tags in Orlando,
then, we can contextualize each mention of a place name and explore the
axes of geographical representation that will be useful to CWRC-affiliated
researchers and in the delivery of CWRC materials. The CWRC team needs
to test spatial data infrastructure that can map diverse projects and varying articulations of spatial experience. For our initial explorations, we
therefore selected two axes of representation that would be of broad interest to literary scholars: the travel or migration of writers or groups of
writers; and trends in writers' geographical subject matter (that is, places
represented in writing).

Creating the Maps

The methodology for generating the maps discussed here involved several
stages. First, Orlando data was queried according to various parameters,
drawing on the semantic tags discussed above, such as "return all biographies in a given range of birth dates," "return all excerpts containing
a given keyword," or, "return all excerpts containing 'Scotland' within
discussions of violence or politics." Second, once the queried data was

retrieved it was fed into a pre-processing stage in which geographical data was extracted, contextualized, and stored separately. By contextualization we mean specifically the association of geographical data with a declared temporal axis, or—when no date was mentioned in the precise context— with a speculation as to temporal location. We processed all place names returned by these search parameters into the form of events with spatial and temporal co-ordinates. In so doing, we avoided the necessity of visualizing all of Orlando's spatial information in a single, temporally conflated map. In the absence of temporal information embedded in the spatial data itself, we drew on the fact that Orlando's documents organize information in roughly chronological order to provisionally infer the temporality associated with a place by extrapolating from adjacent dated material. Based on this process of inference, each instance of geographical information produced by the initial extraction process was associated with a specific date or range of dates, the writer's name, and the subject discussed, as well as the complete excerpt of the prose under each location as mentioned in Orlando.

A third step consisted of matching place names to latitude and longitude information. In advance of mapping, however, the existing spatial data needed to be enhanced. The mapping systems with which we experimented cannot produce a map from a simple place name like "London," as it is not in itself geo-referenced, that is, related to a location on the earth. This is not a trivial process, even for materials in which the different forms of "London" have already been distinguished from one another. Automated services for geo-referencing place names exist, but they produce a certain number of false or (in other respects) inadequate matches and so require considerable manual checking and cleanup. Within CWRC, new place data will be geo-referenced at the time of creation; the hundreds of thousands of place names contained in the CWRC data donations and seed data projects will undergo this process.

For the purposes of these experiments, we geo-referenced the Orlando data with a Python script that uses GeoPy, a geo-referencing tool box that allows users to "locate the coordinates of addresses, cities, countries, and landmarks across the globe" by acquiring data from third party services such as Google Maps and GeoNames. Thus, an enriched subset of the Orlando data was created without modifying the original text base. By processing the contextual semantic information contained in Orlando's custom tags, this subset of data was used to create geographical visualizations of travel and migration events, of writing about place that can be explored and faceted by means of semantic tags.

We considered a number of mapping tools—such as Exhibit (Huynh), OpenLayers (MetaCarta), Google Maps (Google), ArcGIS (Esri), and HyperCities (UCLA)—experimented with several, and achieved varying degrees of success depending, respectively, on the intuitiveness of their navigation, their ability to read and plot geo-referenced data, and the quality of the visualizations they produced. The maps discussed here were produced using the Map View component of the open source Exhibit 2.0 software produced by the SIMILE project (MIT) and more recently sustained by Google. Exhibit enables the creation of dynamic websites with various views for rendering spatial data within a browser.

Because the place tagging is so dense, we found it essential to work progressively. Initially, we experimented with relatively small subsets of the Orlando materials in order to make the maps readable and meaningful. Later, we narrowed down references to a group of writers, specific countries, or a set of subjects. Figure 1.1 offers a bird's eye view of a sample map, the basis for successive visualizations discussed below. It shows places mentioned in the Orlando biographies for the writers born in each century from 1500 to 2000. As Figure 1.1 makes clear, a single map showing all places mentioned in all of the biographies during this time span would contain a dizzying overabundance of data.

Visualizations

Consider the visualization we produced of the travels and global influence of Mary Ward (1585–1645), a Roman Catholic at a time when people of this faith were a persecuted minority in England, whose lifelong ambition was to found a non-enclosed religious order for women modelled after the all-male Jesuits.

Figure 1.1
Subsets of Orlando places:
biographies of writers born between
1500–1599, 1600–1699, 1700–1799,
1800–1899, and 1900–2000 (from
top to bottom).

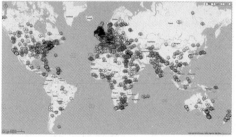

Figure 1.2 Places related to Mary Ward's travels and global influence.

This map produced many hits in England, numerous hits in continental Europe, and a few hits worldwide (see Figure 1.2).

Figure 1.3 shows Ward's extensive travels around Europe: an extraordinary testimony to one woman's influence at a time when travel was slow and dangerous.

Figure 1.4 indicates a concentration of hits in northern England (which reflects the semi-underground life lived by Catholics during the time of Ward's adolescence) and a cluster of hits in London.

Zooming in further in the Exhibit view reveals the various addresses or names of public buildings associated with Mary Ward. Most, but not all, of these addresses and buildings still exist today, which affirms the desirability of certain kinds of mapping technologies for smart phone applications.

If is it possible to produce a map with this degree of detail from the life of a single writer as described in Orlando, imagine the potential for further visualizations. Maps produced from combining multiple writers into a single visualization would reveal a great deal about the relationships between groups of writers and the changing uses of space within the city of London, for example. Imagine the thickly populated general maps of eighteenth-century writers' London or twentieth-century

Figure 1.3
Places related to Mary Ward's travels and influence in Europe.

Figure 1.4
Places related to Mary Ward's travels and influence in England.

writers' London. Theoretically, the degree of possible granularity knows no bounds.

The availability of map resources is a relevant issue. How badly does CWRC, in particular, need online historical maps? The interlayering of maps from different centuries enabled by the HyperCities platform, for example, produces beautiful contrasts and juxtapositions, but spatial relations are not the focus of most CWRC projects. What emerged from our initial round of experiments is that spatially mapping events from roughly the same period does not necessarily provide insight into changing historical patterns in relation to place and space.

Even without the benefit of historical maps against which to view the spatial data, mapping and then comparing Orlando's eighteenth-century London and nineteenth-century London (Figures 1.5 and 1.6) clearly indicates the speed with which the boundaries of the city were moving outwards and the changes made, for instance, by roads taking over from the River Thames as transport corridors. Similarly, mapping and then comparing Orlando's seventeenth-century and nineteenth-century Britain indicates the ways in which literary activity shifted as the centres of population shifted from the old agricultural centres to the new industrial centres.

The outlying markers in the map of Mary Ward's travels (Canada, the United States, India, and Australia) shed light on two further considerations. They show the extent to which the context leveraged from markup is always already embedded in the specifics of the author's life and works, and must therefore be understood as part of an ongoing process of humanistic interpretation and situated representation, rather than a positivist index of certain relations. These hits on Ward's map (Figure 1.2) reflect the information provided in Orlando's entry on Ward that the order she founded flourishes today in those places.

The way Orlando's material on Mary Ward figures on our map highlights one of the crucial aspects of the kind of mapping that will be involved in CWRC as a whole. There are, as mentioned above, rare projects involved in CWRC that focus on the idea of space and have mapping as a central component; however, for the bulk of CWRC projects, and certainly for donated data projects that predate the Collaboratory, these

Figure 1.5
Places in London associated with writers of the eighteenth century in Orlando.

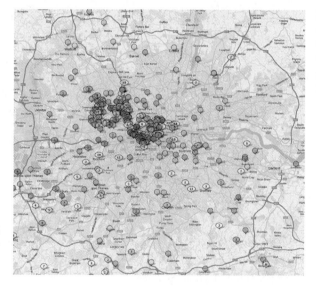

Figure 1.6
Places in London associated with writers of the nineteenth century in Orlando.

concerns are not central to the research aims that inform the way that spatial information is collected. The implications of this are twofold. First, there will be many cases, such as that of Mary Ward's global reach, when spatial information is not as granular as it might be in a dedicated GIS project, which could lead to surprising results. Second, there will be an inherent unevenness in the granularity of the spatial data across the project as a whole. Some projects will dedicate considerable effort to linking spatial and temporal data to enable precise rendering of materials on maps that will support exploration of research questions developed with spatial analysis in mind. Other projects will produce spatial data more casually, in keeping with standard biographical, critical, or bibliographical methods. Thus, CWRC maps rendered from data produced across the Collaboratory will differ considerably from maps created by single projects. Although the format of the data will be interoperable, it will vary considerably from data produced by a single project with uniform principles, aims, and methods in the production of spatial data. While all maps require interpretation, CWRC's maps will, for this reason, require careful readerly analysis. Hence, the rhetoric of the interface will need to signal that the map is not a finished product but an interpretive tool, one of several offered by the Collaboratory.

This species of map will differ considerably, for instance, from those facilitated by the Neatline project: "beautiful, complex maps and narrative sequences from collections of archives and artifacts...maps and narratives with timelines that are more-than-usually sensitive to ambiguity and nuance....Neatline lets you make hand-crafted, interactive stories as interpretive expressions of an archival or cultural heritage collection" (Scholars' Lab). Not all visualizations within CWRC will offer the highly interpretive, detailed, and exquisitely curated spatial and temporal representations of materials produced by a single scholar or co-ordinated team effort in a project to which mapping is central, but the ability to bring together sets of materials and to visualize their spatial data—the unexpected conjunction of materials—may garner serendipitous results. Moreover, embedding such visualizations within an extensive and multi-faceted knowledge environment, so that one can move between the visualizations and other lenses on a given set of materials, means that the mappings will offer a "dynamic rendering of culture," which humanities scholars prefer over "static ones" (Corrigan 80–81). As John Corrigan affirms, "Complex data is dynamic data...It is data that is characterized by interaction between its various parts, which massage each other

Figure 1.7 Places associated with the seventeenth-century Society of Friends in Orlando.

continually in ways that alter our understanding of what we are looking at" (80–81).

The diversity of project aims and data granularity drives home the importance, indeed the necessity, of allowing the reader to move from a map to the source data that lies behind it. Whereas a number of impressive mapping projects associated with writing, such as Gregory Prickman's the Atlas of Early Printing, provide maps that represent data without giving access to the specific source information that underlies each point in a map (as is typical of printed maps), users of CWRC maps will need to be able to access the text that is the source of the visualization in order to determine the relevance of particular points on a map, and subsequently the nature of the connection to the place in question. Information pertaining to provenance also may prove particularly important in this context. Given the inevitability of divergent practices with respect to spatial data on different projects, it will be important to allow those who are creating spatial visualizations of CWRC materials to filter out certain sets of information deemed incompatible with the terms of their inquiry.

Another issue of concern is the way insufficiently specified places— or the combination of varying levels of granularity in a single spatial visualization—can yield misleading results. This can be seen clearly on a map showing the travels of seventeenth-century Quakers.

Figure 1.7 shows at a glance how widely these intrepid women penetrated the eastern seaboard of colonial North America, travelled from Newfoundland in the north to Jamaica and Barbados in the south. It also shows their travels in Europe and eastwards to Greece, Turkey, and Jerusalem, as well as all over England and Ireland. Like Mary Ward, these members of the Society of Friends were driven by the determination to spread their faith worldwide.

But this map also indicates hits in the American Midwest, where no Quakers, indeed no Europeans at all, had reached during the seventeenth century. It is not in the Midwest but in "America" generally that the Orlando text base says many Quakers travelled and preached. Likewise, it is not in Saskatchewan but in "Canada" generally that Mary Ward's order flourishes today (see Figure 1.2). The fact that we are using a map based on current political boundaries as the basis for our visualization is historically insensitive and makes Saskatchewan the generalized geographical centre of Canada at a time in history when such a notion was nonsensical. This problem would be partially resolved by using historical maps that represented the boundaries of Canada as they existed in Ward's lifetime, or the parts of the United States frequented by Europeans during the early activities of the Quakers. If the results for Mary Ward were shown on a historical map rather than a modern map, the "centres" of Canada and the United States (at least from a colonial perspective, on colonial maps) would lie much further to the east and the degree of misplacement would be lessened. Nation or country place names would still produce generalized results that are very misleading if represented by points, but the approximation to more distinct regions would be more evident.

Ward's case would remain problematic, however; the Canada in which her order currently flourishes is indeed present-day Canada that spans from east to west coast, though that was not the Canada of Ward's time. As a result, no single visual representation of Canada could satisfactorily represent Ward's influence. The example of Ward gives rise to potent questions. How, for instance, might one map First Nations settlements

Figure 1.8
Enlarged portion
of map of Society
of Friends.

and activities as opposed to colonial activity, and how might one represent
First Nations conceptions of space at varying points in history?

Both Ward's case and that of the Quakers emphasize the problems of
representation that emerge from mapping information of varying degrees
of particularity within the same environment, and the tension between
concepts of the spatial or geographical, on the one hand, and the national
or political, on the other. They remind us of the constructedness and
historical contingency of visual representations of place and space, and
invite us to explore ways that we might combine existing conventions of
representation, such as the usual pins, lines, polygons, and gradients, to
represent different, and at times conflicting, spatial references and asso-
ciations contained in Orlando's prose and in Orlando's markup.

If one looks at parts of the Quaker map in larger scale (Figure 1.8),
one sees generic designators of a country alongside more precise hits on
particular places within those countries. This combination can produce
misleading ahistorical results: in earlier periods, for instance, current
nations such as Germany and Italy were not united political entities.

The constructedness of space, as well as its constitutive aspects
within literary culture and the production of subjectivities and sensibili-
ties through literature, is especially relevant to Orlando and CWRC whose

Figure 1.9
Scotland as a literary
setting.

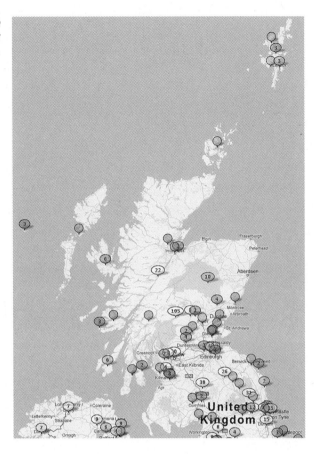

teams are particularly interested in the possibilities for mapping place in
both historical time and imaginative literature.

Figure 1.9 maps Scotland as a setting for writing (fiction and non-
fiction). It indicates the extent to which, within texts, more places are
mentioned in general terms than in Orlando's discussions of writers'
lives, which frequently supply the name of a town, village, castle, or farm-
house. Hence, many texts make reference simply to Scotland, or to the
romantic regions of the Scottish Highlands or Scottish Borders, providing perhaps a fictitious place name within those areas. Again, a range of
visualization strategies could designate different levels of granularity on
a single map and help distinguish particular locations from generalized

areas, thereby creating a hermeneutic layer that represents less specific fictional regions. These layers are akin to "the spaces—Foucault's hetero-topias—that cannot be mapped, such as the marketplace, the theatre, the fairground, and the ship" (Jenstad 117) that Janelle Jenstad identifies as challenges to mapping early modern London in ways that are responsive to the needs of literary scholars. Although such mapping presents dif-ficulties, there is real potential for this kind of visualization to assist in understanding some of the characteristics of the representation of space, and of particular spaces, in literature.

Conclusions

Knowing what we want to map and, as far as possible, how we want to map our materials will be a great advantage to cwrc. When Orlando began, the kind of web-based mapping systems available today did not exist and, although we tried to anticipate what would be required for map-ping, we struggled to sufficiently disambiguate place names for delivery and searchability as text. It is not surprising, then (despite the pains-taking application of spatial metadata throughout the text base), that an extensive cleanup of place tagging was required to create the relatively straightforward maps represented in this chapter.

The challenges described here are by no means unique to this par-ticular mapping project. They invoke the impact of drawing on uneven spatial data, in terms of its granularity (such as North America versus Halifax, Nova Scotia) and density (such as cwrc items that only have a few places mentioned in their metadata in contrast to a piece of travel writing in Orlando that already has extensive tagging). There is yet a further source of unevenness within cwrc: differences in the extent to which contextualizing semantic data is present within and across proj-ects in the Collaboratory. A challenge for both cwrc and Orlando is the sheer density of spatial data across the collections, especially in relation to major population and publishing centres such as London, Toronto, and Montreal. An ideal mapping interface would allow efficient processing and visualization of large quantities of spatial data in a web environment, easy faceting according to a range of criteria, and manual sifting of results, plus quick reference to the source text.

Our early experimental work tackles only a few of the more obvious complexities of spatial and temporal mapping. We are also keenly aware that our pragmatic experimentation with existing open source tools means that, to date, we have relied on existing conventions for representation of space that may be inherently out of step with the nature of our undertaking. As Johanna Drucker urges, humanities visualization needs "interpretations that arise in observer-codependence, characterized by ambiguity and uncertainty, as the basis on which a representation is constructed" to create "a map whose basic coordinate grid is constructed as an effect of these ambiguities" (Drucker par. 2). The systems with which we have experimented thus far cannot begin to support such a nuanced model of spatial visualization. How best to address the mapping needs of literary scholars within CWRC, given the available resources, continues to drive our research. We look forward to learning what affordances other spatial visualization systems, such as Neatline with its attempt to incorporate an interpretive, humanistic perspective, can offer, and how we might adapt them to the kind of collaborative, spontaneous, serendipitous mapping environment that CWRC hopes to support. CWRC also hopes to incorporate more focused, curated mapping work. Creating even a relatively simple environment within which scholars of wide-ranging perspectives can play with place and space as part of their respective investigations will help advance scholarly reflection on mapping itself and discovery of what kinds of mapping are most conducive to scholarly analysis and interpretation in the field of literary historical studies. But we know we still have considerable ground to cover.

WORKS CITED

Digital Sources

Arcgis. http://www.esri.com/software/arcgis

Brown, Susan, and Patricia Clements et al. "Tag Team: Computing, Collaborators, and the History of Women's Writing in the British Isles." *Computing in the Humanities Working Papers* (April 1998). http://projects.chass.utoronto.ca/chwp/orlando

Brown, Susan, Patricia Clements, and Isobel Grundy, eds. *Orlando: Women's Writing in the British Isles from the Beginnings to the Present.* Cambridge: Cambridge University Press, 2006–2012. http://orlando.cambridge.org

Coleman, Nicole, Dan Edelstein, and Paula Findlen. Mapping the Republic of Letters. Stanford University. https://republicofletters.stanford.edu

Drucker, Johanna. "Humanities Approaches to Graphical Display." *DHQ: Digital Humanities Quarterly* 5.1 (2011). http://www.digitalhumanities.org/dhq/vol/5/1/000091/000091.html

GeoNames. http://www.geonames.org

"geopy—A Geocoding Toolbox for Python." Google Code. https://github.com/geopy/geopy

Google Maps. http://maps.google.ca

Huynh, David François. Exhibit. Massachusetts Institute of Technology. http://www.simile-widgets.org/exhibit

HyperCities. University of California, Los Angeles. http://hypercities.com

MetaCarta. OpenLayers. Open Source Geospatial Foundation. http://openlayers.org

Prickman, Gregory. The Atlas of Early Printing. University of Iowa Libraries. http://atlas.lib.uiowa.edu

Scholars' Lab. Neatline: Plot Your Course in Space and Time. University of Virginia Library. http://neatline.org

The simile Project. Massachusetts Institute of Technology. http://simile-widgets.org

tei: Text Encoding Initiative. http://www.tei-c.org/index.xml

Thomas, William G., iii, Richard G. Healey, and Ian J. Cottingham. The Aurora Project. University of Nebraska. http://auroraproject.unl.edu/web/railroads.xhtml

Print Sources

Bol, Peter K. "What Do Humanists Want? What Do Humanists Need? What Might Humanists Get?" *GeoHumanities: Art, History, Text at the Edge of Place.* Ed. Michael Dear, Jim Ketchum, Sarah Luria, and Douglas Richardson. London: Routledge, 2011. 296–308.

Cooper, David, and Ian N. Gregory. "Mapping the English Lake District: A Literary gis." *Transactions of the Institute of British Geographers* 36 (2011): 89–108.

Corrigan, John. "Qualitative gis and Emergent Semantics." *Spatial Humanities: gis and the Future of Humanities Scholarship.* Bloomington: Indiana University Press, 2010. 76–88.

Gregory, Ian. "Exploiting Time and Space: A Challenge for gis in the Digital Humanities." *The Spatial Humanities: gis and the Future of Humanities Scholarship.* Ed. David J. Bodenhamer, John Corrigan, and Trevor M. Harris. Bloomington: Indiana University Press, 2010. 58–75.

Jenstad, Janelle. "Using Early Modern Maps in Literary Studies: Views and Caveats from London." *GeoHumanities: Art, History, Text at the Edge of Place*. Ed. Michael Dear, Jim Ketchum, Sarah Luria, and Douglas Richardson. London: Routledge, 2011. 112–19.

Warf, Barney, and Santa Arias. "Introduction: The Reinsertion of Space in to the Social Sciences and Humanities." *The Spatial Turn: Interdisciplinary Perspectives*. Ed. Warf and Arias. London: Routledge, 2008. 1–10.

MODELLING COLLABORATION
IN DIGITAL HUMANITIES SCHOLARSHIP

Foundational Concepts of an EMiC UA *Project Charter*

Paul Hjartarson, Harvey Quamen, Andrea Hasenbank,
Vanessa Lent, & EMiC UA*

In the humanities, Ms. Mentor regrets to say, things are murky from the start. As underlings in the academic hierarchy, graduate students are supposed to be humbly grateful for all the training they can imbibe. Sometimes they're paid, but often they receive only an inside-the-book acknowledgment....Generous mentors can create once-in-a-lifetime opportunities. Stephen Ambrose's students, for instance, spent summers retracing the steps of Lewis and Clark with their professor—sharing discoveries over campfires first, and later in books and articles. Theirs was a genuine community of scholars.

—Ms. Mentor [Emily Toth], "Who Owns Your Mind?"
Chronicle of Higher Education

What is collaboration, exactly? Where in the spectrum from broad, indirect and tacit indebtedness to explicitly joint work do we locate research in the humanities, especially in light of computing? What conclusion do we draw from the attested benefits of collaboration?

—Willard McCarty, *Humanities Computing*

Introduction

"As scholarship goes multimedia," Andrew Bretz, Susan Brown, and
Hannah McGregor argue in *Lasting Change: Sustaining Digital Scholarship
and Culture in Canada* (2010), "it is also going collaborative. Knowledge
and knowledge production are more extensively networked than ever
before and are deeply embedded socially. The digital turn has led to
the advent of increasingly large-scale and ambitious projects within the
humanities" (18). Funding large, interdisciplinary digital humanities
(DH) projects is certainly a challenge. The problem of funding, however,
pales in comparison to a bigger challenge: developing viable models of
collaboration. If the Editing Modernism in Canada (EMiC) knowledge network, for example, of which our group at the University of Alberta (EMiC
UA) is part, wants researchers—faculty and students—in a number of
disciplines to "collaborate, edit, learn" ("About Us"), it needs to develop
working environments in which ground rules are collaboratively developed and clearly articulated and in which all project members can thrive.
The turn to the digital is occurring at a time when universities in general,
and humanities departments in particular, face unprecedented budgetary
challenges, when student debt is rising, when the job market for recently
graduated PHDs is far from encouraging, and when both junior and
senior faculty feel pressured to do more with less. Is it possible for anyone
in the humanities to "thrive" in such circumstances?

Even if we could isolate these issues, there are challenges enough.
One challenge is working across traditional disciplinary boundaries
within the humanities themselves—between English and theatre or art
history, for example—a difficulty that should neither be overlooked nor
underestimated. Collaborating within a discipline is no easy matter; it
involves not only adjusting to another researcher's personality, understanding the subject in question and each other's work habits, but also
trusting that the additional work necessitated by collaboration is more
than offset by the reward. Collaborating on a digital humanities project,
however, involves working not just across disciplinary boundaries but
also at what Brown terms "the interface of the digital-humanities divide"
(218). Assessing the current state of digital humanities scholarship,

Brown argues that "it will be a major and crucial undertaking to imbue technical systems for the humanities with sensitivity to the complexities of language and discourse, an undertaking in which humanists need to be involved" (218). The final phrase of that sentence underscores both the urgent need for humanists to engage in digital scholarship and their reluctance to do so. Brown adds, "Since digital modes of scholarly production are highly experimental, working at the interface of the digital-humanities divide constitutes, in itself, research, provided that the two aspects of the research seriously engage with one another. This includes archival development, creating generalized digital tools for access or analysis, or developing new pedagogies or critical literacies" (218). Brown's statement is conditional: if humanists and computer scientists "seriously engage with one another," then work at the interface/divide will be "highly experimental" and will constitute research in itself.

This conditional statement is key: serious engagement at the interface/divide of digital humanities is as difficult as it is important. Why? Because the digital humanities discipline is literally—if not for the work of Mary Louise Pratt—what one might term a "contact zone," a many layered, conflicted, and overdetermined "pressure point" between the humanities and the sciences. Pratt's term, developed in an analysis of colonial relations, is admittedly out of place here; what is more, it has been redeployed in so many different contexts, and used so frequently, that it has lost both specificity and analytical purchase.[1] In *Imperial Eyes: Travel Writing and Transculturation* (1992), Pratt defines contact zones as "social spaces where disparate cultures meet, clash, and grapple with each other, often in highly asymmetrical relations of domination and subordination—like colonialism, slavery, or their aftermaths as they are lived out across the globe today" (4). Although the humanities and sciences are "disparate cultures" that "meet, clash, and grapple with each other," comparing that struggle with "colonialism, slavery, or their aftermaths" is certainly questionable. Nonetheless, here we use Pratt's notion of a contact zone to problematize the space of collaboration, to highlight the tension between "interface" and "divide."

There are certainly asymmetrical relations of power at work in this "space," and the inequalities between the humanities and sciences are compounded by the power imbalance among graduate students, post-doctoral fellows, contract faculty, untenured and tenured faculty from various disciplines working side-by-side within a collaboratory. The term *collaboratory*, a neologism that combines *collaboration* and *laboratory*, itself originates in the sciences; its use by digital humanities scholars is another sign of a paradigm shift in progress. The presence of students and postdoctoral fellows in digital humanities collaboratories serves as a reminder that the challenge is to create a space not just for collaborating across disciplines but for mentoring and completing program require-ments as well. The premise here is that working "for" someone, as a "research assistant," a long standing practice in the humanities, does not in itself, create the conditions necessary either for collaborating or mentoring, nor does it address a related issue, that graduate students, postdoctoral fellows, and contract faculty may only work on projects for a relatively short period of time. How does one mentor—can one mentor or be mentored—in a "contact zone"? Is collaboration itself possible in these conditions?

In this chapter, members of the Editing Modernism in Canada research collaboratory at the University of Alberta report on our attempt to develop a viable model of collaboration. How can we produce a model for consent and collaboration that recognizes the disparate forms and conditions of labour connected to humanities research and presentation? EMiC UA has opted to develop a project charter on the iterative model advanced by Stan Ruecker and Milena Radzikowska and adapted for use by the Implementing New Knowledge Environments (INKE) project. Since this work is ongoing, this chapter is necessarily an interim report on ongoing discussions. When we began work on the project charter, EMiC UA consisted of nine researchers: two tenured faculty members, Paul Hjartarson and Harvey Quamen; an archivist, Raymond Frogner; and six graduate students, five in English—Rebecca Blakey, Kristin Fast, Andrea Hasenbank, Hannah McGregor, and Nick van Orden—and one, Matt Bouchard, in information studies. Postdoctoral fellow Vanessa Lent joined us in January 2012. We also work with a number of researchers— Gregory Betts, Wayne DeFehr, Joseph MacKinnon, Linda Morra, Shirley

Neuman, and Paul Tiessen, for example—who may or may not ultimately join the collaboratory. Although most EMiC UA members are based at the University of Alberta, Raymond Frogner works in the Archives, Collections and Knowledge Division, BC Archives in Victoria, and Matt Bouchard is a doctoral student at the University of Toronto. (In October 2013, Hannah McGregor, who was a doctoral student at the University of Guelph, returned to the University of Alberta and to EMiC UA as a SSHRC postdoctoral fellow.) EMiC UA is engaged in three editorial initiatives: the Wilfred and Sheila Watson projects; the Manifestos project; and the Martha Ostenso project. Our mainstay, however, is the Editing Wilfred Watson Archive project. This is the initiative we are using to create digital infrastructure; it is also the initiative we are using to think through the project charter.

Although we have been worrying about the issues of collaboration and documentation for some time, our decision to propose a paper for the second Canadian Writers Research Collaboratory (CWRC) conference, held at Ryerson University in October 2011, signalled a commitment to devote collective time and energy to these issues. Once our proposal was accepted, our three-person group met regularly—approximately once a week over the summer—to push our thinking on these issues. Developing a viable model of collaboration across the digital divide, a model that integrates mentoring into the collaboratory, we believe, is vital not just for our own work but for digital humanities projects generally. What rules of engagement might make collaboration and mentoring possible? Other members of EMiC UA joined us from time to time—as a break from scanning, to offer other perspectives on the matters at hand, or simply out of curiosity—and we reported on our work at regular meetings. In the weeks leading up to the conference, we devoted two regular EMiC UA meetings to debate project charter issues. Given the range of issues a project charter needs to address—from the nature of collaboration itself and the need for documentation to transparency in decision making and what we have tentatively termed "play nice" principles—we decided to focus the Ryerson iteration of our charter on what we term the "trust" cluster of principles: collaboration, credit, communication, and documentation.

Collaboration (or, "What's in It for Me?")

The obstacles to serious and sustained work at the digital humanities interface are formidable. Collaboration is not for everyone and, in the humanities as presently constituted, collaboration is invariably neither the sole nor primary mode of research (or teaching). Although the English and Film Studies Department at the University of Alberta is home to the Orlando Project, to Streetprint, and now to CWRC, DH projects remain a marginal form of departmental research, and collaboration—much like interdisciplinary research itself—is invoked frequently in applications for research funding and less in everyday practice. Given the relative absence of collaboration as a tradition in literary scholarship and the likelihood that collaborative work will remain in a minority relation to solitary research and the monograph, EMiC UA's first commitment, for the foreseeable future, is necessarily to collaboration itself: "Principle: We will work collaboratively, that is, we want and need to learn from one another." Why collaborate? Collaboration is not a component of graduate research programs—students cannot, for example, collaboratively complete master's or doctoral theses—and the humanities, unlike the sciences, have yet to develop widely recognized protocols for evaluating conference presentations, articles, or books produced by multiple authors. If, however, research is inter- or multidisciplinary, collaboration is, or perhaps should be, the preferred model. Moreover, if that research is conducted at the digital humanities interface, it is necessarily collaborative.

The painstaking work involved in editing the letters exchanged by Wilfred Watson and Sheila Watson from 1956 to 1962, for example, centres on an ongoing dialogue between the literary scholars most familiar with the Wilfred and Sheila Watson archives and the digital specialists who can model and implement digital archives and editions. Virtually every editorial decision we make has a technological implication; every technological decision, an editorial consequence. It is worth noting, too, that the dialogue itself is both facilitated and shaped—not always in a positive way—by the technologies (wikis, Skype, Google documents, metadata entry websites) we find ourselves using.[2] Although each group may believe that at the digital humanities interface its particular questions should take precedence—that the issues valued by literary scholars outrank digital concerns or that technical issues trump all others, for example—collaboration works through dialogue. As Linda Hutcheon and Michael Hutcheon point out, "It is no accident that the conversation or dialogue model is a dominant one in theories of collaboration" (1367).[3]

Since the mid-1990s, the computer software community has developed a philosophy known as Extreme Programming or xp. Extreme Programming weaves together principles, practices, and values into strategies that lead not only to better software but to better teams as well. Although concepts like pair programming, frequent software releases, and short development cycles are the popular and well-known components of xp, its ramifications are larger and much more radical. "Extreme Programming," writes xp guru Kent Beck, "is about social change. It is about letting go of habits and patterns that were adaptive in the past, but now get in the way of us doing our best work. It is about giving up the defenses that protect us but interfere with our productivity" (1). A similar attitude has informed our thinking about project charters.

Extreme Programming has been designed to help manage change. We might mistakenly believe that computer software is wholly mathematical, or inflexible when faced with the inexorable laws of logic, or that somehow it magically achieves stasis and stability on its own. None of these views is accurate. The stereotypical view of the retrograde humanities, however, is also fading. Humanists are no longer as technophobic as they once were; literary scholars no longer proclaim Luddism as a virtue, even when we lack technical knowledge, and less and less do we exhibit the ambivalent, oxymoronic personality that Tony Davies once referred to as being a "pioneer of the old" (74). "Everything in software changes," Beck reminds us, and his caveat resonates for the humanities too: "The requirements change. The design changes. The business changes. The technology changes. The team changes. The team members change. The problem isn't change, because change is going to happen; the problem, rather, is our inability to cope with change" (11). Adaptation and flexibility are so important to the xp community that Beck has adopted one of its popular mantras as the subtitle of his book: *Embrace Change*.

The conceptual framework within which xp operates is identical to that found in our project charter—practices shaped by both principles and values. "Principles," Beck argues, "are domain-specific guidelines for life"; "values are the large-scale criteria we use to judge what we see, think, and do"; and "practices are the things you do day-to-day"— observable "evidence of values" (13–15). In xp, principles such as "good communication" inform practices such as "conversation over written communication"—the latter is "inherently more wasteful" and is only "one-way" (Beck 23)—which in turn demonstrate team values of humanity, respect, diversity, and sharing. Embodying those ideals in the daily routines and dynamics of programming teams is xp's secret, manifesting itself in a variety of strategies recognizable to humanists—things like constant and iterative revision (called "refactoring" in programming circles), continual and repeated exposure to both public and peer feedback ("frequent releases"), and even collaboration ("pair programming"). In turn, those team-based strategies affect individual team members' attitudes, inspiring confidence and the willingness to accept responsibility ("Responsibility cannot be assigned; it can only be accepted" [Beck 34]), losing the fear of failure ("When you don't know what to do,…risking failure can be the shortest, surest road to success" [Beck 32]), and promoting "the rare ability to recognize simplicity" [Chromatic, section 5.1]).

In terms of collaboration, perhaps one of the most interesting principles of xp is to "Adopt Collective Code Ownership," the goal of which is to "spread the responsibility for the code to the whole team" (Chromatic, section 6.3). One way to achieve collective ownership is through the practice of pair programming—the coding equivalent of collaborative writing. Two team members sit down at the same computer, sharing the job of writing the day's computer code. They pass the keyboard back and forth between themselves, taking turns writing and thinking and designing. The concept of the team supplants that of the individual; the group trumps the solo author. If one team member believes that a particular programming strategy is neither correct nor desirable, then the pair must find a mutually satisfying solution. "Collective code ownership requires teamwork" is the mantra. "Pair programming makes two people responsible for each line of code in the system, increasing the sense of team ownership" (Chromatic, section 6.3). If we import xp principles directly and literally into the humanities, we might suggest that (at least) two people should be responsible for each sentence, image, slideshow, and multimedia file. Collective ownership, carefully conceived and mutually understood, fosters the emergence of quality. Individual ownership, on the other hand, often devolves into a political struggle for control. The problem with individual ownership, xp says, is that "to make a change in one piece, you must ask permission of its owner...[but] she may be on vacation, get hit by a bus, or be so swamped with other work that she has no time to make your changes. Collective code ownership gives you the power to make necessary changes yourself, wherever they are needed" (Chromatic, section 6.3).

The challenge of dh collaboration prompted Ruecker and Radzikowska to develop the concept of an iterative "project charter," a contract that team members develop and sign in the early stages of their work together and revise as the project evolves, as digital humanities projects invariably do. That charter articulates the principles, policies, and practices governing collaboration. The practice of jointly develop-ing a project charter has been adopted by a number of digital humanities groups. Ruecker himself refers to successive iterations of charters for the projects in which he has participated as "the history of his mistakes" and states that he aspires "to make only new mistakes" (Ruecker, personal communication). However self-deprecating Ruecker's comments, they suggest something of the challenges he has faced. Project charters, how-ever, also document successes. When one of Ruecker's research groups developed a policy that stipulated, "As projects progress to new phases, each team member will have the right of first choice over whether or not to continue with the project," Ruecker and Radzikowska report, "we sud-denly found that many of the reasons for not providing source files simply disappeared" (291–92). Collaboration is grounded in the willingness to share resources, materials, findings, and outcomes; that sharing, in turn, depends on trust. Unfortunately, in the academy, trust invariably seems in short supply.

No group feels the lack of trust more acutely, perhaps, than gradu-ate students, postdoctoral researchers, contract faculty, and emerging scholars, arguably the most vulnerable members of any collaboratory. Can these contributors trust faculty members to recognize their hard work, to involve them as co-authors—in short, to give them, as Jessica Schagerl puts it, a place at the table? Can vulnerable participants collaborate fully without exploitation? Can they place their trust in fellow students and other contract faculty? Interestingly, Schagerl opens her article on mentoring in *Retooling the Humanities: The Culture of Research in Canadian Universities* with a quote from Ms. Mentor, aka Emily Toth:

> Sometimes Ms. Mentor has to burst hopes, shred bubbles, and be the Grinch. While it is true that scholarly types can be generous, open-minded souls who'll share software, footnotes, and recipes for cat treats—they can also backstab, withhold, and compete to leave you penniless, naked, and shivering in the cold (metaphorically speaking). (95)

Schagerl goes on to address the tenuous position of the emerging humanities scholar (graduate student, postdoctoral fellow, contract or junior faculty) in the current university environment. She calls for a shift in perspective at disciplinary and institutional levels to match the current goals of funding organizations such as the Social Sciences and Humanities Research Council of Canada (SSHRC).

At present, an emerging scholar who is contemplating interdisciplinary and collaborative work—attractive to granting organizations—needs to weigh the possibility that such work will not be valued by "department hiring committees and...promotion and tenure committees" (Schagerl 107). As a possible solution to this dilemma, Schagerl suggests that humanities "research culture" take "the everyday practice of mentoring" as "its central retooling strategy" (110). Schagerl's vision of mentoring moves beyond a traditional one-on-one relationship between senior and junior colleagues to a model composed of intergenerational, interdisciplinary, and collaborative networks. She dismantles the stereotype of the isolated humanities scholar and instead reminds us that each emerging scholar already has a "network of professional relationships, some of which may indeed mimic sanctioned power structures but others that are informal, collaborative, and participatory" (Schagerl 104). In redefining the boundaries of mentorship, Schagerl conjures the dynamics of the networked and collaborative digital humanities project. Additionally, such mentorship brings with it membership in a community whose support begins at the intellectual level and extends to often unaddressed emotional and interpersonal issues. Such a mentorship model might help address the anxieties inherent in the figure of the transient emerging scholar who, driven by the vagaries of the current postsecondary economy, shifts institutions every few years. Instead of viewing such movement as entirely negative, one might, following Schagerl, view it as enabling the scholar to develop a vital set of networks that "should be valued in the context of knowledge exchanges and effective linkages increasingly promoted by SSHRC" (Schagerl 102).

Collaborating necessarily involves taking calculated risks. The purpose of project charters is to establish rules of engagement and to manage expectations. While charters may mitigate the risk of collaborating, they certainly do not eliminate all risks. Project charters address factors identified by Daniel Coleman and Smaro Kamboureli in *Retooling the Humanities* as foci for discussion about the future of humanities research, including funding pressures, mentorship models, the tension between solitary and collaborative work, and the idea of interdisciplinarity as a whole. In the collaboratory, multidisciplinary framework of the digital humanities, project charters are one strategy for "retooling" the humanities. Project charters are at once a response to some of the troubling aspects of the current research paradigm and an attempt to work within its structures.

Credit

Our work on an EMiC UA project charter is an attempt to think through issues of work—labour and organization—deliberately, in ways that are frequently overlooked in the digital humanities, as well as in ways that are underserved by traditional models of scholarship in literature and the other humanities. Much as our approach to collaboration comes out of the need and desire to learn from one another, our approach to credit comes out of the need to recognize our respective contributions to generating the outcomes of the project. We anticipate that work from Editing the Wilfred Watson Archive project will branch out into a range of venues, as a variety of shifting subgroups of our members come together to work out problems and address topics arising from this core research. As we work theoretically and editorially to recuperate archival texts and to reassert the social networks of textual production in a digital medium, we have committed to emphasizing the mutually supporting roles of our own group members.

Weaving through these questions of venue, group, and contribution is the undeniable value of credit as academic currency. In an attempt to balance the multiple roles and contributions of project collaborators, EMiC UA has adopted a set of policies that allow for leading contributors to be recognized for their work on particular subprojects while also securing the foundational importance of the entire group to all work emanating from our collaboratory. We intend to expand existing publication practices in the humanities to give equal recognition to all collaborators as authors. Hence, the list of authors on our published work always includes the group as a whole. Policy: EMiC UA will be credited as an organizational author on all publications derived from collaboratory work. This approach allows individual co-authors to list work on a curriculum vitae in the traditional academic manner, while also directing interested parties to the project website to learn more about specific contributors and their roles. The author note, typically used to provide institutional or biographical details, offers a space to expand upon the roles of contributors. The acknowledgements section, typically used to credit funding bodies or other forms of research support, can be reworked as a space to elaborate networks of contribution.

This set of policies and practices creates a concentric model of credit, wherein "primary contributors" or co-authors are always recognized as working within a body of knowledge enabled by the work of the group as a whole. In this model, the project website becomes a primary signifier of credit; rather than simply recording a static directory of personnel, the website becomes a fluid document of participation and activity.

Documentation

The need for documentation is grounded in several realities: that DH projects change significantly as they develop; and that DH projects committed to mentoring are likely to experience a significant change in membership over time. Documentation, the encapsulating of knowledge and wisdom into a collection of human readable files, has its parallels in the coding world, too. Often seen under the guise of "commenting," the concept refers to the inclusion of human readable snippets of text that are interwoven into computer code itself, offering telltale signs about the genesis, history, or arcane logical gymnastics at work in the code itself. And, perhaps surprisingly, code documentation has spawned a controversy—is it a good thing or a bad thing?—that might help humanists arrive at better strategies for documenting projects.

Robert C. Martin, author of *Clean Code: A Handbook of Agile Software Craftsmanship*, takes the radically negative stance that documentation is bad. Code ought to be self-explanatory, he maintains. It should express its intent with direct and obvious simplicity. Martin's militant position, although surprising and perhaps counterintuitive, holds a useful lesson for humanists, however:

> Comments are not like Schindler's List. They are not "pure good." Indeed, comments are, at best, a necessary evil. If our programming languages were expressive enough, or if we had the talent to subtly wield those languages to express our intent, we would not need comments very much—perhaps not at all.

> The proper use of comments is to compensate for our failure to express ourself in code. Note that I used the word failure. I meant it. Comments are always failures. We must have them because we cannot always figure out how to express ourselves without them, but their use is not a cause for celebration. (53–54)

The problem with comments, says Martin, is that they go stale, cover up bad code, and shift us into a mode of describing when instead we should be fixing. "They lie," he says flatly (Martin 54).

Even Martin concedes that comments are necessary at times, but his caveats about when and how to comment properly and usefully can illustrate the issues for humanists who are grappling with the problematics of project documentation for the very first time. Martin articulates the mismatch between author and audience that is all too familiar to humanists. He is wrestling with the polysemous nature of language (that is, code). And humanists might read in Martin's screed a number of other interesting theoretical maneuvers: that documentation serves as the Derridean "dangerous supplement" (Derrida 158) to language's inadequacy, that it is the suturing of a cognitive rift, that it is a second attempt at ideological interpellation.

And so, contra Martin, in the cultural divide between the *D* and the *H* of digital humanities, there is room for precisely the kind of documentation that he has described. Documentation is not the problem: it is both a solution and an opportunity. Digital humanists, increasingly working at the level of code, might not actually have the requisite literacy that Martin assumes is present in his programming teams. Brown's observation that "working at the interface of the digital-humanities divide" is productive "providing that the two aspects of the research seriously engage with one another" (218) means, for us, that humanists cannot sustain long-term DH projects if they refuse to engage—or even to learn anything at all about—topics like computer programming, markup languages, or interface design. Conversely, programmers cannot sustain DH projects in the long term without either taking the concerns of humanists seriously or understanding how and why humanities scholarship develops as it does. Altering practices on both sides of the divide might be the foundation that makes sustainable DH work possible. For example, Martin cites a few snippets of Java code and asks an intriguing question, but one that he sees as an either/or dichotomy:

> Which would you rather see? This:
> ```
> // Check to see if the employee is eligible for full benefits
> if ( ( employee.flags & HOURLY_FLAG ) &&
> ( employee.age > 65 ) )
> ```

Or this?

```
if ( employee.isEligibleForFullBenefits() ) (Martin 55)
```

"It takes only a few seconds of thought to explain most of your intent in code," Martin says (55). But humanists new to the DH world might easily benefit from both the English comment and the helpful clarity of an aptly named method. The best answer might be a combination of the two options Martin cites: both clear code and documentation.

A set of "best practices" in DH documentation, then, might be a hybrid form of the "typical practices" from both sides of the digital humanities and project documentation itself, the discursive common ground. Documentation is an information interchange, not compensation for failure. Documentation is shared culture. As DHers, we need not only to promote code literacy on the part of our humanist colleagues but also to encourage an understanding of humanist scholarship on the part of programmers. If documentation, as Martin insists, marks the failure of intent to match expression, then shared practices about documentation and discussions about the values that they embody might be the best way not to mind—that is, to mend—the gap between the digital and the humanities. Martin's caveats remind us about the various kinds of documentation that digital humanities projects need to generate and the different audiences for whom those documents are intended. Well-written internal documentation, for example, should assist new team members by providing the record of a project's history and its evolution ("The team changes. The team members change," reflects Beck [11]). Code comments included for reasons that are legal, clarifying, informative, or expressive of some kind of incomplete intent are wholly worthwhile, Martin maintains. Warnings against potential consequences and leaving "to do" notes for other programmers is useful, too.

In the early months of scanning correspondence in the Wilfred Watson fonds, Nick van Orden worked with Joe MacKinnon, our most experienced scanner, to develop a document they titled "How to Scan like a Rock Star." When Rebecca Blakey joined the project, she not only scanned with van Orden and MacKinnon but consulted their documentation, and has since updated it. When scanning moved from Wilfred Watson's correspondence to his notebooks and journals, our scanning techniques needed to change and the documentation required updating. We recently installed updated scanner software that may well require changes in both scanning and documentation. Strong documentation enables the Watson project to build on the knowledge developed by previous group members; what is more, that documentation, we hope, keeps us true to our earlier decisions and commitments.

Strong documentation is also essential to recognizing the contribution of each member of the collaboratory to project milestones and outcomes: letters and journals scanned; a metadata entry site developed and tested; memoranda of agreement negotiated and signed; metadata entered; texts transcribed, optical character recognized, or proofread; lines of code written or bugs fixed; files backed up; images colour-corrected and cropped; new staff members trained. Another principle we have developed is that "a task is not completed until the documentation is shared." Strong documentation will derive not just from reports filed but also from data collected as part of the workflow. Accurate documentation is necessary not only to give credit where credit is due but also to support applications for funding, to report to granting agencies on work completed, or to substantiate statements made in letters of reference and elsewhere. This chapter itself, part of what members of the collaboratory term the "Ryerson iteration" of the EMiC UA charter, is itself part of our documentation process (as are other papers published by EMiC UA members).

Communications

If dialogue and documentation are essential to collaboration, then communication needs to begin "at home," among members of the collaboratory itself. Our subgroup is recommending that EMiC UA keep its administrative structure as "horizontal," that is, non-hierarchical, and as simple as possible: "horizontal" to facilitate dialogue among group members and simple to minimize bureaucracy and to give EMiC UA the flexibility it needs to respond quickly to changing conditions and opportunities. Communication at home means access to working documents and as much transparency in decision making as possible. We need to communicate not only with other members of the collaboratory but with EMiC UA partners. The EMiC knowledge network is more parent than partner, so if communication begins at home, then EMiC itself is part of that home, as are the literary executors of the Wilfred and Sheila Watson estates. EMiC UA partners include CWRC, the University of Alberta Libraries, and the John M. Kelly Library at St. Michael's College in Toronto. Our commitment to disseminate our work as widely as possible is a commitment to interdisciplinarity, that is, to present our work at gatherings of all disciplines represented on the project, not just to members of our own disciplinary groups.

If, as Schagerl argues, new forms of mentorship are needed, then DH projects may have a role to play in "retooling the humanities." For graduate students, postdoctoral fellows, and contract faculty, the value of collaboration extends well beyond traditional notions of training. In addition to training in research and methodology, team members learn to communicate and collaborate within an interdisciplinary environment. In "An Addiction from Which We Never Get Free"—the title is Bill Reading's characterization of thinking—Rey Chow reflects on the nature of "humanistic knowledge" in the age of information. "If the tendency of information is to render knowledge infinitely disposable," Chow asks, "what are the possibilities of a nondisposable knowledge? Does nondisposable knowledge still exist and how may it be preserved? Is there something about the reading, writing, and thinking habits that scholars have cultivated for centuries that may still be relevant here?" (52). Thinking itself, Chow argues, may be at once the most vital and elusive thing we need to "redeem" in the age of information. "Such a redemption," she argues,

> can take the form of reconceptualizing how the humanities—the writings, images, and sounds that constitute all those treasured records from the past— may become dialogue partners with non-humanistic fields. Such a dialogue, involving the understanding of how knowledge boundaries become established

in the first place, would not only help contextualize the more narrow conception of the humanities and restore the latter's proximities and affinities with the other human sciences. It would also make possible cross-disciplinary, cross-referential kinds of writing and reading that would have as their preoccupation not the defensive or nostalgic perpetuation of a particular kind of conceptual arrangement, but rather the intelligent construction of possible movements and passages among different conceptual arrangements. (53)

Digital humanities projects not only open a dialogue between the humanities and "non-humanistic fields," they also enable the "cross-disciplinary, cross-referential kinds of writing and reading" necessary to redeem humanistic thinking in an age of disposable information.

These concerns with collaboration, interdisciplinary dialogue, and communication are not, of course, unique to the digital humanities. Linda Hutcheon and Michael Hutcheon's article "A Convenience of Marriage: Collaboration and Interdisciplinarity," for example, documents the experience of working collaboratively as married colleagues across disparate fields. When their research necessitated a further reach of knowledge and experience, they extended this collaboration to a group of four graduate students. Their article highlights the challenges and benefits of such interdisciplinary work and addresses many of the same issues of the collaborative collective within the context of a non-digital project. Since the completion of the research and subsequent publication of their findings, the graduate students reported that "the professional skills learned in this collective process of researching, writing, and adapting have stood them in good stead in their subsequent (and differing) careers" (Hutcheon and Hutcheon 1371). Further, Hutcheon and Hutcheon assert that, although the collaborative process was at times slower than expected, the overall results for those involved were invaluable: "everyone was forced to think differently, to listen more carefully and more critically, to look for new ways to integrate insights" (1371). The collaborative process created an environment of "collective respect for personal and disciplinary differences and evolved a kind of 'rhetoric of dissensus' that permitted, indeed demanded, continued discussion"

(Trimbur 609). The collaborative process fosters an environment of innovative communication between disciplines. Communication becomes even more crucial in DH projects. Clear communication within digital humanities teams is essential in alleviating the "tension that can exist between programmers and non-programmers, the varying perspectives of different disciplines, a lack of common language and understanding of the project between team members" (Siemens 229). A project charter sets in place the policies and practices necessary to foster effective communication among team members. Our hope is that such interdisciplinary and intergenerational communication results in scholarship that challenges the status quo and sets a standard for similar projects that will continue to enhance, evolve, and ultimately enrich the culture of humanities thinking.

Conclusion

At this stage in our discussions regarding the EMiC UA project charter, we have more questions than answers. Perhaps we will always have more questions. Perhaps it is the dialogue itself—the ongoing discussions regarding the project charter as an enabling form of communication among members of the group—that is important. Certainly, communication plays a significant role in the trust cluster as we have been mapping it. At some point in our work together, we realized that collaboration and credit are the key issues we need to address if we are to sustain our work together over the long term. Those two principles, we also began to realize, are forces held in uneasy tension. As one group member put it, the more one invests in collaboration within the humanities, particularly as a graduate student, postdoctoral fellow, contract faculty, or emerging scholar, the more one is made aware of the need for the academic currency of individual credit. Prioritizing individual credit, however, can leave a researcher wanting the advantages of collaboration, the risks notwithstanding, and prompt her to undertake more collaborative work. Collaboration and credit function as two poles dominating and shaping the field in which we work, and the result is a constant flux of attraction and repulsion. Between these poles, we hold on to documentation and communication as ways of tracking the movements and relationships within our collaboratory, of balancing this dynamic, and propelling our work forward.

EMiC UA Project Charter "Trust Cluster": Collaboration, Credit, Documentation, and Communication

The Editing Modernism in Canada project seeks to place graduate education at the centre of its work. In collaboration with the University of Victoria's Digital Humanities Summer Institute, it provides training in the digital humanities; through its partnership with Trent University's Public Texts program, it offers courses in the theory and practice of editing; and through funding provided by a SSHRC Strategic Knowledge Cluster grant, it offers funding, including postdoctoral fellowships, to students who choose to edit Canadian texts. Early in its work, the EMiC UA research group resolved to build on EMiC's foundational commitment to the training and mentorship of graduate students and other emerging scholars by developing a collaborative environment in which those scholars could function as full members of a research team and receive credit appropriate to their work on projects. To that end, EMiC UA placed a high priority on developing a project charter; we soon realized, however, that the task would prove as difficult and demanding as it was crucial to our work. This document is a work in progress. Because our work is in its early stages, it is grounded more in principles than in policies and practices. As our work develops, these principles will give rise to policies and practices; moreover, all principles, policies, and practices will be more fully tested and revised in our day-to-day operations. This ongoing revision we understand as the heart of an iterative project charter. The present document is part—a small part, at that—of a larger whole. The focus here is on "trust" because it is essential to equitable collaboration. We have also worked on a "play nice" cluster, that is, principles we think should govern our collective commitment to tasks, deadlines, and conflict resolution.

I. Collaboration

PRINCIPLE	POLICY
We will work collaboratively. That is, we want and need to learn from one another.	
As a DH "collaboratory" in a university setting, we place a high priority on fostering graduate student development in all areas (including in the acquisition of collaborative skills).	Research assistants are eligible for EMiC UA and EMiC Dalhousie funding to attend training institutes (Digital Editing and Modernism in Canada [DEMiC] and Textual Editing and Modernism in Canada [TEMiC]) and to present conference papers as part of one or more of the project groups.
Collaborators are people who sign the charter. That is, membership in EMiC UA is defined by an individual's acceptance of the principles, policies, and practices of the collaboratory.	Research assistants are encouraged to sign the project charter when they begin their work with EMiC UA and thus become collaborators. They are also encouraged to expand their participation in the collaboratory beyond simply putting in their hours.
We will strive to keep the administrative structure of the collaboratory as simple and as "horizontal" (that is, non-hierarchal) as the needs of the project permit. Given the developmental nature of the work EMiC UA is undertaking, the administrative structure of the collaboratory should be kept not only simple and non-hierarchical, but as malleable and flexible as possible to enable us to respond effectively and efficiently to the many changes development brings.	
We will work within schedules and to deadlines arrived at collaboratively.	
All collaborators have the right of first refusal on ensuing stages of the project.	

II. Credit

PRINCIPLE	POLICY
All work undertaken to advance EMiC UA projects is equally deserving of credit. (Giving credit speaks to the ethos of the project itself.)	EMiC UA will be credited as an organizational author on all publications; additionally, we will use the naming of authors, notes, and acknowledgements as differing ways of attributing credit on all publications.
We recognize the need for credit as a part of academic advancement. (This follows from our commitment to mentoring and to our support for the completion of academic programs as part of EMiC UA project work.)	All participants will be listed on the project website, including roles and dates; the website provides an ongoing record of contributors and their contributions.

III. Documentation

PRINCIPLE	POLICY
Collaboration is rooted in clear documentation, both as a means of understanding one another's work and as a means of distributing credit.	A task is not completed until the documentation is shared.
Documentation is necessary not only for the purpose of informing other group members and continuing workflow, but in support of grant applications and reports.	
We will document our work as it arises from the rhythms of the project. (Documentation will be geared around project planning, dissemination, and reporting.)	
Documentation is meant as a support; therefore, documentation responsibilities will be kept to a minimum (so that the project work can carried out efficiently) while ensuring that a sense of the project's development is recorded (so we can see how the project evolves).	
All documents, including working documents, generated by the group are always accessible to current group members.	The primary site for documentation is the wiki.

IV. Communication

PRINCIPLE	POLICY
We will strive for transparency in decision making and communication.	
We will strive to disseminate our work as widely as possible.	We will strive to produce open source code and style sheets whenever possible.
We will strive to reflect the interdisciplinary nature of our work in the way we disseminate it.	

AUTHORS' NOTE

* This document is the work of many hands. Kristin Fast, Andrea Hasenbank, and Paul Hjartarson took the lead in developing the Editing Modernism in Canada University of Alberta (EMiC UA) project charter and in writing the paper presented at the CWRC conference held at Ryerson University in October 2011. At one time or another, most members of EMiC UA, including Matt Bouchard, Harvey Quamen, Joseph McKinnon, and Charlotte Nobles, participated in our meetings, and all members, including Hannah McGregor, discussed both the charter and the draft prior to its presentation at Ryerson. Andrea Hasenbank, Paul Hjartarson, Vanessa Lent, and Harvey Quamen took the lead in revising both the paper and the project charter for publication. We would also like to acknowledge the invaluable advice offered by Lynne Siemens of the University of Victoria and Stan Ruecker of the IIT Institute of Design in Chicago, and the support of Dean Irvine, director of EMiC, and Susan Brown, director of CWRC. The shortcomings of this chapter, however, are entirely our own.

NOTES

1. Mary Louise Pratt's concept of contact zones gained currency less through her book *Imperial Eyes: Travel Writing and Transculturation* than through her essay "Arts of the Contact Zone," published in *Profession* (New York: MLA) in advance of the book. The article focuses on writing and literacy.

2. The use of technology in the practice of collaboration warrants further discussion. We find ourselves both liberated and constricted by the tools we choose to use to connect with one another, which facilitate, complicate, and prevent various relationships and processes.

3. Although collaboration is at the heart of research in the digital humanities, it is both an issue and a practice discussed in numerous contexts. In addition to the article by Linda Hutcheon and Michael Hutcheon, see, for example, articles by Ede and Lunsford, and by Gilman.

WORKS CITED

Beck, Kent, with Cynthia Andres. *Extreme Programming Explained: Embrace Change*. 2nd ed. Boston: Addison-Wesley, 2005.

Bretz, Andrew, Susan Brown, and Hannah McGregor. *Lasting Change: Sustaining Digital Scholarship and Culture in Canada*. 2010. http://www.cwrc.ca/wp-content/uploads/2011/05/Lasting-Change-Knowledge-Synthesis.pdf

Brown, Susan. "Don't Mind the Gap: Evolving Digital Modes of Scholarly Production across the Digital-Humanities Divide." *Retooling the Humanities: The Culture of Research in Canadian Universities*. Ed. Daniel Coleman and Smaro Kamboureli. Edmonton: University of Alberta Press, 2011. 203–31.

Chow, Rey. "'An Addiction from Which We Never Get Free.'" *New Literary History* 36.1 (2005): 47–55.

Chromatic. *Extreme Programming Pocket Guide*. Sebastopol, CA: O'Reilly Media, 2003.

Collaboratory. *Wikipedia: The Free Encyclopedia*. http://en.wikipedia.org/wiki/Collaboratory

Davies, Tony. *Humanism*. 2nd ed. New Critical Idiom Series. New York: Routledge, 2008.

Derrida, Jacques. *Of Grammatology*. 1967. Baltimore: Johns Hopkins University Press, 1997.

Ede, Lisa, and Andrea J. Lunsford. "Collaboration and the Concepts of Authorship." PMLA 116.2 (2001): 354–69.

Editing Modernism in Canada. Project website. http://editingmodernism.ca

Gilman, Sander L. "Collaboration, the Economy, and the Future of the Humanities." *Critical Inquiry* 30.2 (2004): 384–90.

Hutcheon, Linda, and Michael Hutcheon. "A Convenience of Marriage: Collaboration and Interdisciplinarity." PMLA 116.5 (October 2001): 1364–76.

MacKinnon, Joseph, Nicholas van Orden, and Rebecca Blakey. "How to Scan Like a Rock Star." EMiC UA Working Document.

Martin, Robert C. *Clean Code: A Handbook of Agile Software Craftsmanship*. Boston: Prentice-Hall, 2009.

McCarty, Willard. *Humanities Computing*. Basingstoke: Palgrave Macmillan, 2005.

Ms. Mentor [Emily Toth]. "Who Owns Your Mind?" *Chronicle of Higher Education* 21 May 1999: n. pag.

Pratt, Mary Louise. "Arts of the Contact Zone." *Profession* (1992): 33–40.

———. *Imperial Eyes: Travel Writing and Transculturation*. New York: Routledge, 1992.

Ruecker, Stan. Personal communication. 16 July 2012.

Ruecker, Stan, and Milena Radzikowska. "The Iterative Design of a Project Charter for Interdisciplinary Research." *Proceedings of the 7th ACM Conference on Designing Interactive Systems*. New York: ACM, 2008. 288–94.

Schagerl, Jessica. "Taking a Place at the Table." *Retooling the Humanities: The Culture of Research in Canadian Universities*. Ed. Daniel Coleman and Smaro Kamboureli. Edmonton: University of Alberta Press, 2011. 95–112.

Siemens, Lynne. "'It's a Team If You Use 'Reply All'": An Exploration of Research Teams in Digital Humanities Environments." *Literary and Linguistic Computing* 24.2 (2009): 225–33.

Trimbur, John. "Consensus and Difference in Collaborative Learning." *College English* 51.6 (October 1989): 602–16.

AN INTERACTIVE,

MATERIALIST-SEMIOTIC ARCHIVE

Visualizing the Canadian Theatrical Canon in the Simulated Environment for Theatre

Sasha Kovacs and Jennifer Roberts-Smith, Teresa M. Dobson, Sandra Gabriele, Omar Rodriguez-Arenas, Stan Ruecker, Stéfan Sinclair, Shawn DeSouza-Coelho

Introduction

In its 2011 season, Toronto's Soulpepper Theatre Company contributed to a notable and "problematic," to cite *Globe and Mail* critic J. Kelly Nestruck, revival movement in the history of Canadian theatre ("Canadian Revivals"). The two "revivals" mounted by the company, Guillermo Verdecchia's *Fronteras Americanas* and Judith Thompson's *White Biting Dog*, were both Governor General's (GG) Literary Award–winning plays, which, despite their past successes and their status in the Canadian theatrical canon, had rarely, if ever, been revived on such a scale. This, in itself, was not surprising; as Nestruck observed, "in the country's theatre ecology, second productions have always been harder to get than first productions...And revivals of older plays? For a long while, they were even rarer" ("Canadian Revivals"). What was surprising was the intervention of Soulpepper's productions into the traditional construction of the Canadian theatrical canon as a body of printed, rather than performed, works. In a gesture that we argue demonstrates what Ric Knowles has called a materialist-semiotic approach to theatre, Soulpepper publicized its revivals as re-presenting important past performances, rather than re-producing important published works.[1] That gesture reflected an increasing interest—in theatrical and scholarly circles alike—in the challenges of preserving and recovering the non-textual elements of theatrical performance. If the canon is performative, how can one archive it for posterity, and who should be the archivist(s)?

We propose that as printed text becomes increasingly unsatisfying as a means of archiving a theatrical canon, the digital Simulated Environment for Theatre (SET) provides some useful functions to supplement textual records. In particular, SET enables a materialist-semiotic perspective on the archive by accommodating both print-based and performative records. The precursor to SET was Watching the Script, a project we initiated in 2003 that aimed to enrich the ways in which plays could be read. It allowed users to see text displayed in proximity to an abstract visualization of "characters" (coloured dots) in "space" (a two-dimensional grid), thereby positioning users as watchers, rather than readers, of script (Roberts-Smith et al., "Visualizing Theatrical Text"). In 2008, when a domain expert in theatre joined our research team, we began to ask how the performative function of theatrical text might be visualized in relation to material theatrical phenomena that exist in time and space (Roberts-Smith et al., "Visualizing Theatrical Text"). The SET project was conceived to address that very question. In doing so, the project aimed to provide a useful tool for three constituencies of users: theatre creators, especially directors interested in virtually sketching their concepts before or during production; theatre educators, who might use the system to extend their own approaches to teaching the semiotic relationships between dramatic texts and performative contexts; and theatre researchers, who might visualize the insights into historical performance available in a range of theatrical and paratheatrical records (Roberts-Smith et al., "Visualizing Theatrical Text"; "Visualizing Theatre Historiography").

In the experimental process of visualizing theatrical action in the SET system on the basis of records of two historically distinct productions of one play—Judith Thompson's *White Biting Dog*—we realized that SET could function as a dynamic tool to record not just discrete productions, but also production histories, and to mark the historiographic contingencies of any visual representation of performance. This realization gave rise to concrete outcomes: specifically, SET functions for visualizing the sources that had led us to the theatrical representations we authored (Roberts-Smith et al., "Visualizing Theatre Historiography"). At the theoretical level, we began to ask what our virtual mapping of documented production histories of a canonical text was doing to the text's hegemonic hold on or authority in performance creation and analysis. In this chapter, we offer an extended discussion of the Soulpepper revivals' challenge to the prevailing concept of the Canadian theatrical canon; the theoretical questions raised by the revivals in relation to theatre archiving practices current among other contemporary theatre practitioners; and, using our visualization of the production history of *White Biting Dog* as an illustration, the potential for the SET system to visualize those challenges and questions in materialist-semiotic terms. We argue that SET, when used as an archival tool, has the potential to visualize the undoing of the authority of text in the project of theatrical canon formation.

Soulpepper Theatre 2011:
Reviving, Revising, and Questioning the Canon

To return to Soulpepper's "problematic" revivals, it was neither surprising that *Fronteras Americanas* and *White Biting Dog* had rarely been revived in large-scale productions, nor was it surprising that Soulpepper chose to revive Governor General's Literary Award–winning plays. When it was first founded, Soulpepper mounted "only classical plays and modern classics" (Wasserman 22) and, unlike the "alternative movement" that preceded Soulpepper, the company unapologetically refused to produce new Canadian work.[2] The nationalism at Soulpepper's core was located instead in its self-designation as a "classical repertory theatre company" with a mandate to "tell the world's greatest stories in vital Canadian interpretations" (Soulpepper, "The Company/The Soulpepper Difference"), which implied that Soulpepper's performance methods, rather than the scripts it chose, were Canadian. This conception of "Canadian" theatre (which is not unique to Soulpepper) has led to criticism, articulated most recently by Kamal Al-Solaylee, former theatre critic for the *Globe and Mail*, who says, "we continue to operate in a theatrical milieu where our deference to the classical (and largely European) repertoire is coupled with undervaluing our own dramatic articulations. And, increasingly, that disconnect is making our largest theatres appear out of touch" (58).

Perhaps in response to such criticism, after three seasons that did not include a single Canadian work, Soulpepper has consistently mounted homegrown Canadian plays as among "the world's best" stories (Soulpepper, "Archives"). Typically, these plays have been past critical and box office successes, many of which have won Governor General's Literary Awards, and consequently have seemed unproblematic candidates for inclusion as Canadian "classics" in the Soulpepper repertoire.[3] Nonetheless, Nestruck notes in a generally negative review of the 2011 production of *White Biting Dog*:

> While it's unlikely that Soulpepper picks its Canadian programming by throwing darts at a list of past winners of the Governor General's Award for Drama, it can sometimes seem like that's the case. Sticking to plays that have previously made the GG grade has served the company well in the past, with the Eric Peterson-John Gray hit *Billy Bishop Goes to War* and Sharon Pollock's *Doc*. But this season it's proved more problematic. ("White Biting Dog")

More than one critic, bemoaning the shortcomings of Soulpepper's productions of both *Fronteras Americanas* and *White Biting Dog*, took the opportunity to assert that "much canonized Canadian drama was weaker than its reputation" (Robert Cushman qtd. in Nestruck, "Canadian Revivals"). Nestruck cites, for example, Christopher Hoile's astonishment that "such an 'absolute mess' could have ever won the G-G" and the *National Post*'s Robert Cushman, who went so far as to question the existence of "the supposed Golden Age of English Canadian drama" (qtd. in Nestruck, "Canadian Revivals"). What was problematic about Soulpepper's 2011 revivals was the canonical status of the plays, a status that was called into question when Soulpepper's productions demanded that they demonstrate theatrical value as well as the literary value that had been conferred upon them by publishing houses, anthologists, and literary awards.

While not all critics assessed *Fronteras Americanas* and *White Biting Dog* as harshly as those quoted above, Soulpepper's 2011 revivals seem to have opened a critical debate about the nature of the Canadian dramatic canon and the process by which it has been defined historically. Nestruck lauded this opportunity for "critics and audiences to get in on the game of canon-building that academics have hitherto monopolized" ("Canadian Revivals"), but he was not the first to draw attention to the historical centrality of text in this "game." As Denis Salter has noted, the Massey Commission, which in 1951 reported to the federal government on the state of Canadian culture, expressed the hope that the production of more plays would translate into a more clearly defined Canadian nation with a robust cultural community at its core. The commission proposed that the development of a vital theatrical culture depended upon the establishment of a "national repertoire of Canadian-made plays on Canadian topics in a Canadian idiom and presented in a recognizable Canadian style" (qtd. in Salter 82). Alan Filewod further observed that "the notion of a dramatic literature [was] the first condition of an autonomous national theatre" ("Undermining" 1). The Massey Commission achieved much of its desired aim. The commission's position, for example, informed the practices of founding editor Don Rubin of the *Canadian Theatre Review* (*CTR*) (Filewod, "Undermining" 1)—established in 1974, *CTR* still publishes "at least one significant new script per issue" ("Canadian Theatre Review")—as well as the mandates of Canadian theatrical publishing houses, which contribute to the commission's hoped for "substantial body of proven plays (Canadian classics in other words) to which artistic directors would automatically turn when planning their upcoming seasons" (Salter 82).

The alternative theatre movement of the 1970s, with its early emphasis on collectively created works, has been read historically as a protest against regional theatres' failure to get "in touch" with Canadian voices (a failure that has been blamed on the British organizational model inherited from Vincent Massey, along with his aspirations for a Canadian literary canon).[4] More recent scholarship, however, has challenged the "mythological nature of [that] history" (Barton, "Creating Spaces" viii), which did not account for the "nuances" at work within the "analytical category" (Knowles, *Reading* 130) it sought to define. To take one salient example, Tarragon Theatre, although usually classified as an influential member of the alternative movement, has in many respects maintained Massey's view of textual production as key to the success of Canada's theatrical development (Filewod qtd. in Barton viii).[5] It is likely not coincidental that both *Fronteras Americanas* and *White Biting Dog* were developed at Tarragon.[6] Bill Glassco, director of the original 1984 production of *White Biting Dog*, founded Tarragon "partly in reaction to what he saw as 'slapdash production standards'...at the Factory Theatre Lab" (Knowles, *Reading* 132). Glassco sought to elevate the status of theatre by investing in Canadian playwrights, and his theatre's loyalty to writers remains integral to its public profile.[7] Today, Tarragon Theatre is the kind of Canadian theatrical institution envisaged by Massey: one with a focus on literary production, whose premieres of new Canadian plays typically coincide with their publication.[8]

If the original Tarragon productions of *Fronteras Americanas* and *White Biting Dog* were "literary" in the sense that they grew out of aspirations for and have contributed to a printed literary canon, both plays nonetheless owe their status as Soulpepper's "Canadian classics" as much to their Tarragon productions as they do to their literary histories. Indeed, the publicity surrounding Soulpepper's 2011 productions indicated, directly and indirectly, that the original Tarragon productions were central to Soulpepper's decision to mount the plays. In the case of *Fronteras Americanas*, which won both a Chalmers Award and a Governor General's Literary Award after a successful run in Tarragon's Extra Space in January–February 1993 (Wasserman 309), Soulpepper announced, "Soulpepper Associate Artist, Guillermo Verdecchia, and director Jim Warren, are collaborating once again, after eighteen years, to introduce the Governor General's Award–winning *Fronteras Americanas* to new audiences" (Soulpepper, "Press Releases"). With this announcement,

Soulpepper positioned itself as renewing access to a classic stage production for audiences who missed the 1993 production.

Similarly, Nancy Palk, who directed the 2011 production of *White Biting Dog*, was quoted on Soulpepper's website:

> I was at the opening night of *White Biting Dog* in 1984 at Tarragon, and it was one of those wonderful fantastic opening nights...I've always been just crazy about it [the play]....Not only does it make a lot of sense for Soulpepper to be doing it because of Judith [Thompson]'s stature in Canadian theatre but also because Judith, Joe [Ziegler] and I all went to theatre school together. As did Louise Guinand, the lighting designer and Christina Poddubiuk, the costume and set designer. It really makes sense from the company's historical point of view. (Soulpepper, "White Biting Dog")

The memory of the 1984 production was at the forefront of Palk's mind as she approached her own production. Palk recalled a "fantastic" opening night, while Verdecchia and Warren revisited a previously successful production; both revivals were framed by Soulpepper as attempts to return in some way to a performed ideal, rather than a textual one. This was arguably a radical and progressive departure from traditional constructions of the Canadian canon, and one that reflected a movement (pace Nestruck) in both critical and academic circles. As Bruce Barton asks, "why not push hard on (even against) the historical preoccupation with a Canadian dramatic canon?" ("Evoking Theatre" 1).

Soulpepper's desire to revive performance history was as evident on stage as it was off stage, and (perhaps ironically) seems to have been the focus of much of the criticism of its 2011 revivals. In the one-man show *Fronteras Americanas*, for example, the playwright himself played the roles of "Wideload" and "Verdecchia," as he had done in the original production.[9] Despite major advances in the field of visual projection, Soulpepper also simulated the same kinds of performance technologies that were used in the 1994 production (the original production was innovative for its use of PowerPoint "slides"). It is not surprising, then, that the 2011 production of *Fronteras Americanas* was criticized for smelling "to high heaven of the early 1990s" (Nestruck, "Remount without a Cause").

Palk's *White Biting Dog* likewise referenced the play's Tarragon premiere, most vividly in Poddubiuk's evocation of Sue LePage's original set. Poddubiuk adapted LePage's rendering of the Bloor Street Viaduct, using the crisscross pattern that had appeared on LePage's arched, ceiling level "girders" as an element of the posts, which suggested both the bridge and the corners of the protagonist's home in the 2011 production. This design gesture arguably extended the original production's manipulation of stage reality, suggesting that Palk and Poddubiuk took seriously the principle (as Poddubiuk explained to Palk) that "it's not realism" (Soulpepper, "White Biting Dog"; see also our comments in "Visualizing Theatre Historiography").[10] Like the design of *Fronteras Americanas*, however, Poddubiuk's set was the focus of complaints that *White Biting Dog* was dated. For Cushman, for instance, the allusion of the bridge was unnecessary on the grounds that it was no longer a "practicable endeavour" to jump off the Bloor Street Viaduct, which has incorporated a suicide barrier since 2003; and he was unimpressed by the set's unrealistic blending of bridge and apartment, complaining that "Christina Poddubiuk's set does not seem to have mortgaged any appearance of domesticity for the sake of providing an upper level for the first brief scene on the bridge" ("Theatre Reviews").

Most likely, Nestruck, Cushman, and others were troubled by Soulpepper's canonization of *Fronteras Americanas* and *White Biting Dog* precisely because the company strove to excavate and enact a performance history and, in doing so, it projected a "false" universalism. Soulpepper seems to have assumed that the works in its canon had, as Knowles puts it, "universal meaning that is available for interpretation by audiences anywhere" and "that artistic inspiration transcends what are considered to be the accidentals of historical and cultural context, that it speaks across various kinds of difference to our common humanity" (Knowles, *Reading* 9). By drawing attention to the historical and cultural contexts of their premieres (in literal rather than conceptual terms—again, consider the decision to simulate early PowerPoint slides rather than explore newer technologies), Soulpepper revealed those contexts as anything but accidental and in turn called into question the universality of the inspirations that should have transcended them. Perhaps counterproductively, Soulpepper's move towards a canonization of performance—rather than published text—was the very gesture that challenged the notion of a Canadian theatrical canon.

Archiving Performance from an Interactive, Materialist-Semiotic Perspective

At the risk of buttressing the ivory tower of canon making that Nestruck has denounced, we would like to suggest that Soulpepper Theatre Company, by positioning its 2011 revivals as re-presentations of canonical performances, implicitly embraced what Knowles has called a "materialist semiotics" of the Canadian theatrical canon. Knowles borrows from theories of cultural materialism and theatre semiotics to analyze the ways a performance "text," which he defines broadly to include script, "mise en scene, design, actors' bodies, movement and gestures, etc." (Knowles, *Reading* 19), is a "product of a more complex mode of production" than its literary counterpart, one "that is rooted, as in all cultural production, in specific and determinate social and cultural contexts" (Knowles, *Reading* 10). He proposes three central "poles" in his triangular model of performance analysis: "performance text," "conditions of theatrical production," and "conditions of reception" (Knowles, *Reading* 19). These poles, Knowles asserts, work dynamically and relationally to create meaning (19) and, if we apply them in an analysis of Soulpepper's 2011 productions of *Fronteras Americanas* and *White Biting Dog*, we find evidence of all three in each play's production history.

Soulpepper's revivals were based on past performance "texts." Both revivals re-enacted past conditions of production in their use of theatre technologies, actors, and design gestures. Further, in the publicity framing the revivals, the conditions of their original reception were invoked. In drawing attention to these factors, Soulpepper staged what might be characterized as living histories: the productions and the publicity surrounding these performances operated as embodied archives of definitive previous performances. The company (perhaps unintentionally) drew attention to the shaping influences of the process of production—in this case historical influences—and consequently characterized the production histories of their revivals as among the texts, conditions of production, and reception that defined the 2011 performances.

To further complicate theoretical matters, this method of reproducing the Canadian canon—by engaging the written text as well as the material and cultural conditions that surrounded the text's original theatrical production—is as much anti-historical as it is a historicizing gesture. As Joseph Roach points out, "performance, like memory, operates as both quotation and invention" (33). Or, in Richard Schechner's formulation, because performance is repeated, it is "always subject to revision" and "reinvention from the second time to the nth time" (Schechner 36–37). Performance cannot occur the same way twice, even if a "constancy of transmission" (Schechner 36–37) implies a desire for exact reproduction. Hence, Soulpepper's 2011 revivals cited their originals, but also—and inevitably—foregrounded the differences between the revivals and their originals. In so doing, Soulpepper's Canadian canon became a process rather than an artifact, a gesture of canonization from the present rather than a presentation of a canonical object.

We must reiterate that Soulpepper's re-characterization of the Canadian theatrical canon was not necessarily unique. In fact, the company was one of several to stage revivals in recent seasons (Nestruck, "Canadian Revivals"). Moreover, Soulpepper may not subscribe to the notion of re-characterization that we posit here. If, however, we regard re-characterization as a shift in thinking about the Canadian theatrical canon that affirms the processes over the artifacts of canonization, then—with further apologies to Nestruck—Soulpepper's revivals may be seen as part of a broader movement in theatre studies to reconsider the nature and potential function of performance histories. Roach has been a leader in this movement; also key is Diana Taylor's formulation of the tensions between the archive (the written record) and the repertoire ("embodied practice/knowledge" [19]), both of which she sees as recording vestiges of past performances. It is perhaps not irrelevant, in light of Barton and Knowles's politically inflected accounts of the development

FILM PROJECTION / SOUND	TEXT / SONG	MOVEMENT
At the Toronto Warehouse:	*NEIGHBOUR sings a song in conjunction with a recording of her voice.*	*Off in a corner, barely visible at first, three women insinuate themselves into the room through a movement phrase that involves circulating from pillar to pillar.*
A percussive drumbeat begins to fill the room. A black and white triptych of a desert road is projected on the east wall while a colour image of shimmering city lights is projected onto the opposite wall.	NEIGHBOR *(singing)* Told you once, I told you twice, I've told you a thousand times. I told you once, I told you twice, I've told you a thousand times.	
	FATHER *(enters the space and addresses the audience)* Tell me something: Where do you think you belong? Let me rephrase: What nationality are you?	

Figure 3.1

Image of one page from Bluemouth Inc.'s archive of *What the Thunder Said*, with columns for "film projection/sound," "text/song," and "movement" as performed "At the Toronto Warehouse" (23).

FILM PROJECTION / SOUND	TEXT / SONG	MOVEMENT
At the AT&T Office Space:	American? Too vague. Dig deeper, try to feel the patriotism boomerang through time. Imagine yourself as your earliest ancestor. Wade past any forced allegiance to whoever let your forefathers and their loved ones survive. Try to find the essence of who you are. Close your eyes and ask yourself, 'Where do I belong?'	*Composition for Just Close Your Eyes.*
One of the white walls that made up the room in The Prologue is dismantled and carried to the far end of the room. Projected onto the dismantled wall is a black and white triptych of a desert road.	NEIGHBOUR *(singing)* It's time for a change, It's time for a change, It's time for a change...	
The Isadora software, operated in performance.		

Figure 3.2

Image of one page from Bluemouth Inc.'s archive of *What the Thunder Said*, with columns for "film projection/sound," "text/song," and "movement" as performed "At the AT&T Office Space" (24).

of Canada's theatrical canon, that Taylor's work is concerned principally with the politics of printed documentation and draws on de Certeau's analysis of archival knowledge's "immunization against alterity" (Taylor 19) to argue that the "degree of legitimization of writing over other epistemic and mnemonic systems" (Taylor 18) is largely the vestige of a colonial history.

Nonetheless, what a materialist-semiotic approach to canonization gains in richness and democracy it loses in stability, thoroughness, and detail; like all repertoires, the current "revival" movement remains a changing, incomplete, and approximate—perhaps even generalized—record of the past. Companies currently producing non-textual performance have been particularly conscious of the challenge of archiving their repertoires. Bluemouth Inc., for example, whose *What the Thunder Said* is a site-specific, participatory piece that changes with every venue, has produced a printed archive documenting performances in two different environments. It is presented in columns, one of which shows "Stage Directions: 2003 Production (rear unit of a Dufferin Street warehouse between Queen and King Streets, the west end of Toronto)," and another "Stage Directions: 2006 Production (stripped office space, historic AT&T building, lower Manhattan" (Bluemouth Inc. 21). Because of the limitations of print, overlay is impossible, so Bluemouth Inc. foregrounds sequentially the differences in material conditions that affected their final performance (see Figures 3.1 and 3.2).

In addition to stage directions, text, and "movement scores" (Bluemouth Inc. 24), Bluemouth Inc.'s non-traditional archival prompt book includes images of the "Isadora software operated in performance" (Bluemouth Inc. 24), photographic representations of several actors in performance (Bluemouth Inc. 28), and "textual commentary" from company members who self-reflexively evaluate the performance process (see Figure 3.3).

The design of Bluemouth Inc.'s script illustrates the methodology of its archival practices: "the text-performance-audience interaction should not be considered in a vacuum, but rather as an event embedded in a complex matrix of social concerns and actions, all of which 'communicate' or contribute to giving the theatre experience its particular

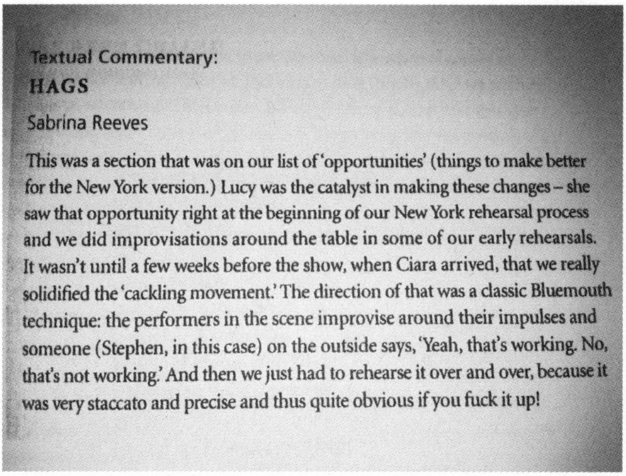
Textual Commentary:
HAGS
Sabrina Reeves

This was a section that was on our list of 'opportunities' (things to make better for the New York version.) Lucy was the catalyst in making these changes – she saw that opportunity right at the beginning of our New York rehearsal process and we did improvisations around the table in some of our early rehearsals. It wasn't until a few weeks before the show, when Ciara arrived, that we really solidified the 'cackling movement.' The direction of that was a classic Bluemouth technique: the performers in the scene improvise around their impulses and someone (Stephen, in this case) on the outside says, 'Yeah, that's working. No, that's not working.' And then we just had to rehearse it over and over, because it was very staccato and precise and thus quite obvious if you fuck it up!

Figure 3.3
Image of one page from Bluemouth Inc.'s archive of *What the Thunder Said*, showing a section of Sabrina Reeves's "textual commentary" (39).

'meaning' to its participants" (Carlson 5). This practice might equally be characterized, in Knowles's terms, as a cultural materialist approach to the printed archive. Although Bluemouth Inc.'s publication defines the parameters of its text, its conditions of production, and its reception, it also acknowledges the "invention" (Roach's term) in each performance by including records of two separate performances, and it engages its readers in an active process of reconstituting the performances it documents. Hence, this archive resists standardization and any implication of repeatability; instead, it offers its readers a set of choices from which to select and make new meanings. In a gesture paralleling its expectations of live audiences, Bluemouth Inc. asks readers to participate in constituting the meaning of its archive.[11]

Bluemouth Inc.'s interactive, materialist-semiotic approach to archiving its repertoire is equally current in the present Canadian performance ecology, where there has been an upsurge in archives that resist the legacy of literary canonization. Recently, a number of these archives have been collected in Barton's *Canadian Devised Theatre: Reluctant Texts from Exuberant Performance*, which he describes as "selections of documents that, arguably, first and foremost perform the limitations of print" ("Evoking Theatre" 1). With the emergence of the rich "devised theatre" tradition from which Barton's "texts" are drawn, the efficacy of the textual "canon" seems likely to become increasingly obsolete.

According to Barton,

> "devised theatre" is both a broadly defined and notoriously elusive category that incorporates a wide range of different objectives, techniques, and styles. However, in general, the terms identify an approach to theatrical creation and performance for which text is not accorded primary or "sacred" status—indeed one in which text may be secondary in terms of its authority within the developmental process and secondary in terms of the order in which the performance elements may be selected and incorporated into the final production. Rather, in devised theatre the elements of visual and aural presentation, as well as the work's engagement with narrative, equally emerge out of a set of processes that are based on interdisciplinarity, movement, improvisation, physical discipline, and the set of creative instruments understood and experienced as instinct and intuition. ("Evoking Theatre" 1)

Barton affirms the need for archives that do not purport to capture, reproduce, or define the essences of live performances, but instead offer experiences of meaning-making that are in some way analogous to the experiences they document. That analogy, as Bluemouth Inc.'s archive and Barton's collection illustrate, can be accomplished by means of an active exploration of the parameters (defined as narrowly and as vividly as possible) that generated the original "texts" and their conditions of production and performance. This conception of the archive is politically inflected insofar as the reader or researcher, the director, designer, or performer (in Soulpepper's case), the audience or critic (in Nestruck's view) contributes to a creative and cultural process of meaning-making.

White Biting Dog: Archiving the Repertoire

As the shortcomings of printed text as a means of archiving a theatrical canon become increasingly evident, the digital Simulated Environment for Theatre offers some useful functions with which to supplement print-based records. SET approaches the archive from a materialist-semiotic perspective, potentially foregrounding the archival function of the

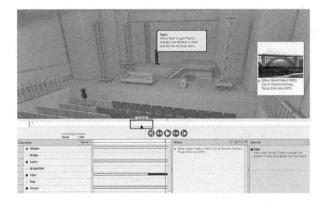

Figure 3.4
An excerpt from the opening sequence of Judith Thompson's *White Biting Dog*, as performed by Soulpepper Theatre in 2011. SET's Reading, Character, and Stage Views are linked by the central Line of Action and can be optionally annotated.

repertoire (to return to Taylor's term) by taking account of the shifting relationships between Knowles's poles of performance "text," conditions of production, and reception. Its interface offers three "Views," or distinct areas, linked by means of a central "Line of Action" analogous to a timeline. The Reading View contains text and annotations in parallel, two-dimensional panels. The Character View provides a list of characters and indicates which characters are on stage—speaking or silent—at any given point in a text or performance. The Stage View shows a scaled, three-dimensional model of a performance environment, populated by abstract avatars that can be moved around in the space, and optionally annotated with text or images (see Figure 3.4).

Changes to any one view are automatically reflected in the other views, and both text and staging can be played back simultaneously in real time. Additionally, SET permits users to navigate through the three-dimensional space of the Stage View and adopt the perspective of any character avatar or audience member at any point in space, as an analogue for the various perspectives experienced by performers and audiences during live theatrical events (see Figures 3.5A, 3.5B, and 3.5C).

SET also emphasizes the agency of the user in constituting the meaning of a performance, since all of SET's functions are user controlled (though the interface can be used in playback mode to view what others have created). Users can input and edit texts, create and upload three-dimensional models of performance environments, move character

Figures 3.5a, 3.5b, and 3.5c
Excerpts from the opening sequence of Judith Thompson's *White Biting Dog*, as performed by Soulpepper Theatre in 2011. SET allows users to adopt the perspectives of audience and character avatars.

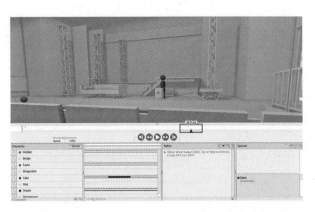

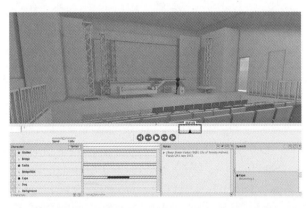

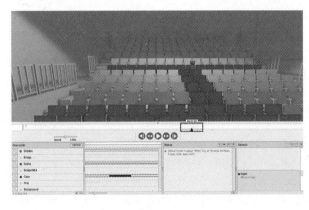

avatars around in the models, annotate all elements of the environment, link text and annotations to stage action, and control the pace and perspective of performance in playback. Although its two principal interpretive modes—data creation and data playback—are interactive, SET also can produce more stable artifacts akin to written and material archives, since data can be exported in publication mode as read-only files or as playback movies. Lastly, because it is a virtual environment, SET can offer hypothesized and hybridized performance histories, allowing users not only to archive aspects of a performance (real or imagined), but also to visualize the genealogies of a performance history.

Our team already has theorized the potential for these functionalities to enhance approaches to theatre history and historiography (Roberts-Smith et al., "Visualizing Theatre Historiography). In practising this research methodology—by inputting and analyzing the materials from the production histories related to the canonical texts performed at Soulpepper—we also came to realize that SET has the further potential to assemble a corpus of performances of individual plays that make up the canon. SET can house not only a play script, but also the various visualizations of that play script's theatrical history, the archival documents that validate that history, and the ephemeral memories that reshape theatrical knowledge. The analysis of electronic corpora, what Douglas Biber describes as "large systematic collections of spoken and/or written text stored on a computer," has been used for decades to consider the "lexical and grammatical variations" (20) of language use. Applying a similar methodology to a visualized performance corpus in SET might help articulate the "proof" that accounts for the place of individual plays or groups of plays in the "substantial body of proven plays" (Salter 82) constituting the Canadian canon.

Visualizing the Performance "Text"

Perhaps the most obvious advantage to using the SET system as an archive is that its Stage View foregrounds the ways in which a theatrical "text" is constituted mutually by a variety of textual and non-textual theatrical elements. For example, neither the 1984 nor the 2011 production of *White Biting Dog* performed its text as it was first published in 1985 or in subsequent editions. All three versions of the play (1984, 1985, and 2011) begin with accounts of Cape's attempted suicide. In the 1984 production, however, Cape reported his suicide attempt in a direct address to the audience that was significantly longer than the first published version of 1985; and, in 2011, the sequence was cut and altered so that Cape turned to the audience later and the exchange between Cape and the dog was enacted instead of reported. This alteration signalled that the 2011 production defined reality (or unreality, as Palk and Poddubiuk might put it) differently from the 1984 production and from the 1985 edition. In 1984, when eye contact and direct communication between character and audience was established immediately and the conversation with the dog was reported, the audience might have believed that the play-world operated according to the same rules as ordinary reality, and that Cape had imagined the dog; the 1985 text implied this same effect in fewer words. In 2011, however, Cape did not begin in direct address, and the dog spoke for itself. Immediately, the rules of the play-world (where dogs could speak) were significantly different from the rules of ordinary reality. But, when Cape turned to address the audience directly and viewers were suddenly defined as occupants of his unreal world, the ordinary reality the audience thought it occupied became as susceptible to redefinition as the play-world. If Cape could see the audience and viewers could see him and hear the dog, then either their sanity was as much in question as Cape's or all reality—fictional and non-fictional—was radically perceptual. This significant development in the performance "text," which relied on contrasting manipulations of space between productions—at times within a single production—is entirely occluded by the print transmission of the script. In contrast, since materialist-semiotic visualization tools permit users to organize space and time as well as the written word, SET can illustrate the ways in which the 1984 and 2011 productions constructed the materialist-semiotic performance "text" differently to define on- and off-stage realities (see figures 3.6, 3.7A, and 3.7B). (See also our comments on this sequence in Roberts-Smith et al., "Visualizing Theatre Historiography.")

Figure 3.6
Cape reporting his conversation with the dog to the audience in the 1984 Tarragon Theatre production of *White Biting Dog*. In Sue LePage's set, the Bloor Street Viaduct is suggested by girder-like structures at ceiling level.

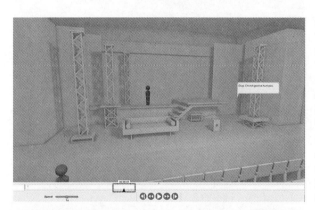

Figure 3.7A
The dog speaking in the 2011 Soulpepper Theatre production of *White Biting Dog*. In Christina Poddubiuk's set, the Bloor Street Viaduct is suggested by posts that operate as bridge girders in this sequence and later as the corners of Cape's apartment.

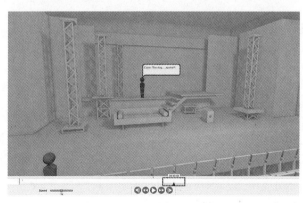

Figure 3.7B
Cape turning to the audience at "the dog spoke!" in the 2011 Soulpepper Theatre production of *White Biting Dog*.

Figure 3.8
Sue LePage's set for the 1984 Tarragon Theatre production of *White Biting Dog* included a ramp through the audience connecting the stage to the lobby.

SET's attempts to visualize textual multiplicities extends and amplifies similar materialist-semiotic gestures made in print-based archives such as Bluemouth Inc.'s archival prompt book; here, SET visualizes "textual" conditions of performance in a vivid dimensional image of the media in which they were first experienced (space and time) that is not accessible in print.

Visualizing Conditions of Production

As Jonathan Dollimore and Alan Sinfield put it, "texts [are] inseparable from the conditions of their production and reception in history [and are] involved, necessarily, in the making of cultural meanings which are always, finally, political meanings" (qtd. in Knowles, *Reading* 13). The three-dimensional models we created for our visualizations of the 1984 and 2011 productions of *White Biting Dog* not only illustrated significant differences in set design, which Knowles would classify as an element of the extended theatrical "text," they also drew our attention to some of the conditions of production Knowles emphasizes. In particular, the "stage and backstage architectures" (Knowles, *Reading* 19) of the Tarragon Theatre and the Young Centre for the Performing Arts (the home of the Soulpepper Theatre Company) had political implications

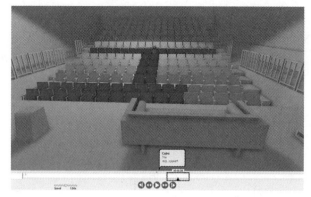

Figure 3.9
View from the stage
of the Michael Young
Theatre, where there
was no architectural
possibility of connec-
ting audience to
lobby in the 2011
Soulpepper Theatre
production of *White
Biting Dog*.

we had not previously considered. In the 1984 set, a ramp or walk-
way (representing the sidewalk outside Cape's home and used for stage
entrances and exits) extended out from the stage, through the audience,
and into the lobby of the Tarragon Theatre (see Figure 3.8).

This was a political design gesture, which implicated the audience in
the psychological deterioration of the play's characters (see Nunn 28) in
a manner arguably consistent with Thompson's work in general. In contrast, the 2011 Soulpepper production routed actors around the audience
seated in the Young Centre's Michael Young Theatre (Roberts-Smith et
al., "Visualizing Theatre Historiography"). In fact, it was not feasible to
build a ramp from the Michael Young Theatre stage through the audience to the Young Centre lobby (see Figure 3.9).

Before we visualized the sets, we had not interpreted the architecture
of either Tarragon Theatre or the Michael Young Theatre as politically
inflected; in practice, however, their respective layouts limited the range
of meanings that could be articulated theatrically.[12] Of course, we are not
suggesting that Soulpepper's production of *White Biting Dog* was a critical failure due solely to the theatre's architectural differences from the
original venue of Tarragon Theatre's Mainspace. Rather, what a comparative visualization illustrates is that one (of many) often-overlooked
circumstances of production inhibited the replication of a previous
canonical performance. As stated earlier, Soulpepper posited a kind
of "cultural modelling" in relationship to canon formation and envisaged a "replication" of past performance conditions of Thompson's play

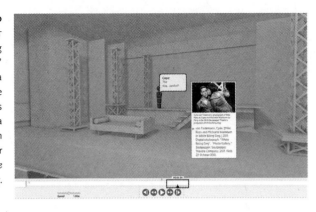

Figure 3.10
Section of the SET interface showing "the dog spoke!" annotated with a photographic image of Mike Ross as Cape and Michaela Washburn as Pony in the 2011 Soulpepper production of *White Biting Dog.*

(Sela-Sheffy 150). In SET's comparative visualization, such a transhistorical notion is shown to be fallacious. In fact, SET foregrounds the material factors that make such an attempt impossible. SET shows the way in which performance, as Knowles formulates, ultimately is always susceptible to change (and varied critical reception) depending on the conditions of production (paramount, in this case, the contingencies of space).

While SET is useful in serendipitously illustrating the changeability of theatrical production, we nonetheless are aware that SET visualizes some of Knowles's conditions of production differently from others, and in so doing may imply a hierarchy of importance among those conditions. Whereas spaces are simulated in SET's three-dimensional stage view, other conditions—"actor, director, designer training and traditions, rehearsal process, working conditions" (Knowles, *Reading* 19)—can only be visualized as two-dimensional annotations in SET's interface. Some of these are paratheatrical activities, either physically or chronologically distant from any given performance of a play—designer training or the rehearsal process, for example—and, as such, they exceed SET's central mandate to archive the experience of live performance and hence are relegated appropriately to two-dimensionality. Others—actors' bodies in particular—are central to a materialist-semiotic understanding of performance experience; we might even contest Knowles's classification of the actor's body as a condition of production rather than an element of the performance "text." Up to this stage of project development, our approach to avatar design has been to deliberately avoid representing the individual

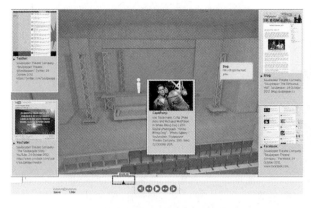

Figure 3.11
A visualization of the 2011 Soulpepper production of *White Biting Dog* annotated with publicity materials hyperlinked to original online sources.

identities of actors (Ruecker et al.). Instead, we offer highly abstract representation of characters that are distinguished from one another only by colour, size, and human or non-human form, and optionally annotated with supplemental photographs of actors playing characters (see Figure 3.10; Roberts-Smith et al., "Visualizing Theatre Historiography").

Visualizing Conditions of Reception

SET's annotation function also has been useful in visualizing Knowles's third "pole" of theatrical analysis, conditions of reception, which include "publicity/review discourse, front of house, auditorium, and audience amenities, neighborhood, transportation, ticket prices, historical/cultural moment of reception, etc." (Knowles, *Reading* 19). Above, we have discussed the impact of publicity and reviews on the reception of Soulpepper's productions of *Fronteras Americanas* and *White Biting Dog*; records of all the sources we cite could be provided as annotations to simulations of the performances, with annotations referring to online sources hyperlinked to the originals (see Figure 3.11).

To deconstruct and illustrate the politics of those reviews, SET can visualize the difference Cushman notes between the cultural historical moments of the 1984 and the 2011 productions of *White Biting Dog*—specifically, the addition of the suicide barrier to the Bloor Street Viaduct. Until the suicide barrier was added in 2003, the Viaduct had remained

Figure 3.12A Side view of the Bloor Street Viaduct in 1920.
[City of Toronto Archives, fonds 1244, item 2473]

Figure 3.12B *Side view of the Bloor Street Viaduct in 1984.*
[City of Toronto Archives, fonds 268, file 7, item 11]

Figure 3.12c
Bloor Street Viaduct
after the 2003
addition of a suicide
barrier designed by
Dereck Revington.
This architectural
project was titled *The
Luminous Veil.*
*[Photo by Dereck
Revington]*

visually consistent for the better part of a century (note especially the crisscross pattern in its girders; see Figures 3.12A, 3.12B, and 3.12C).[13]

For audience members familiar with the cityscape of Toronto, the adverse effect of the suicide barrier upon the plausibility of the play's action may have been as salient as it was for Cushman. Similarly, members of the 2011 audience who, like Palk and her team, had seen the 1984 production of *White Biting Dog* may, like Cushman, have been especially conscious of the way in which the viaduct's new architecture affected the 2011 production's ability to construct a relationship between the stage

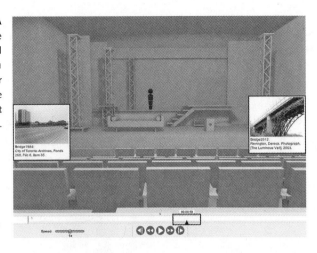

Figure 3.13A
A visualization of the cultural historical moments of a 2011 audience member who remembers the Bloor Street Viaduct of 1984.

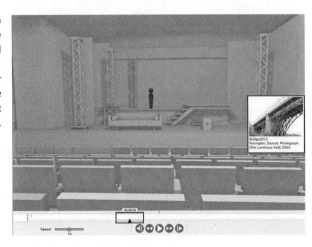

Figure 3.13B
A visualization of the cultural historical moments of a 2011 audience member who never visited the Bloor Street Viaduct of 1984.

world and the world outside the theatre. As Cushman suggests, the reality of the suicide barrier effectively fictionalized the opening event of the play, and consequently historicized the play as an artifact from a pre-barrier era. Of course, not all audience members would have responded as Cushman did, especially those who were not familiar with the history of the bridge. To distinguish between individual audience members' experiences and memories, SET also allows users to collapse annotations when they are not relevant (see Figures 3.13A and 3.13B).

The user's ability to include annotations and construct visualizations moves the scope and range of set's documentation of production histories beyond the theatrical context itself; it offers the ability to account for how specific historical differences (produced in this case by age, geography, and cultural experience outside the theatrical space) can affect and indeed constitute an audience member's relationship to a particular production. This approach to documenting reception is yet another complex functionality of set; it implicitly asks the user to reject the bias of transhistoricism, which, as Knowles asserts, typically characterizes assessments of a play's canonicity. set offers a function whereby users are encouraged to account for the historical context within which a play is produced and received, the cultural markers it refers to, and the ways in which distinct (even unique) sets of memories and experiences produce a play's multiple meanings in performance. This function supplements and redefines the relationship to canonical text and canonical performance (in Soulpepper's formulation) by foregrounding the relationship to a corpus of knowledge and experience that exists within and outside of the theatrical space, both simultaneous with and asynchronous to any individual performance experience.

Multiplicity, Imagination, and Interactivity

In addition to potentially contrasting memories of the pre-1984 Bloor Street Viaduct, viewers of the 2011 production of *White Biting Dog* may also have had contrasting memories of the 1984 Tarragon production of Thompson's play. One way to illustrate the influence of such memories upon the reception of the 2011 Soulpepper production might be to create a hybrid model of the 2011 and 1984 sets illustrating Poddubiuk's response to LePage's design gesture (see Figure 3.14). We created such a model when first testing set's functionality.

While this image does visualize conditions of reception, it is also, as we argue above, an imaginary space that allows users to ask speculative questions about a hypothetical performance that was not actually experienced. Indeed, in its "ability to alter and experiment with attested

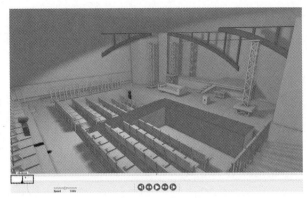

Figure 3.14
Section of the SET interface showing bridge girders and ramp from Sue LePage's 1984 design for *White Biting Dog* superimposed on Christina Poddubiuk's 2011 design.

historical performance environments...SET allows us to ask, in a relatively quick and inexpensive way, 'what if?'" (Roberts-Smith et al., "Visualizing Theatre Historiography"). To augment Knowles's rubric, we might call this kind of visualization an immaterialist semiotic, one that draws attention to the instability of performative meanings—not just under different performance conditions, as does Bluemouth Inc.'s archive, and not just under different conditions of reception, as does our comparison in Figures 3.13A and 3.13B, but also according to the creative agency of the archivist. This chapter argues for the impact of *White Biting Dog* through the lens of SET's publication mode—in particular its capacity to capture stable images of different states of our visualized archive of the 2011 production—and by exporting those images for examination outside of SET. But users with access to a copy of SET could add or remove representations of any element from any of Knowles's three poles of materialist-semiotic analysis at will, thereby changing the archive to reflect differences in individual audience members' recollections, interpretations, and applications of the performance after the event. Since any given visualization of a performance is only optionally recorded and exported as a "publication" in the SET system, the approach to archiving employed here is, to use Taylor's term again (with some qualification), reportorial. Whereas Taylor expresses serious concern about the lack of embodiment in digital environments and their consequent inability to participate in epistemologies of performance (Taylor 16), SET offers users not the embodied experience of audience or performer, but the embodied experience of the archivist. Its users are required to create and interact with records of performance, and thereby are involved in the process of performing the archive. In SET, the archive is primarily practised rather than written or read; its users are inescapably both the subjects and the objects of the histories they generate. In this way, SET perhaps resists the politics of colonialism implicit in the typographical historical canon that is fixed and instead proposes an archive that can visualize the dynamism of transmission, revision, and alteration. There is, however, a cost to the application of SET: an acceptance of the particularities of the digital environment that, along with its vast ability to collect artifacts ranging from the historical to the speculative, also demands that representations be schematic and reduced to the scale of display.

Archiving the Archive

Despite our emphasis on the repertoire over the written archive, probably the most vivid contrast between SET and other digital performance simu-lation systems (such as Virtual Vaudeville, Ortelia, or Theatron 3) is the presence of theatrical text as a constant feature of its interface (Roberts-Smith et al., "Visualizing Theatre Historiography"). The emphasis that SET's Reading View inevitably places upon an analogue for printed edi-tions arguably perpetuates the received ideas about the literary nature of the Canadian canon that scholars such as Knowles, Barton, and Salter have aimed to complicate. Like Bluemouth Inc.'s archive, or Barton's collection of performance texts, SET is as invested in the stability of its records as it is in enabling a range of interpretive interactions with those same records. Because SET is a repository rather than a collection, how-ever, it can also offer a meta-archival layer of visualization, potentially characterizing the archive itself as susceptible to a materialist-semiotic analysis. On the most literal level, SET can provide transparent docu-mentation of the provenance of the records it synthesizes in the form of annotations (see, for example, our bibliographic citations for photographs in Figures 3.10 and 3.12A–C). It also permits analyses of records, such

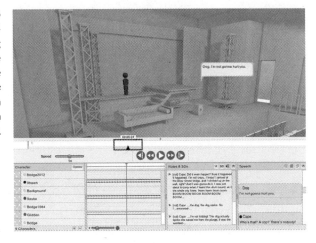

Figure 3.15
Our model of Sue LePage's set for the 1984 Tarragon Theatre production of *White Biting Dog*, annotated with a section of LePage's technical drawings showing her designs for the bridge girders and an image of the bridge they represent.

Figure 3.16
The invisible off-stage dog speaking to Cape in 2011. The text cut from the 1984 version of *White Biting Dog* is shown in an annotation in Text View.

as our models of the sets for *White Biting Dog*, to be annotated with the sources on which they are based (see Figure 3.15).

SET can also visualize the relationships between complementary or even contrasting records in an archive, showing, for example, changes made by the 2011 production to the text recorded in the 1984 prompt book of *White Biting Dog* (see Figure 3.16).

Most interestingly for our purposes, however, the visual separa-tion of the Reading View and the Stage View in SET's interface implies the same disparity between the typographical and performance tradi-tions, or between the archive and the repertoire, in Canadian theatre that recent scholarship and criticism have noted. That separation highlights the written word as susceptible, like other moments captured in the archival records of production, to repertorial change over time. Although SET does not yet offer a means of visualizing cause and effect, future iterations might do so and, if they do, we might use SET to visualize the intervention that Soulpepper's productions have made in the print-based Canadian theatrical canon (Roberts-Smith et al., "Visualizing Theatre Historiography"). It might even be possible in SET, by manipulating emphases in the Reading and Text Views, to show the repertoire influencing the archive, and vice versa.

Conclusion: Archiving a Corpus Rather Than a Canon?

As theatre historian Alan Filewod proposes, "the thesis that theatrical governance and canonicity are indexical of nationhood has collapsed to the point where it has widely been critiqued as an instrument of historical racism and class hegemony" (Filewod, "Named in Passing" 118). Indeed, to talk of the Canadian canon today is to discuss a "transhistorical textual community" that many might assert is necessarily obsolete in the wake of our acknowledgement that "texts do not have a single, authoritative meaning, however much the established spokesmen for the canon at any given moment may claim that is the case" (Alter 5). Despite these theoretical advances, the critical responses to Soulpepper's productions of both *Fronteras Americanas* and *White Biting Dog* confirm that canonicity—an idea with lingering resonance—arguably could be used to discredit the worth of historical performance traditions when they no longer speak to current arbiters of taste. Rather than deny the value of printed texts that undoubtedly have affected the collective memory of theatregoers, we propose that SET can assemble various performance texts, visualize the ways they constitute meaning, and potentially analyze those materials as a corpus. We hope this kind of archive might facilitate an understanding of Canadian theatre as more than a "substantial body of proven plays," as Salter has suggested was characteristic of Massey's theatrical federalism (82). Rather, this corpus might visualize the synergies across a play's production and reception histories as a vehicle for witnessing and experiencing the operations of nationhood that are, to quote Filewod again, "enacted in the imagined theatre" (*Performing Canada* 1).

AUTHORS' NOTE

This research was funded by an Image, Text, Sound, and Technology Grant and a Standard Research Grant from the Social Sciences and Humanities Research Council of Canada. We are grateful to Eleanor Antoncic and Sue LePage (Tarragon Theatre); Drew Baker (Theatron 3); Toby Malone, Christina Poddubiuk, and Kelly Read (Soulpepper Theatre Company); Dereck Revington (University of Waterloo); the City of Toronto Archives; and the L.W. Conolly Theatre Archives (University of Guelph).

NOTES

1. Ric Knowles, in his analysis of the establishment of the English-Canadian canon, confirms the historical contexts that shape Nestruck's assertion: "before 1980 few Canadian scripts received a second production" (Knowles, "Voices (Off)" 91). Knowles suggests that the "quixotic and unpredictable" nature of the Canadian dramatic environment ("Voices (Off)" 91) led to the development of three "national anthologies" that sought to stabilize the dramatic canon. One of these, Jerry Wasserman's two-volume anthology, *Modern Canadian Plays*, which features the work of Judith Thompson (*Lion in the Streets*) and Guillermo Verdecchia (*Fronteras Americanas*) in its fourth (2011) edition, "shaped curricula" and "heavily influenced subsequent scholarship" (Knowles, "Voices (Off)" 95). André Loiselle's assertion that the anthology was the most distinguished of a group first published in the mid-1980s (n. pag.) points to the continual praise bestowed upon this text. Thompson's *White Biting Dog* appears, perhaps not coincidentally, in a 2003 collection of her work introduced by Knowles, entitled *Late 20th Century Plays*. Nonetheless, the production histories of *White Biting Dog* and *Fronteras Americanas* are far from extensive. There is a discrepancy between the discourse of the canonization project (see below), which for the first time made these texts accessible and soon widely taught, and the theatre community's allegiance to that project. Though *White Biting Dog* did have a subsequent production in 1990 at the Grand Theatre (dir. Maya Ardal) after its 1984 premiere at Tarragon Theatre (dir. Bill Glassco), and though it returned to Tarragon on its ten-year anniversary in 1994 (dir. Morris Panych), before its Soulpepper revival the play never reached large audiences. Similarly, after the 1993 premiere of *Fronteras Americanas* at Tarragon (dir. Jim Warren), Theatre Aquarius produced the play in 1995 (dir. Christopher McHarge) and the only other production, prior to Soulpepper's, was at the Adelaide, Australia 9's Nexus Multicultural Arts Festival (dir. Sam Haren) (for references regarding this production history see Ardal; Glassco; Haren; McHarge; Panych; Warren). According to the Canadian Actors' Equity Association's classification system, which ranks theatres according to box office potential, the

2011 productions of *White Biting Dog* at the Young Centre's Michael Young Theatre (category D) and *Fronteras Americanas* at the Young Centre's Marilyn and Charles Baillie Theatre (category A) promoted both plays to higher ranked venues than previous productions (CAEA).

2. Eugene Benson and L.W. Conolly suggest that the "alternate theatre in Canada emerged in the 1960's" and was "prompted by a changing political climate at home and a groundswell of interest in Canadian history, culture, and institutions" (85). They identify Toronto Workshop Productions (TWP) under the leadership of George Luscombe as the "forerunner" (Benson and Conolly 86) to this movement. Other significant companies include Factory Theatre Lab (now Factory Theatre), Tarragon Theatre, and Theatre Passe Muraille (TPM). For a more thorough discussion of the history and characteristics of this movement, see Denis Johnston's *Up the Mainstream: The Rise of Toronto's Alternative Theatres*. For a more detailed analysis of Tarragon's position within that framework, see Johnston's *Diverting the Mainstream: Bill Glassco and the Early Years of Tarragon Theatre*.

3. Since 2007, Soulpepper has mounted David French's *Of the Fields, Lately* (Chalmers Award for Best New Canadian Play, 1974), *Salt-Water Moon* (Nominee for the Governor General's Literary Award for Drama, 1985), and *Jitters*; John Gray's *Billy Bishop Goes to War* (Chalmers Award for Best New Canadian Play, 1982; Governor General's Literary Award for Drama, 1982); John Murrell's *Waiting for the Parade* (Chalmers Award for Best New Canadian Play, 1977; Governor General's Lifetime Artistic Achievement Award, 2008); and Sharon Pollock's *Doc* (Chalmers Award for Best New Canadian Play, 1984; Governor General's Literary Award for Drama, 1986).

4. The development of a number of regional theatres in major urban centres throughout Canada was part of the "monument complex" or "edifice complex" at work in the late 1950s to the early 1970s Canadian theatrical ecology (see Kilbourn et al.). Public investment in theatre buildings and infrastructure (Arts Club Theatre, Vancouver Playhouse, Theatre Calgary, Citadel Theatre, Globe Theatre, Royal Manitoba Theatre Centre, Neptune Theatre, Theatre New Brunswick) was made in the wake of the Massey Report of 1951, which also led to the establishment in 1957 of the Canada Council for the Arts (a government subsidy system to the arts). Many of the regional theatres are characterized conventionally as endorsing "conservative repertoires, a mistrust of Canadian drama, middle-class audiences, and a marked tendency to prefer foreign, usually British, artistic directors" (Filewod, "Erasing" 202). Alan Filewod notes that the alternative houses of TPM, TWP, and Tarragon, in the late 1960s to the mid-1970s ushered in a "historical crisis" by "overshadow[ing]" and "challeng[ing]" regional theatres with an "experimental" and "nationalistic" fervour that has been characterized as a kind of "cultural heroism" ("Erasing" 202). See Filewod, "Erasing Historical Difference"; Knowles, *Reading the Material Theatre*; and note 5 below for a more complex discussion of the methodological dangers of this "mainstream/alternative paradigm" (Filewod, "Erasing" 202).

5. Knowles notes, "most scholars in recent years have become uncomfortable with a 'mainstream-alternative' binary" (*Reading* 130). He goes on to articulate Tarragon Theatre's specific "discomfort" with the "alternative label": "Although Tarragon has always been anxious to position itself 'on the cutting edge,' and although its play development mandate and relatively small budget set it apart from the Regional Theatre network from the beginning, the theatre has produced in its policies,

procedures, physical arrangements, public profile and production history a discourse of stability, balance, comfort and quality that sets it apart from organizations such as the Factory Theatre, with its discourse of excitement, adventure, and risk" (Knowles, *Reading* 130).

6. *Fronteras Americanas* premiered at Tarragon Theatre's Extra Space after development workshops at the Canadian Stage Company and Tarragon (Wasserman 309).

7. Tarragon Theatre currently supports twelve playwrights in residence (Tarragon Theatre, "Playwrights-in-Residence").

8. *Fronteras Americanas* was published by Coach House Press in 1993. It premiered at Tarragon Theatre in January–February of that year. Similarly, *White Biting Dog* premiered in January of 1984 and the first edition appeared that same year. More recent examples include Erin Shields's *If We Were Birds* (premiere in 2010; publication by Playwrights Canada Press in 2011) and Brendan Gall's *Wide Awake Hearts* (produced in 2010; publication by Coach House Press in 2010 in Gall's collection *Minor Complications*).

9. There is a difficulty in using an alternate actor, since this one-man show is a personal story and features a character named Verdecchia. Verdecchia himself, however, has expressed a desire for alternate casting scenarios: "I'd love to see—some day, I hope—a production of *Fronteras Americanas* that is transgendered and cast with an Asian actor, or something. I'd really like to see somebody take the border theme to the nth degree" (qtd. in Wasserman 310). This suggests that the 2011 casting of Verdecchia was deliberate.

10. On Thompson's style and its relationship to Tarragon Theatre's aesthetic, see Knowles ("Introduction"). By 1995, all of Thompson's plays (save for the "anomalous" productions of *The Crackwalker* and *Habitat*) had premiered at Tarragon (Knowles, "Introduction" xiii). More recently, *Palace of the End* received its premiere at the Canadian Stage Company in 2008, but it is not surprising that in her early career Thompson maintained a close link to Tarragon because her aesthetic, which stretches the limits of naturalism in subtle ways, became a signature of sorts for Tarragon Theatre. Following Glassco, Tarragon's second artistic director Urjo Kareda claimed a "mysterious richness" in his theatre's naturalistic plays (qtd. in Knowles, *Reading* 136). Though Thompson's work often is described as "magic realism" (see, for example, Maufort), her work still "rarely break[s] through" the "boundaries of naturalism" (Knowles, *Reading* 136). See also our comments below on Poddubiuk's set.

11. See Keren Zaiontz's analysis of *What the Thunder Said*, which discusses the ways Bluemouth Inc. "integrates spectators into the performance event" (10). This remains a salient feature of Bluemouth Inc.'s work: in its more recent production of *Dance Marathon* (which premiered at Harbourfront Centre's World Stage in 2008–09), the audience actively competed in the performed "marathon."

12. For more on the way in which SET can instigate the exploration and comparison of performance environments, see Roberts-Smith et al., "Visualizing Theatre Historiography."

13. The Bloor Street Viaduct also has a significant Canadian literary history, which unfortunately lies beyond the scope of this chapter. See, for example, Michael Ondaatje's novel *In the Skin of a Lion*.

Al-Solaylee, Kamal. "Dead White Guys: European Classics Still Dominate Canadian Theatres." *Walrus* September 2011. http://walrusmagazine.com/articles/2011.09-theatre-dead-white-guys

Alter, Robert. *Canon and Creativity: Modern Writing and the Authority of Scripture.* New Haven, CT: Yale University Press, 2000.

Ardal, Maya, dir. Graphic poster for production of *White Biting Dog*, by Judith Thompson. Grand Theatre, London, ON, 1990. L.W. Conolly Theatre Archives, University of Guelph Library, Guelph, ON.

Barton, Bruce. "Creating Spaces." *Developing Nation: New Play Creation in English-Speaking Canada.* Ed. Barton. Toronto: Playwrights Canada Press, 2009. v–xxii.

———. "Evoking Theatre: From Reluctance to Exuberance." *Canadian Devised Theatre: Reluctant Texts from Exuberant Performance.* Ed. Bruce Barton, Natalie Corbett, Birgit Schreyer Duarte, and Keren Zaiontz. Ottawa: Borealis Press, 2008. 1–5.

Benson, Eugene, and L.W. Conolly. *English-Canadian Theatre.* Toronto: Oxford University Press, 1987.

Biber, Douglas. "Corpus Linguistics and the Study of Literature: Back to the Future?" *Scientific Study of Literature* 1.1 (2011): 15–23.

[Bloor Street Viaduct in 1920]. City of Toronto Archives, fonds 1244, item 2473.

[Bloor Street Viaduct in 1984, Side View]. City of Toronto Archives, fonds 268, file 7, item 11.

Bluemouth Inc. "What the Thunder Said." *Canadian Devised Theatre: Reluctant Texts from Exuberant Performance.* Ed. Bruce Barton, Natalie Corbett, Birgit Schreyer Duarte, and Keren Zaiontz. Ottawa: Borealis Press, 2008. 18–57.

Canadian Actors' Equity Association (CAEA). "Canadian Theatre Agreement for 2009–2012." *Equity Online.* http://www.caea.com

Canadian Theatre Review. Website. University of Toronto Press Journals, 2011. http://www.utpjournals.com/Canadian-Theatre-Review.html

Carlson, Marvin. *Places of Performance: The Semiotics of Theatre Architecture.* New York: Cornell University Press, 1993.

Cushman, Robert. "Theatre Reviews: Savage Whimsy in *White Biting Dog* and Cirque's *Totem.*" *National Post* 26 August 2011. http://arts.nationalpost.com/2011/08/26/theatre-reviews-savage-whimsy-in-white-biting-dog-and-cirques-totem

DeSouza-Coelho, Shawn. [Bloor Street Viaduct, Street View.] Toronto, Ontario, 2012.

Dondis, Donis A. *A Primer of Visual Literacy.* Cambridge, MA: MIT Press, 1973.

Glassco, Bill, dir. *White Biting Dog*, by Judith Thompson. Set Sue LePage. Perf. Jackie Burroughs, Clare Coulter, Hardee T. Lineham, Stephen Ouimette, Larry Reynolds. Archival VHS, Private Collection, Tarragon Theatre, 1984.

Filewod, Alan. "Erasing Historical Difference: The Alternative Orthodoxy in Canadian Theatre." *Theatre Journal* 41 (May 1989): 201–10.

———. "Named in Passing: Deregimenting Canadian Theatre History." *Writing and Rewriting National Theatre Histories.* Ed. S.E. Wilmer. Iowa City: University of Iowa Press, 2004. 106–26.

———. *Performing Canada: The Nation Enacted in the Imagined Theatre.* Textual Studies in Canada Monograph Series: Critical Performance/s in Canada. Kamloops, BC: Textual Studies in Canada, 2002.

———. "Undermining the Centre: The Canon According to CTR." *Theatre Research in Canada / Recherches théâtrales au Canada* 11.2 (1990): 1–4.

Haren, Sam, dir. *Fronteras Americanas*, by Guillermo Verdecchia. Perf. Alirio Zavarce. Nexus Cabaret, Lion Arts Centre, June 2001. *Theatre Australia.*

Johnston, Denis. *Diverting the Mainstream: Bill Glassco and the Early Years of Tarragon Theatre.* N.p.: n.p., 1988. [Available at Tarragon Theatre].

———. *Up the Mainstream: The Rise of Toronto's Alternative Theatres.* Toronto: University of Toronto Press, 1991.

King's Visualization Lab. "Theatron Final Report." *Theatron 3: Educational Undertakings in Second Life.* English Subject Centre, The Higher Education Academy, Council for College and University Education, 2009. http://www.english.heacademy.ac.uk/ explore/projects/archive/technology/tech23.php

Kilbourn, William, Jean Roberts, David Gardner, David Peacock, Claude Des Landes, and Walter Learning. "The Canada Council and the Theatre: The Past Twenty-Five Years and Tomorrow." *Theatre Research in Canada / Recherches théâtrales au Canada* 3.2 (1982). http://journals.hil.unb.ca/index.php/TRIC/article/view/7487

Knowles, Ric. "Introduction: Judith Thompson in Criticism." *Judith Thompson: Critical Perspectives on Canadian Theatre in English.* Ed. Knowles. Vol. 3. Toronto: Playwrights Canada Press, 2005. vii–xv.

———. *Reading the Material Theatre.* Cambridge: Cambridge University Press, 1994.

———. "Voices (Off): Deconstructing the Modern English-Canadian Dramatic Canon. *Canadian Canons: Essays in Literary Value.* Ed. Robert Lecker. Toronto: University of Toronto Press, 1991. 91–111.

LePage, Sue, des. Technical drawings for *White Biting Dog*, by Judith Thompson. Tarragon Theatre, Toronto, ON, 1984. L.W. Conolly Theatre Archives, University of Guelph Library, Guelph, ON.

Loiselle, André. Review of *Modern Canadian Plays*, ed. Jerry Wasserman. *Theatre Research in Canada / Recherches théâtrales au Canada* 16.1 (1995). http://journals.hil.unb.ca/ index.php/tric/article/view/7190/8249

MacDorman, Karl F., Robert Green, Chin-Chang Ho, and Clinton T. Koch. "Too Real for Comfort? Uncanny Responses to Computer Generated Faces." *Computers in Human Behaviour* 25.3 (2009): 695–710.

Marshall, Raymond, stage manager. Prompt script. *White Biting Dog*, by Judith Thompson. Tarragon Theatre, Toronto, ON, [1984]. L.W. Conolly Theatre Archives. University of Guelph Library, Guelph, ON.

Maufort, Marc. "Exploring the Other Side of the Dark: Judith Thompson's Magic Realism." *"Union in Partition": Essays in Honour of Jeanne Delbaere.* Ed. Gilbert Debusscher and Maufort. Liege: L3-Liege Language and Literature, 1997. 191–200.

McHarge, Christopher. House Program, Theatre Aquarius Production of *Fronteras Americanas*, by Guillermo Verdecchia, 1995. Theatre Aquarius Archives, University of Guelph Library, Guelph, ON.

Nestruck, J. Kelly. "Canadian Revivals on the Rise." *Globe and Mail* 23 September 2011. http://www.theglobeandmail.com/arts/theatre-and-performance/nestruck-on-theatre/ canadian-revivals-on-the-rise/article617676/

———. "Remount without a Cause." *Globe and Mail* 12 May 2011. http://www. theglobeandmail.com/news/arts/theatrefronteras-americanas-remount -without-a-cause/article2020028/

————. "*White Biting Dog*: These People Need to Be Saved. So Does the Production."
Globe and Mail 19 August 2011. http://www.theglobeandmail.com/arts/theatre-and-performance/white-biting-dog-these-people-need-to-be-saved-so-does-the-production/article629793/

Nunn, Robert. "Spatial Metaphors in the Plays of Judith Thompson." *Judith Thompson: Critical Perspectives on Canadian Theatre in English*. Ed. Ric Knowles. Vol. 3. Toronto: Playwrights Canada Press, 2005. 20–40.

Ondaatje, Michael. *In the Skin of a Lion*. Toronto: McClelland and Stewart, 1987.

Ouzounian, Richard. "Is Tarragon Dropping of Healey Play Dramatic Cowardice?" *Toronto Star* 3 February 2012. http://www.thestar.com/article/1126131--is-tarragon-dropping-of-healey-play-dramatic-cowardice-ouzounian

Palk, Nancy, dir. *White Biting Dog*, by Judith Thompson. Set Christina Poddubiuk. Perf. Gregory Prest, Fiona Reid, Mike Ross, Michaela Washburn, Joseph Ziegler. Soulpepper Theatre, Toronto, ON. 15 August 2011.

Panych, Morris, dir. Performance file for *White Biting Dog*, by Judith Thompson. Tarragon Theatre, Toronto, ON, 1994. L.W. Conolly Theatre Archives, University of Guelph Library, Guelph, ON.

Quick, Andrew. *The Wooster Group Workbook*. New York: Routledge, 2007.

Revington, Dereck. [Photograph: *The Luminous Veil*.] 2003.

Roach, Joseph. *Cities of the Dead: Circum-Atlantic Performance*. New York: Columbia University Press, 1996.

Roberts-Smith, Jennifer, Shawn DeSouza-Coelho, Teresa Dobson, Sandra Gabriele, Omar Rodriguez-Arenas, Stan Ruecker, Stéfan Sinclair, Annemarie Akong, Matt Bouchard, Diane Jakacki, David Lam, and Lesley Northam. "Visualizing Theatrical Text: from Watching the Script to the Simulated Environment for Theatre (SET)." *Digital Humanities Quarterly* 7.3 (2013).

Roberts-Smith, Jennifer, Shawn DeSouza-Coelho, Teresa Dobson, Sandra Gabriele, Stan Ruecker, Stéfan Sinclair, Alexandra (Sasha) Kovacs, and Daniel So. "Visualizing Theatre Historiography: Judith Thompson's *White Biting Dog* (1984 and 2011) in the Simulated Environment for Theatre (SET)." *Digital Inquiry into Textual Relations: Research and Teaching with Online Tools*. Ed. Susan Brown and Stan Ruecker. Spec. issue of *Digital Studies/Le champ numérique* 3.2 (2012).

Ruecker, Stan, Ali Grotkowski, Sandra Gabriele, Jennifer Roberts-Smith, Stéfan Sinclair, Teresa Dobson, Annemarie Akong, Sally Fung, and Omar Rodriguez. "Abstraction and Realism in the Design of Avatars for the Simulated Environment for Theatre." *Visual Communication Journal* 12.4 (2013): 459–72.

Salter, Denis. "The Idea of a National Theatre." *Canadian Canons: Essays in Literary Value*. Ed. Robert Lecker. Toronto: University of Toronto Press, 1991. 71–90.

Schechner, Richard. *Between Theatre and Anthropology*. Pennsylvania: University of Pennsylvania Press, 1995.

Sela-Sheffy, Rakefet. "Canon Formation Revisited: Canon and Cultural Production." *Neohelicon* 29.2 (2002): 141–59.

Soulpepper Theatre Company. "Archives." Soulpepper Theatre Company, 2011. http://www.soulpepper.ca/the_company/archives.aspx

————. "The Company/The Soulpepper Difference." Soulpepper Theatre Company, 2011. http://www.soulpepper.ca/the_company/the_soulpepper_difference.aspx

————. "Press Releases." Soulpepper Theatre Company, 2011. Accessed 8 March 2012. http://www.soulpepper.ca/media/press_releases.aspx

———. "*White Biting Dog*: Artist Profile." Soulpepper Theatre Company, 2011. Accessed 29 September 2011.

Tarragon Theatre. "Playwrights in Residence." Tarragon Theatre, 2012. Accessed 29 February 2012.

———. "Production History." Tarragon Theatre, 2012. Accessed 29 February 2012.

Taylor, Diana. *The Archive and the Repertoire: Performing Cultural Memory in the Americas.* Durham, NC: Duke University Press, 2003.

Thompson, Judith. *Late 20th Century Plays, 1980–2000.* Toronto: Playwrights Canada Press, 2003.

———. *White Biting Dog.* Toronto: Playwrights Canada Press, 1985.

von Tiedemann, Cylla. [Digital Photograph, Mike Ross and Michaela Washburn in *White Biting Dog*, by Judith Thompson.] Photo Gallery, Soulpepper Theatre Company, 2011. http://www.soulpepper.ca/performances/11_season/white_biting_dog.aspx#overview

Warren, Jim, dir. *Fronteras Americanas*, by Guillermo Verdecchia. Set Glenn Davidson. Perf. Guillermo Verdecchia. Tarragon Theatre, Toronto, ON, October 1993.

———. *Fronteras Americanas*, by Guillermo Verdecchia. Set Glenn Davidson. Perf. Guillermo Verdecchia. Soulpepper Theatre Company, Toronto, ON, May 2012.

Wasserman, Jerry, ed. *Modern Canadian Plays.* 4th ed. Vol. 2. Vancouver: Talonbooks, 2001.

Worthen, William. *Drama: Between Poetry and Performance.* Malden, MA: Wiley-Blackwell, 2010.

Zaiontz, Keren. "The Instability of Walls, Pillars, and Floors in Bluemouth Inc. Presents *What the Thunder Said.*" *Canadian Devised Theatre: Reluctant Texts from Exuberant Performance.* Ed. Bruce Barton, Natalie Corbett, Birgit Schreyer Duarte, and Keren Zaiontz. Ottawa: Borealis Press, 2008. 8–17.

"TALK TO THE WORK"

Applying ISTC Identifiers to the Digital Edition of the Canadian Bookman (1909–1941)

Ravit H. David

Introduction

There is growing international awareness of the political and cultural importance of offering access to digital resources and developing practices for their preservation. How to determine the identity of digital documents and data, however, and semantic relationships other than identity (including similarities and partial identities of various kinds, especially when rights may exist) rarely receives attention and remains an undertheorized subject.

Colleagues who research good practice in the construction of projects in the digital humanities suggest one possible reason for this neglect. They point out that for the majority of academics who write books or other textual materials, dissemination of their work other than through print media is new terrain and considered outside the authors' domain (Warwick et al. 90). Rarely are authors and publishers concerned with accessibility and discoverability; rather, academic librarians are seen as largely responsible for ensuring discoverability of a scholar's work.

Authors and publishers expect librarians to create metadata records that link a scholarly work to the host institution's integrated library system (ILS), perhaps highlight the work as a "special item" in its online public access catalogue (OPAC), and to link further to a library resource guide.

Academic authors need to reconsider how they reach potential readers, and this means thinking beyond mounting content on a server in the hope that Google users will know what to do next. In order to draw attention to one's scholarly labour and to have one's labour revealed in searches across the web, digital identifiers become as important as name and title. This chapter offers conceptual and pragmatic perspectives on the potential and benefits of such identifiers at the work level for digital projects in the humanities. More specifically, it considers how the new International Standard Text Code (ISTC) system may be used to manage e-content by offering functionality and potency for securing discoverability, stability, and sustainability of archival projects, scholarly digital editions, and sole databases in the humanities. As a test case, the chapter draws on the Canadian Writing Research Collaboratory's (CWRC) digital edition of the *Canadian Bookman* (1909–1941), a specialized periodical dedicated to promoting the literary and artistic culture of Canada. The ISTC system not only enhances usage of the periodical, it also signifies semantic and other identities, as well as relationships between these identities. I close this chapter with suggestions for further research into the nature of digital work, including bibliographic versus ideational identification and the need to supply enriched metadata and proper identifiers so that readers can have comprehensive access to a work's identity.

What Is a Digital Identifier?

A digital identifier must be unique, and its uniqueness must be unambiguous; it must identify one and only one object in a given space. The purpose of using identifiers as labels for digital objects is to establish a one-to-one correspondence between the members of a set of labels and the members of the set counted and labelled (Paskin, "On Making" 29). Norman Paskin defines an identifier as "a tool for naming content objects as first-class objects in their own right with a mechanism to make these names actionable through 'resolution,'" but cautions that such naming is not enough, as "managing resources interoperability requires appropriate metadata. Creating a mechanism to provide a description of what is identified in a structured way allows services about the object to be built for any purpose" ("Digital Object" 98). In other words, the management of content in digital environments requires the existence of not only unique, persistent, and reliable identifiers, but identifiers that are able to distinguish each piece of content, as well as any associated services (for example, access rights and copyright) that might be activated.

Currently, standards exist or are in development for managing Internet resources, including uniform resource names (URN), uniform resource locators (URL), and resource description frameworks (RDF) for metadata. These resource mechanisms provide infrastructure for managing resource discovery and distribution, but are not sufficient to manage intellectual content and associated rights in complex digital collections that involve various levels of contribution.

An identifier is an important feature of any model of information ontology.[1] First, and most important, when international systems—such as the digital object identifier (DOI) system—are used to assign identifiers to digitized works, infrastructure administrators and technical staff no longer struggle to unify metadata standards that originate from different resources and are created by different people using different schemas. In many cases, such as CWRC—an online infrastructure project designed to enable unprecedented avenues for digital studies in and about Canada— the platform hosts projects from Canadian universities in both official languages, English and French. Normalization of CWRC's metadata likely would require the involvement of professional cataloguers who were willing compromisers. In fact, an international object identifying system, under which all contributors may register their content, would be a more efficient way to overcome metadata differences.

Further, international identifier systems provide a more stable, persistent element than metadata. Although metadata may change, digital identifiers are registered in external agencies and are not affected by any changes that take place in the database. The stability of digital identifiers creates a foundation for the maintenance of reliable linking and traffic building and eases the management of copyright. Often, for instance, securing copyright for digital scholarly editions is labour intensive—especially when dealing with older materials—and necessitates a management system at the site level to guarantee that all materials destined for online undergo the proper copyright clearance process. Moreover, digital identifiers make it easy to cite a work (regardless of its physical home) and serve as a version control (if it is assigned a checksum function). Digital identifiers employ a system of bibliographic identification that allows object identifiers to resolve dynamically into the correct URL as materials move. Thus, internal construction on the hosting platform should not affect the discoverability of the objects across the web, even in cases where they have been physically dis- or re-located.

The importance of unique identification has now been recognized by the digital preservation community (Jones and Beagrie 98), and the key to digital preservation lies in interoperability across media or formats, technology platforms, and linguistic and semantic barriers. An international system of identification, then, is a way to ensure preservation. For instance, if CWRC's infrastructure is a project's home, then registering the works of the project through an international system of DOIs with an external agency would be a major step towards preservation by ensuring consistency of the digital object identity, format, and size. While the DOI would have no connection with the actual content of the work, it can and should testify to the integrity of the files. Thus, an identifier's meaning is what Matthew G. Kirschenbaum and his co-authors define as "a further layer of computational abstraction that we can leverage against the first in order to reach a more informed evaluation about the state of the digital materials in question" (8). Indeed, persistence is synonymous with future interoperability. In other words, any data put online should be able to identify a work, its creator, and its content, and provide a means to access it or some service about it both in the present and future (Paskin, "Digital Object" 101). Further, in the case of works under copyright or some sort of digital rights management restrictions, identifiers and metadata are of paramount importance. The DOI would name the object and identify it as a unique entity, while metadata would describe the concept of the object. Assigned to objects of intellectual property, these identifiers would enable connections to be denoted on intellectual and physical levels (Paskin, "Components").

The Crisis of Book Identifiers

The world of digital publishing is currently experiencing identity problems that also concern various conditions that apply to non-commercial digital content made available online by libraries, computational humanities projects, and other sources. When the publishing industry first set out to transform print content into digital content, it automatically adopted the international standard book number (ISBN). The ISBN is a unique, numeric, commercial book identifier based on a nine-digit standard book numbering (SBN) code created by Gordon Foster in 1966. In the early days of e-publishing, publishers thought of e-books as the digital equivalents of their print counterparts. By December 2010, however, with the proliferation of media platforms, the International ISBN Agency had reached the conclusion that "given the complexity of the current e-book supply chain, the traditional model of publisher-assigned ISBNs is no longer adequate. An enhanced framework may be required for product description and the requirements of new intermediary stakeholders will need to be considered in formulating any solution."[2]

The practice of using ISBNs to identify e-books varies. At times, ISBNs properly identify a product or version of an e-book; sometimes they identify only a file format; in other instances, the same ISBN is assigned to both the print and e-versions of a book. The failure of the old ISBN system to keep up with the multiple conversions that occur during the distribution of present-day titles makes its reception and survival vulnerable. Separate ISBNs do facilitate the discoverability of various file formats and resolve digital rights management issues, but they do not link different versions of an e-book title. Currently, to avoid fragmentation, publishers count on libraries and electronic platforms to employ internal work identifiers or an ISBN database to match and link the various forms of a given work. Interoperability is limited, however, and identifiers and databases do not enable cross-platform discoverability. In fact, in its present state the ISBN identifier of e-books actually impedes content: if an ISBN does not identify different versions and editions of books, then an understanding of the life cycle of a book—from print to digital, and from digital to various digital packages and formats—is unavailable. If that life cycle is not available to readers, the book's identification is unavailable as well.

Between Book and Work: The ISTC Is Born

Traditional cataloguing theory has a rich history of developing and refining the concepts of textual production and reception, a vital distinction in a world where "book" may begin to take on new meanings in the digital world.[3] Indeed, a digital project may involve more than one print book, more than one work (for example, a digitized print book or a born-digital text), or a cross-media conversion of a text. In his 2001 publication, *The Nature of "A Work": Implications for the Organization of Knowledge*, Richard P. Smiraglia uses semiotics to advance the understanding of the social role of works and, building on Birger Hjørland's epistemological stances, he delineates the spatial separation between "text," "document," and "work": "A text is the set of words that constitute a writing. A text is not the same as a document, which is the physical container (an item) on which the text is recorded....A work is the set of ideas created probably by an author or perhaps a composer, or other artist, set into a document using text, with the intention of being communicated to a receiver....A work may have many texts and may appear in many different documents" (*Nature* 3–4). Smiraglia goes on to point out the necessity of establishing and tracking relationships between works. He divides these relationships into two categories: equivalence relationships that exist among copies of an item (for example, a book and its microform reproductions); and derivative relationships that exist among variations of a work (for example, editions and translations) ("Progress" 345). Smiraglia further delineates derivative relationships as either derivations or mutations:

Derivation may take one or more forms: 1. Simultaneous editions; 2. Successive editions; 3. Amplifications; or, extractions....In these categories the work derives culturally over time, but ideational and semantic content do not change. Mutations may take one or more forms as well: 1. Translations; 2. Adaptations; 3. Performances. In these categories the ideational and semantic content have mutated to some degree. The relations among the exemplars of a work constitute a network of textual identity. ("Works as Signs" 199–200)

As Smiraglia notes, because works are used to communicate new knowledge and exist in a social world, a work's meaning is not chained to an "existential anchor" ("Works as Signs" 193)—it is subject to ever-changing reception principles and continuous reinterpretation in evolving cultures. Simply, a work is an instantiation—a manifestation of a specific point in time—or, as Susan Schreibman writes, any text (or paratext[4]) is "a temporal artefact reflecting both the prehistory of the most contemporary instantiation of the work and a post-history of previous instantiations" (291).

These theoretical underpinnings developed independently of the commercial book trade, but they became practical as it became clear that ISBNs were no longer adequate descriptors of commercial e-books. Users and the publishing industry grew increasingly frustrated by the fact that e-books do not fit the mould of discrete objects imposed by the ISBN system—e-books neither maintain their integrity, nor lend themselves in a simple way to conventional citation systems. As a result, the publishing industry began investigating other ways to identify e-books, and the ISTC soon emerged as a possible solution. ISTC is a new identifier for the book industry and has great potential for non-commercial text-based digitization projects. Whereas an ISBN provides a unique identity in the supply chain for each product format, either as a physical product (a hardback or paperback) or digital product or format (a downloadable audiobook or PDF e-book), an ISTC identifies the underlying creative textual work and the discrete results of creative and/or intellectual effort expressed as text. These works may include illustrations, but works that are predominantly illustrations—books of photographs with minimal text—are not eligible for ISTC. Graphic versions of novels, comics, cartoons, and manga are eligible, but the ISTC identifies only the textual element of these works, not the images.

The ISTC standard is governed in a manner similar to ISBN. The International ISTC Agency licenses registration agencies to manage the allocation of identifiers. One notable identifier is the "derivation" field. For the purposes of assigning an ISTC to a work, a derivation (or a derived work) is one that is sufficiently different to be distinguishable from manifestations of the work from which it is derived. For instance, a numbered edition of an original work (a second edition, for example) is a derivation. There are various derivation types: abridged, annotated, compiled, critical, excerpted, expurgated, nontext added or revised, revised, translated, adapted, unspecified (Holdsworth 13–14).

Although ISTC was released at the end of 2009, its implementation has been slow. This is unfortunate, as it is a promising identifier that is able to characterize relationships between works. In fact, relationships between different ISTCs provide as much value as the ISTC identifier itself, as they create connections between various life stages of a work and can facilitate the clustering of works. In the publishing world, for instance, an ISTC for an illustrated edition of a work and an ISTC for the original work can create a relationship that would easily reflect the insertion or deletion of non-textual components. Due to the flexibility of its ONIX (ONline Information eXchange)-based schema, ISTC can be extended to digital projects outside the commercial world, and the relationships that ISTC establishes would prove invaluable to humanities scholars seeking to follow texts through various permutations and adaptations. One need only think of a popular work such as Lewis Carroll's *Alice in Wonderland* to recognize the potential of such an identifier. Discovery of all the projects that make use of different elements or editions of such a work to create a new instantiation of part or all of its identity would change the face of *Alice* scholarship. A determined scholar might, for instance, track the work from its original (pre-digital and pre-ISBN) publication through the hundreds of editions, expansions, contractions, and adaptations of *Alice in Wonderland* over the past century (from annotated, critical, abridged, and illustrated editions to film script to stage play).

The ONIX-based schema of the ISTC (see Appendix, this chapter) has two distinct advantages for the humanities scholar in that is does not establish preference for one version over another, and it does not relegate the identity of a work to a specific home. Instead, the ISTC system connects and associates works strictly according to content. As a global unique identifier, an ISTC makes it clear to users which expression of the work is being used where and by whom—without prejudice. The ISTC also frees readers, scholars, and editors from the mistaken perception of print editions as always being the "source" or "original work," a perception that is no longer tenable in the twenty-first century.[5]

Identity and Sameness: The Canadian Bookman as a Test Case for ISTC Registration

The *Canadian Bookman* was a specialized periodical with a focus on books and authors, literary criticism, publishing, bookselling, and libraries. The *Bookman* commenced publication in 1909 in Toronto as a monthly review of contemporary literature devoted to the interests of the Canadian book buyer. It published until 1914 and re-emerged in 1915 as the *Canadian Bookseller and Library Journal*. It changed its name to *Canadian Bookman* in 1919 and published continuously until the October–November issue of 1941.

The *Canadian Bookman* digital edition project is hosted by CWRC and uses ISTC registration to accomplish two primary objectives. The first objective is to enable cross-platform discovery of the project, in which readers are exposed to related projects and other digital copies of the *Canadian Bookman* available on the web. The second objective of ISTC registration is to describe the serial's paratextual elements, specifically advertisements, in order to move beyond basic encoding strategies to represent the relationship between works and advertisements.

Periodical publishing was profoundly affected by mass production during the rise of modernism. Publishers then (as now) had to increase advertising space to lower the price of subscriptions and widen the dissemination of periodicals. This created an economic dependency on advertising revenues. Drawing on Jerome McGann's assertion that both the work's words ("linguistic codes") and its physical features (the "bibliographical code") (56) transmit meaning, CWRC's *Canadian Bookman* project contends that advertisements exceed their commercial dimension to become an intrinsic textual feature of the periodical.

The functioning of advertisements as optical codes that guide reading has long been overlooked. Indeed, modernism tended to privilege the notion of an autonomous work and focused primarily on aesthetic features. The dismissal of advertisements as insignificant has resulted in the removal of advertisements from some modernist literary periodicals during the process of library rebinding. That incision prevents today's readers from accessing the vast bibliographical knowledge that positions the literary work as a historicized object, as well as an aesthetic one. For instance, book advertising has changed over time and advertisements show how publishers viewed books in previous decades. Were those publishers selling books as physical objects? The content of books? The emotional experience of reading? Advertisements also act as gateways to the network of publishers, editors, typesetters, and advertising agencies associated with Canadian book publishing. Further, by modifying the original context in which a literary text was read, the work's social dimensions are lost, the reading event—as well as the reader's interpretation of the text—altered. The careers of many Canadian writers began in Canadian periodicals, for example, and advertisements that shared layout with short stories and poems have a bearing on the work, its evolution, and its life span. In fact, the digitization of the *Canadian Bookman*—with a strong research emphasis on the juxtaposition of early literary works alongside advertisements—could reframe the reading event and influence anew the interpretation of literary texts.

In order to transcribe, annotate, and represent advertisements as extra-textual cues, and analyze how they serve to alter the reading event and a reader's interpretation of literary texts, it is necessary to consider layout as a discursive system. Dissecting a periodical's page (including the physical placement of advertisements on the page) will help determine the authoritative value of the physical proximity of advertisements to a literary work and their role in the production of literary meaning. CWRC's *Canadian Bookman* project, in its initial stages, aims to look at the historical and bibliographical information connected to advertisements in each issue of the periodical (specifically, the people responsible for each advertisement, including the publisher, copywriter, printer, and consumers).

Before this in-depth identification of the periodical can take place, however, a full run of the journal had to be located and the paper issues scanned with optical character recognition (OCR) software to convert them into workable files. Some issues of the *Canadian Bookman* were located at the Thomas Fisher Rare Book Library of the University of Toronto and others were found at the E.J. Pratt Library of Victoria University in the University of Toronto. After librarians closely supervised the scanning of the fragile paper issues of the *Canadian Bookman*, the journal was mounted on the *Internet Archive* website (http://archive.org) where only those issues that are out of copyright are available. The CWRC project aims to put the full run of the *Canadian Bookman* online, but there are ongoing Canadian copyright considerations for many of the issues, and all issues from 1923 to 1941 have been dark archived (i.e., the content has been preserved but has not been granted public access) until copyright is secured.

A digital edition of the *Canadian Bookman* will be used for the purpose of researching the relationship between advertisements and related works, and a digital edition with annotations and related research findings and materials will be created. Thus, almost a century after it ceased publication, renewed interest in the *Canadian Bookman* has already begun to create at least three new instantiations of this work. First, a complete run of the journal was scanned for the *Internet Archive* where, unlike the print-based collections, the periodical issues were brought together as a single new digital object. Second, a digital edition of those issues out of copyright now appears on the CWRC website—a new event and format for this periodical that is now partly available via electronic devices. Since neither of these events changed either the content of the work or the texts associated with it, it would be appropriate to assign one ISTC number to both instantiations. Third, the annotated edition that is planned for the complete CWRC edition will derive from the scanned and print-based work.

Several questions arise from these digitizations of *Canadian Bookman*. One must ask, for example, whether these scanned versions should be registered as the original work. There is no easy answer to this probing question. If paratexts inform the work—as I believe they do—scanning and presenting on the web only those periodical issues that are free of copyright shifts the work away from its original, print-based state. But in what way has the periodical been derived from the original? Is it in a manner that justifies a different identifier? Does "original" refer to an individual issue (or the texts within that issue) or the complete run of *Canadian Bookman*? This matter is complicated further by the fact that a significant amount of content in the full run has Canadian copyright issues that may prevent its inclusion in the final digital edition. Moreover, serials differ from monographs, and one may wonder whether separate registration of each issue accurately reflects the intention of its editors (both the editors of the original print run and the current digitization). In other words, how a work is divided and identified has much to do with editorial considerations and not only with the management of digital content.

The digitization of source materials, particularly for long-term curation and distribution in open formats, requires the use not only of regular and progressive naming systems but also unique global digital identifiers. At times, digital identifiers may seem restrictive, especially to users who focus on content over the management of digital objects, for example. And yet, digital identifiers can and should be examined as attributes of textual manifestation. How do digital identifiers fit into frequently debated issues, such as how an infrastructure can be built to support the creation of "true" digital critical editions, and what constitutes a "digital critical edition"? Christine Borgman has noted the continuing importance of access to various editions of a text, commenting that humanities scholars and students make "the finest distinctions among editions, printings, and other variants—distinctions that are sometimes overlooked in the transition from print to digital form" (Borgman 12). In their discussion of multi-texts and digital editions, Christopher Blackwell and

Gregory Crane offer an overview of digital editions and what an ideal digital library infrastructure might provide:

> Digital editions are designed from the start to include images of the manuscripts, inscriptions, other source materials, not only those available when the editor is at work but those which become available even after active work on the edition has ceased....Even if we do not yet have an internationally recognized set of electronic identifiers for manuscripts, the print world has often produced unique names (e.g., LIBRARY + NUMBER) that can later be converted into whatever standard identifiers appear. (Blackwell and Crane par. 62)

Instead of relying on unique names from the print world, as Blackwell and Crane suggest, using a global unique identifier, such as ISTC, at the work level will retain the distinctions among the various versions, editions, and derivations of texts. These identifiers will secure the discoverability of the works on a cross-platform level, since there is no single infrastructure or tool that is used in the field. Moreover, not only will registration of global unique identifiers make use of an identifier system that takes advantage of recent developments in the Semantic Web;[6] it will unveil to the reader all the critical decisions of a scholarly editor and serve to underline the importance of better representing the complicated nature of textual sources, variants, and their textual transmission. Models that advocate for the inclusion of all the raw data (page images and transcriptions, for example), previous editions, and scholarship on which an edition is based illustrate the important need for all digital scholarship—whether it be the creation of an archaeological reconstruction or a digital edition—to be recognized as an interpretative act.

Conclusion

Currently, because of its ability to rise above format, owners, and other issues to represent a more abstract identity of a work and thus enable access to the work's relatives close and far, ISTC is the best option for an international identifier system. Assigning an identifier that is at once international and different from any current mode of automatically assigning object identification in a local database has many advantages.

In the future, it may be that scholarly communities, which include digital humanists, will develop a global unique identifier system that will support more adequately the open access paradigm and the non-commercial nature of their various projects. But until such a system is fully investigated and developed, the global unique identifier registry service ISTC can serve ongoing projects by distinguishing their content from that of previous and future scholarly editions and digital undertakings.

ISTC ONIX Record for the *Canadian Bookman*

```
<ISTCRegistrationRecord>
    <RegistrantsInternalReference/>
    <ISTCRecordType>01</ISTCRecordType>
    <ISTCRequestStatus>01</ISTCRequestStatus>
    <ISTCWorkType>01</ISTCWorkType>
    <Origination>02</Origination>
    <Derivation>
        <DerivationType>02</DerivationType>
        <DerivationNote>A searchable, hypertext edition, enhanced by rich contextual and historical
            information of the print-based serial, The Canadian Bookman.
            The Canadian Bookman was published by the Canadian Authors Association.
            It was a specialized periodical dedicated to promoting the literary and artistic culture of Canada.
            Its focus was books and authors, literary criticism, publishing, book-selling and the library profession.
            The Bookman commenced publication in 1914 in Toronto as a monthly and lasted for one year.
            The periodical re-emerged, briefly, in 1915 as The Canadian Bookseller and Library Journal and, finally,
            took hold as the Canadian Bookman in 1919 to last twenty-two years,
            ceasing with the October/November issue of 1941.</DerivationNote>
    </Derivation>
    <Title>
        <ISTCTitleType>01</ISTCTitleType>
        <TitleText>The Canadian Bookman</TitleText>
        <Subtitle>A hypertext, annotated and enriched edition of the Canadian Bookman</Subtitle>
    </Title>
    <WorkDate>
        <WorkDateRole>02</WorkDateRole>
        <Calendar>00</Calendar>
        <DateFormat>05</DateFormat>
```

1. Warwick, Claire, Melissa Terras, Paul Huntington, and Nikoleta Pappa, "If You Build It Will They Come? The LAIRAH Study: Quantifying the Use of Online Resources in the Arts and Humanities through Statistical Analysis of User Log Data," *Literary and Linguistic Computing* 23.1 (2008): 85–1021. For further discussion of identity conditions, see Renear and Dubin 183; and Guarino 221.

2. In a December 2010 report, the board of the International ISBN Agency described the problem as follows: "Consumers need to know whether a particular title that they want is available as an e-book and, if so, what specific 'content experience' they are buying and whether any particular product is, or is not, capable of delivering the desired experience, regardless of the retail channel or application where they choose to purchase the e-book. Given the complexity of the current e-book supply chain, the traditional model of publisher-assigned ISBNs is no longer adequate. An enhanced framework may be required for product description and the requirements of new intermediary stakeholders will need to be considered in formulating any solution."

3. For the differences between "text," "data," and "document," see Buckland.

4. For a discussion of paratext, see Genette.

5. Paul Fyfe recently suggested that universal identifiers and automated resolutions are the twin arms of a new system of bibliographic control and, as such, they may resuscitate an editorial idealism, since "the automation of correction can displace editorial judgments into the synthetic functions of server polling or algorithms whose logic may be increasingly difficult to extract or kept private by commercial entities" (274). At the same time, Fyfe notes, an international digital identifier suggests editorial forgiveness, where editing can become seamless in a web of copy. Thus, he connects identifiers with the invisible life cycle of a digital work and suggests that identifiers are meaningful not only in supplying metadata for a work but in assigning specific objects. For Fyfe, the work thereby is transformed from an abstraction to an object with a unique name that cannot be duplicated, even in digital reproduction.

6. The Semantic Web relies on rules of inference that create a pathway between different data sets. Instead of looking for specific metadata filled with specific words, the Semantic Web uses objects to find specific data that include the rules of inference-objects that will make it possible for a researcher to find the precise document or data set necessary for a given project. At present, however, encoding language such as Extensible Markup Language (XML) and Text Encoding Initiative (TEI) does not yet respond to technologies and standards that identify the semantics of document contents, even when Document Type Definition (DTD) is available. An additional level of discoverability is needed in order to capture the relationship between entities, RDF for example, or, as suggested here, object identifiers that capture the relationship between objects on a semantic level.

WORKS CITED

Blackwell, Christopher, and Gregory Crane. "Conclusion: Cyberinfrastructure, the Scaife Digital Library and Classics in a Digital Age." *DHQ: Digital Humanities Quarterly* 3 (2009). http://www.digitalhumanities.org/dhq/vol/3/1/000035.html

Borgman, Christine L. "The Digital Future Is Now: A Call to Action for the Humanities." *DHQ: Digital Humanities Quarterly* 3 (2009). http://works.bepress.com/cgi/viewcontent.cgi?article=1232&context=borgman

Buckland, Michael K. "Information as Thing." *Journal of the American Society for Information Science* 42.5 (1991): 351–60.

Fyfe, Paul. "Electronic Errata: Digital Publishing, Open Review, and the Futures of Correction." *Debates in the Digital Humanities*. Ed. Matthew Gold. Minneapolis: University of Minnesota Press, 2012. 259–80.

Genette, Gerard. *Paratexts: Thresholds of Interpretation*. Trans. Jane E. Lewin. Cambridge: Cambridge University Press, 1987.

Guarino, Nicola. "The Role of Identity Conditions in Ontology Design." *Proceedings of the International Conference on Spatial Information Theory: Cognitive and Computational Foundations of Geographic Information Science*. Ed. Christian Freska and David M. Mark. Berlin: Springer-Verlag, 1999. 221–34.

Holdsworth, Michael. *The International Standard Text Code (ISTC): A Work in Progress. A Supply Chain Perspective*. Book Industry Study Group and Book Industry Communication. March 2010. http://www.bic.org.uk/files/pdfs/100401%20ISTC%20for%20BIC-BISG%20obic%20Final%20corrected.pdf

International ISBN Agency. *Summary of Business Requirements Study on ISBNS & E-books*. International ISBN Agency. December 2010. http://api.ning.com/files/LyejPys2drPkZNQ1Pa59D*u-jaHaH24zdVRH3gvMXRmdABiCvPXYKt2bj*qgs*o4Jjj GrNDMNs4IFTFV5ES9N*I8gw5PDYGQ/ISBNebooksstudypublicsummary110105.pdf

Internet Archive. http://archive.org

Jones, Maggie, and Neil Beagrie. *Preservation Management of Digital Materials: A Handbook*. London: British Library, 2001.

Kirschenbaum, Matthew G., Richard Ovenden, Gabriela Redwine, and Rachel Donahue. *Digital Forensics and Born-Digital Content in Cultural Heritage Collections*. Council on Library and Information Resources, Washington, DC. December 2010. http://www.clir.org/pubs/reports/pub149/reports/pub149/pub149.pdf

McGann, Jerome. *The Textual Condition*. Princeton: Princeton University Press, 1991.

Paskin, Norman. "Components of DRM Systems." *Digital Rights Management: Technological, Economic, Legal and Political Aspects*. Ed. Eberhard Becker, Willms Buhse, Dirk Günnewig, Neils Rump. Berlin: Springer-Verlag, 2003. 26–61.

———. "Digital Object Identifiers." *Information Services and Use* 22 (2002): 97–112.

———. "On Making and Identifying a 'Copy.'" *D-Lib Magazine* 9.1 (January 2003). http://www.dlib.org/dlib/april06/paskin/04paskin.htmldoi:10.1045/april2006-paskin

Renear, Allen, and David Dubin. "Towards Identity Conditions for Digital Documents." *Proceedings of the 2003 International Conference on Dublin Core and Metadata Applications: Supporting Communities of Discourse and Practice—Metadata Research and Applications*. Dublin: Dublin Core Metadata Initiative, 2003. 181–89.

Schreibman, Susan. "Computer-mediated Texts and Textuality: Theory and Practice." *Computers and the Humanities* 36 (2002): 283–93.

Smiraglia, Richard P. *The Nature of "A Work": Implications for the Organization of Knowledge.* Lanham, MD: Scarecrow Press, 2001.

———. "The Progress of Theory in Knowledge Organization." *Library Trends* 50.3 (2002): 330–49.

———. "Works as Signs, Symbols, and Canons: The Epistemology of the Work." *Knowledge Organization* 28.4 (2001): 199–200.

HOW TO PLAY WITH MAPS

Bethany Nowviskie

The title of this chapter is a nod to Mark Monmonier's influential 1991 volume, *How to Lie with Maps*, a book that raised the cartographic awareness of a generation of university students, particularly in the social sciences where the stakes can be quite high for uncritical reading of graphs and images. Monmonier examines the complex rhetoric of contemporary mapmaking in the age of print journalism and pre-web mass media. His book provides a cautionary tour through the variety of expressive approaches that cartographers and the designers of geospatial infographics were using on the cusp—but not quite the bloom—of interactive digital mapping. In essence, it is a survey of print-based designs that produce geospatial un-truths in exactly those situations where truth is implied or expected. In other words, Monmonier looks at mappy, newsprint versions of a progression Mark Twain is said to have named "lies, damned lies, and statistics."

But one cannot "play with maps" without playing with the truth. That is because we approach most geospatial visualizations with two strong assumptions that contribute to the power and supposed (strangely unquestioned) universality of digital mapping. The first assumption is that—unless otherwise explicitly signalled as fiction, farce, or allegory—solid, real-world referents underlie everything we see in maps. The second is that certain uniformities of scale and symbology exist within a single map—that is, cartographers maintain reasonable continuities in the relation of design to reality. Mapping embeds the tacit promise that "you are here" means something practical, and that the rules of any game of representation will never be changed in the middle of a street grid.

Humanities scholars know, however, that ludic fictions are among our surest avenues to deep understanding of culture, aesthetics, and the human psyche—to the interpretive outcomes that matter to us. In other scholarly disciplines, "playing" with maps might be seen as junk science or, worse, outright deception and abuse. In contrast, scholars of literature and the arts are free to validate, investigate, and even perpetrate the telling of delightful lies.

In this chapter—originally conceived as a keynote presentation for the Canadian Writing Research Collaboratory conference on space, place, and play—I seek to promote wise foolishness in the spatial humanities. I intend to interrogate the bases of digital mapping and of engagement with geospatial information tools and systems (that is, with analytical GIS) as we have received those technologies from the sciences, and from more mimetic disciplines like landscape architecture and urban planning. Further, I hope to encourage and enable digital humanists to play with maps. By implication, that means to toy with (and maybe even subvert) established technological systems of production and dissemination of digital maps. Those twinned areas of praxis and inquiry, for my purposes, require much attention and work—and there is no denying that play elicits humanists' best work. At the heart of this essay is a set of historical maps by a fourteen-year-old girl from 1820s New England. I will offer Frances Henshaw and her cartographic method as our guide to a twenty-first-century humanities GIS. First, however, I must address an opportunity and its disciplinary context.

It is clear that we operate today from within the arc of a methodological turn in humanities scholarship. The work my colleagues and I in the Scholars' Lab have undertaken recently, from our location in a centre for digital study strategically embedded within the University of Virginia research library, aims to help us round that bend—that is, to prepare our archives and digital services to meet the humanities researchers we see moving, in increasing numbers, away from abstract, theoretical engagement with texts, images, and objects toward hands-on analysis, materialized synthesis, and active representation and manipulation of the cultural record. This work is not uncritical. It is theoretically informed, but it is also procedural and generative—hacked and made. And it is acutely aware of its relationship to traditional methods in the interpretive humanities.

It is no surprise that the methodological turn is happening parallel to (or at least in a kind of parabolic synchronicity) a spatial turn in the humanities. Serious and growing scholarly engagement with GIS was virtually assured when the devices and interfaces of mapping technology became ubiquitous. We carry live links to global positioning systems in our pockets and embed them in our cars, we consult slippy maps on touchscreens before stepping outside for a walk, and we are coming to expect to be able to sort digital search results spatially and to access historical and real-time location information for a wide variety of data. If a particular datum can be mapped, we often feel annoyed when it has not yet been mapped. And although the spatial technologies of everyday life fuel some of our expectations (technologies like networked transportation and social media tools), it now seems obvious to us that mappable data points include more than busses and trains, family and friends, and related objects of our stalker-like affection. How could we, as humanities scholars, not expect that mapped information include our texts and objects of study, in the spatial contexts in which we find or place and interpret them?

The Scholars' Lab at the University of Virginia Library has been busy in this arena. Over the past few years, we have offered a variety of training programs for humanities scholars, software developers, and GIS librarians, including an Institute for Enabling Geospatial Scholarship funded by the National Endowment for the Humanities (NEH). We have collaborated on presentational mapping and analytical GIS projects with University of Virginia faculty and with winners of our graduate fellowships in digital humanities. (In this program, nearly every applicant's research project since 2007 has included some sort of spatial dimension.) We have worked to make our collection of GIS data and scanned historical maps discoverable and freely available for use by scholars and developers in the most flexible way possible. Further, we have undertaken a project called Neatline, a set of open source, Omeka plugins for digital storytelling, funded by the Library of Congress and NEH. We are developing these tools so scholars can create their own selective, content-driven, and highly interpreted geotemporal expressions of collections that may be housed in libraries, museums, and archives, or which they assemble themselves with the aid of our Neatline software.

The Scholars' Lab is a division of a major research library. That means it serves a very broad and interdisciplinary community that stretches well beyond the humanities. But for me, trained as a textual critic, it is important to stop periodically to map our laboratory work in GIS onto my home discipline. It is fair to say that we are making local investments not so much in appreciation of the applicability of GIS to literary and bibliographical inquiry as it stands now, but rather in hopeful preparation: to lay the groundwork for a spatial humanities to come.

A first step for the Scholars' Lab is to establish the following: humanities scholars should not consider cartographic and geospatial technologies only through the lens of more obviously GIS-able disciplines like anthropology and archaeology, or area studies, urban planning, and environmental history. These fields have adopted existing spatial data, tools, and methods—and they have, to varying degrees, either made their peace or already negotiated terms of compromise with a set of limitations and assumptions they have inherited from the sciences. These are assumptions that circumscribe and, from the point of view of literary scholars, may even circumvent the expressiveness of geographic information systems.

To question these assumptions is not to dismiss the fascinating work that is already unfolding when humanities scholars apply established GIS techniques to their research problems. Currently, for example, we are collaborating with University of Virginia classicist Jenny Strauss Clay and two of her graduate students. These scholars are letting Homeric verse drive a GIS analysis to determine feasible routes for travel—by mule—through the terrain of ancient Greece. The project tests Strauss's theory that Homer's catalogue of ships is ordered mnemonically as three distinct and real "itineraries" that would be familiar and memorable to listeners and bards. To that end, the Scholars' Lab is applying a specific GIS technique called least-cost-path analysis, used primarily by governments to lay out highways. The project itself is potentially groundbreaking: it promises not only to elucidate the relationship between orally transmitted verse and real-world geographies, but—if distinct sequences are truly evident—to reveal the locations of lost archaeological sites (Clay). But its GIS methods, in themselves, are not strictly innovative. The story so far of GIS in the humanities is less about transformation and experimentation than about one-way adoption of technologies devised for other disciplines. Why is that?

First, we must acknowledge what has been holding humanists back. In 2008, Martyn Jessop of King's College, London published an article in *Literary and Linguistic Computing* in which he documented what he called an unexpected "inhibition" among digital humanities scholars—a reluctance to engage deeply with geospatial tools and data (Jessop 39). In this piece, Jessop identifies the chief deficiencies of GISes, from the point of view of the humanities, and he addresses the institutional systems that fail to support and promote their use. He notes that digital humanists are deeply engaged with place and space, and not usually daunted by a learning curve; they are, however, hesitant to embrace GIS. This article raises a fundamental question: Why—given the huge blossoming of activity elsewhere in GIS, the deep engagement of the humanities with place and space, and the general technological adventurousness of the digital humanities community—have scholars in our field been so slow to engage with maps?

Jessop offers four possible reasons (42–52), which I will survey here. The first and "most fundamental" addresses the very place of visualization and work with images in the discourse-based research methodology of the humanities. We were never taught (and therefore we are not teaching our graduate students) how to read and create images—much less how to engage intelligently with cartographic representation, old or new.

This is a widely recognized (if seldom addressed) issue in humanities research training, particularly in the fields of literature and history. But less frequently do we address the problem of cartographic awareness in the context of new possibilities afforded to literary scholarship by digital mapping.

The next two reasons involve GIS tools and the data to which we as humanities scholars want to apply those tools. How suitable are current geospatial software packages to the concerns of the humanities, since this software is made and marketed almost entirely within the sciences and quantitative social sciences? Production and reception histories of texts—that is, the history of printing and publishing, the histories of readership—may be reasonably mappable, but, as we know, such bibliographical scholarship is still marginalized in the broader discipline of literary studies. How useful, then, are GIS tools to the interpretive concerns of the majority of literary scholars? How apt are they at reflecting or analyzing the spatial relations of qualities like subjectivity and emotion? Can GIS tools be used to analyze time as it is experienced and expressed in narrative—how do they deal with the complex chronologies we see every day in the documentary record? The answer is "not very well." In fact, it is only recently that time became a factor at all in the geospatial software produced by California-based Environmental Systems Research Institute, a company that controls the market for analytical GIS.

We also we need to ask ourselves to what degree humanities questions and humanities data are at all suited to GIS. Typical GIS tools are geared toward synchronic analysis of incredibly dense data sets, but humanists tend to analyze sparser data, leading to understandings that play out diachronically over time. More importantly for literary scholars, GIS software has been designed to filter out uncertainty and ambiguity. It is built to smooth away wrinkles—to remove their traces as aberrations that are probably accidental, on the way to resolving larger data trends. GIS software does not celebrate, highlight, or dwell in ambiguity.

For Jessop, the broad issue of scholarly communication is also of great importance (46–49)—how we are to fund, produce, evaluate, distribute, and archive innovative geospatial scholarship in disciplines and institutions that are wedded to traditional research practices—a large question whose parameters lie outside the scope of this chapter. One might expect that our uses of GIS, since Jessop's 2008 article, would have become increasingly ludic and experimental. But Ian Gregory and Paul Ell suggest otherwise in their 2007 book, *Historical GIS: Technologies, Methodologies, and Scholarship*. Gregory and Ell state that "the researcher using GIS should be asking, 'What are the geographical aspects of my research question?' rather than [the more open] 'What can I do with my dataset using this software?'" (1), opening their treatment in a manner far too proscriptive for my purposes. Such an approach will be highly effective in applying GIS tools to the precise purposes for which they were designed, but I find it unnecessarily limiting with respect to experimental visualization practices in fields like literary and textual studies.

To summarize my discouraging litany, GIS does not enjoy wide use among humanists for a number of reasons. First, we are not practiced in handling image-based data. Second, there is a fundamental mismatch between our research questions, data, and expectations, and those for which GIS software was designed. As a result, we keep telling ourselves, in what may be a self-defeating way, that in order to use spatial tools and methods we should behave more like scientists. Finally, prevailing institutional structures have neither rewarded nor helped to sustain research in the field of digital humanities.

But we must remind ourselves of the allure of lying with maps and the potential utility of any playful methodology for humanities inquiry. The notion of drawing as a way of thinking—what Johanna Drucker has called "graphesis" or knowledge building through iterative graphical expression—may help energize and shape a literary GIS suitable for humanities research (Drucker 133–36). It might aid us in asserting a role for cartographic design in humanities exegesis, and help us bring spatial approaches and software systems into productive tension with the aims and customs of interpretive (as well as strictly analytical) place-based research. Maps, as literary scholars will want to read and produce them, operate somewhere (perhaps everywhere) on the playful spectrum of lies, damned lies, and statistics. I view this not as something to caution against, de-bug, and filter away, but to enable—particularly if we want to see a locally appropriate upswell of creative and scholarly engagement in

the spatial humanities, complementing the use of geographical information in other disciplines and industries.

We should not focus on maps as finished visualizations, as products
of analysis; rather, we ought to consider mapping a hermeneutic activity, a process or methodology. For literary scholars, geographic specificity
may prove less important than interpretive possibility. We must understand the making of maps and images as iterative and speculative (always
something to be reworked and refined), and never treat maps in the
humanities as monolithic, passively received outputs of GIS algorithms
inaccessible to the typical reader or scholarly end user. Even within a
framework that tacitly assumes a one-to-one correspondence between
representation and real landscape, we can license ourselves to lie—
experimentally, playfully, procedurally, and productively. The digital maps
preferred by scholars of language and literature are not answers. They are
questions. They are invitations.

The historical example of Frances Alsop Henshaw, who was fortunate
to have good teachers, functions precisely in this invitational way. In 1823,
Henshaw was fourteen years old. As the daughter of a reasonably well-to-
do New England merchant, she attended Middlebury Female Academy, a
small school in Vermont. There, she created a document I first encoun-
tered in the library of map collector David Rumsey. It purports to be a
"book of penmanship," but—in addition to the set copy-texts one might
expect to see in a handwriting practice-book—also contains a series of
hand-drawn, delicately coloured maps of what were then the nineteen
United States. Each of these maps—and this is where the penmanship
exercise comes in—is paired with a geometrically designed and highly
embellished prose passage, which Henshaw seems to have copied from
the geography books that were available to her as a schoolgirl in the new
American republic.[1] Henshaw's maps and texts alike are interpretive representations of the geodetic or descriptive literature from which she read
geography. The maps themselves are lovely, but more interesting is their
interplay with texts—both with Henshaw's source documents and with
the words she lays out on the page.

What I find most fascinating about this small book is that Henshaw
seems to have set herself clear cartographic operating constraints. She

writes about geography on pages that hover within a framework of what I can only term aesthetically inflected cardinal co-ordinates. It is not just her maps that can be geolocated. The shape of each of Henshaw's textual passages represents (either conceptually or geographically) the American state it describes, and she frequently positions notes about political and natural boundaries around the text blocks in what would be—to a reader of a map rather than a paragraph—cartographically appropriate margins of the page. In other words, the top margin for her writing is "north," and the gutter of the book (because she writes on rectos only) is the "west."

In some ways, Henshaw's book is utterly unique. But it is also a product of larger trends in the geographic education of women in North America in the early nineteenth century. Middlebury Female Academy was the first school established by famed educational reformer Emma Willard, author of *A Plan for Improving Female Education* (1818) and co-author of a seminal textbook, *Geography for Beginners* (1826). Willard is best remembered today as the founder of the Troy Female Seminary, now the prestigious Emma Willard School for girls in Troy, New York. Beginning in the 1820s, Troy Female Seminary was America's preeminent academy for teachers who went on to spread Willard's approaches to the pedagogy of place and space across the continent. Willard had moved from Middlebury to Troy two years before the date recorded in Henshaw's book, but a reading of her letters and her *System of Universal Geography* (co-authored in 1827 with William Channing Woodbridge) in the context of Henshaw's schoolwork is suggestive of continued influence. The arts-based geospatial exercises Willard developed early in her career as a teacher endured among the instructors she trained and the students she taught—influencing Frances Alsop Henshaw.

Willard's chief pedagogical innovations were two: first, to centre geographical instruction and discovery learning in hands-on activities that had her students creating personalized, localized, graphical maps. And second, to use maps at all, in the teaching of history and geography. Geography had long been accepted as a discipline suited to women's education and was emerging as an important path to literacy and the development of a common national identity in early America (Brückner). In women's educational history, there seems to have been a marked rise, beginning in the 1790s, of cartographic representation mixed with the more conventional alphabets and didactic texts of ladies' embroidered samplers. But until Willard's work in the 1820s, formal geography was taught largely without maps (Schulten 542–45).

The chief geographical textbooks of Willard's day were Jedidiah Morse's *Geography Made Easy* and Noah Webster's collection of grammars and spellers. Both were geared toward purely textual and verbal exercises of memorization. Morse (whose book, I have discovered, served as a primary resource for Henshaw in 1823) offers complex and evocative textual descriptions of places and spaces on the American continent. He relegates maps, however, to an expensive and much less well-circulated supplementary volume. Similarly (as described by literary historian Martin Brückner), Webster's closest gesture toward graphical expression of geography can be found in a prose "map" made entirely of typography—without representational line art—in which the names of American states and European countries are seen in rough spatial relation to each other (Brückner 115).

In contrast, in her early career as a teacher, Willard privileged the visual and asked her students to begin their mastery of American geography not by reading geodetic texts or even by studying maps, but by going outside and drawing. They sketched maps of spaces and places well known to them—their homes, schools, villages, and towns—from which they could work outward. Eventually, with the aid of textbooks and atlases, they moved from local representation to the national and international scene. Crucial to this lesson (and to my understanding of the graphetic possibilities for spatial humanities research) was the persistence of the basic exercise Willard taught: to create graphical visualizations as an aid to developing geospatial memory.

Historian Susan Schulten cites the cartographic impulse of Willard's early pedagogical practice as stemming from a "more general fascination with the idea of graphic representation" (543). This fascination, which evolved and was tested at the Middlebury Female Academy, is everywhere evident in Willard's later textbooks, a body of work that quickly moved from synchronic spatial imagery in geography primers (that is, maps as snapshots in time) to timelines and time-flows, architectures of time and diachronic geotemporal visualization in history books. For her power-ful graphic intervention in a field dominated by prose, Schulten places Willard at "the graphic foundations of American history" (542). This sug-gests a central role for Willard in the complex, shared textual and visual endeavour of nation building that scholars like Brückner describe in the early American republic. Moreover, it is well worth noting (when we con-template our own moment in the spatial humanities) that the use of maps in historical and interpretive texts evolved first through amateur draw-ing exercises—through pedagogical and methodological practice. Willard understood the importance of her contribution. "In history," she said, "I have invented the map" (Willard, Letter. qtd. in Lord 228).

But Willard had her critics. One of them raises issues that strike at the heart of Henshaw's exercise book and the example it offers to modern, spatially minded scholars of the interpretive humanities. In the 1840s, Marcius Willson criticized Willard's textbook maps—which bear the traces of the subjective and personal mapmaking exercises that she undertook with her students—as being "insufficiently geographical" and "focused instead on human events and boundaries" (Schulten 554). In effect, I read Willson as saying, "You put humanities in my geography!" But there is also an element to his critique that may be summarized as "You put space in my time!" Schulten sees Willson's publications as an attack by a rival author on Willard's attempts to "reconceptualize the past on a plane rather than in a narrative" (554).

For such a reconceptualization to work, we have to recognize the necessity of placing emphasis on perspective and dimensionality in both spatial and temporal visualization. In moving fluidly from geography to history, Willard produced not only maps, but what she called fold-out "chronographer" timelines depicting events and cultural influences as a river widening toward the present-day reader at the bottom of the page. She also drew structural "temples of time" that raised architectural col-umns and a pediment of historical personages above the chronographic streams presented as part of the temple's mosaic floor (Schulten 560). In order to work, such visualizations must emphasize the crucial element of the subjective positioning of the viewer or interpreter—in this case through means of exaggerated perspective. In the Henshaw example, the subjectivity of the mapmaker becomes evident through selection and arrangement.

Three hallmarks of Willard's later geographic and visualized historical pedagogy are relevant to the spatial humanities: graphesis (or drawing as a way of knowing); perspective (both conceptual and pictorial); and a necessary, attendant privileging of individualized response—those human events and readings that so troubled Willson. How fortunate that Henshaw's "penmanship" document has survived as an early product of Willard's curriculum and educational philosophy—and with enough identifying information to connect Henshaw to Willard.

Let us consider more closely Henshaw's subjective mapmaking, in text and watercolour, across the American landscape of 1823. Close analysis of this historical document may provoke us to consider what modern mapping technology affords and fails to afford. We must think both analytically—how might GIS help us better understand such artifacts?—and creatively—what might we require of our own tools and data in order to adopt Henshaw's generative, playful methods? Of course, such adoption will hinge on the openness of the academy to sketching and iterative design as legitimate methodologies in digital scholarship.

Henshaw's book begins with penmanship exercises. Its first thirty-five pages contain astronomy, geography, and American history texts that she copied from a pre-1814 printing of Morse's image-free *Geography Made Easy*. It is interesting that Henshaw skips some of Morse's most direct and provocative instructions for the design and reading of maps, found in a section of *Geography Made Easy* that proscribes—again in prose—a symbology for rivers, mountains, forests, harbours, and roads and offers a whimsical notion of cardinality: "In books of geography by the right hand we must understand the east; in those of astronomy, the west; in such as relate to augury, the south; and the writings of poets, the north" (Morse 28). It is worth noting that Henshaw's texts side with the geographers rather than the poets, marking north at the top of the page.

The heart of Henshaw's book, however, is a series of nineteen hand-coloured maps and accompanying texts, at least ten of which were designed to sit in a particular spatial relationship to the American states they describe. The maps are organized on a principle of adjacency, and

Henshaw's choices seem to reflect the conceptual and actual limits of American statehood in the atlases available to her at home and at school—primarily an 1805 edition of Mathew Carey's *American Pocket Atlas* and an 1812 edition of Aaron Arrowsmith and Samuel Lewis's *General Atlas*. She leaves out some defined territories and regions (like the Louisiana Purchase), and may have used a third, as yet unidentified atlas for the state of Indiana.

It would seem that Henshaw deliberately selected, omitted, and recombined maps for representation in her book. In my attempt to codify her activity, I began combing full-text archives and collating passages of her text using Juxta, a textual collation tool we have developed at the University of Virginia. This led to a wealth of information and an ability to draw reasonable conclusions about the sources for Henshaw's prose. Sometimes my textual research methods helped me find a map, or think through the textual history of an atlas. Regrettably, a similar research approach to the geographical imagery in Henshaw's book is almost unimaginable, since we lack sufficiently large, open corpora of scanned historical maps and widely adopted systems for identifying, geo-rectifying, comparing, and collating such maps.

But what if it were possible to analyze Henshaw's geographical imagery spatially? Most of the same protocols and software tools that would promote sophisticated research and identification of historical maps would be of interest beyond cartography and history; they are equally applicable to research problems in book history and graphic design. What might comparative, image-based searches across archives of page scans teach us about the history of ornamentation and typography? What might a process like geo-rectification (the stretching and rubber-sheeting of historic maps made possible by GIS software) reveal when performed across a set of similar textual features—such as the manuscript flourishes that decorate Henshaw's pages? Moreover, would the limits of this activity, limned with GIS approaches and toolsets, help illustrate the limitations of the software we have inherited from the sciences?

Henshaw uses a unique format and design for each pair of text-maps in her book. Two pairs will serve to illustrate her technique, but others are available for scrutiny online, in the open access map library of collector

Figure 5.1
"(Description of)
Virginia," Frances
Henshaw, 1823.
*[Courtesy of David
Rumsey Map Collection.
List #2501N]*

Figure 5.2
"Virginia," Frances
Henshaw, 1823.
*[Courtesy of David
Rumsey Map Collection.
List #2501.012]*

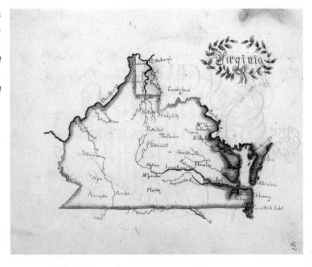

David Rumsey. The first pair of maps presents the state of Virginia in its antebellum contours—that is, before the events of the Civil War provoked the division of Virginia and West Virginia. Near the panhandle appear interesting incongruities—fictions, actually—between political boundaries and watersheds. It is tempting to read an unresolved tension between two conceptual layers or dimensions, as represented on the single plane of Henshaw's map. If she had been limited to modern GIS tools, Henshaw would have been forced to disambiguate her representation into layers, exposing a tension between informational and aesthetic structures in maps that textual scholars would recognize as the longstanding issue of "overlapping hierarchies" in the work of the Text Encoding Initiative (Renear, Mylonas, and Durand).

The textual representation of the state of Virginia shows Henshaw breaking her own rules. Recall her cardinal directions, which place north at the top margin and west in the gutter of each recto leaf. They are augmented by labels for bounding states and bodies of water: "Bounded North by Massachusetts," "south by the Atlantick," and so forth. These cardinal directions hold true across every one of the nineteen texts, even in cases like Virginia, where the shape of the corresponding map prompts Henshaw to choose a landscape orientation for the page. In the text that corresponds with her Virginia map, she offers a fairly unpoetic and disjointed selection of passages from *Geography Made Easy*—capping the penmanship exercise with an elaborate ornamental cherub holding a sweeping ribbon or banner inscribed "Virginia." But the cherub occupies the "northern" field of her page, so Henshaw is unable to position the expected "North by MARYLAND" label appropriately. In other words, the aesthetic force of the textual ornament trumps Henshaw's own conventions of directionality. Maryland is displaced to the west—where it crowds Kentucky toward the south, into a position where one might now seek, and fail to find, Tennessee.

In the case of Ohio, Henshaw's text lacks labelled directionality but may have been designed to echo the rectilinear north and rough diamond-like shape of the southern portions of the state. At least two different editions of *Geography Made Easy*, and—by my analysis—possibly three or more source documents, seem to have gone into Henshaw's

Figure 5.3
"(Description of)
Ohio," Frances
Henshaw, 1823.
*[Courtesy of David
Rumsey Map Collection.
List #2501T]*

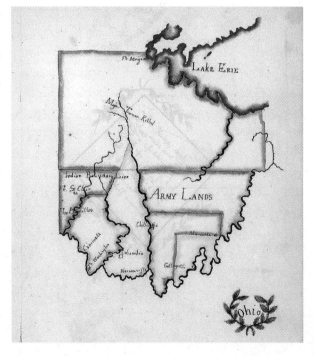

Figure 5.4
"Ohio," Frances
Henshaw, 1823.
*[Courtesy of David
Rumsey Map Collection.
List #2501.018]*

selection and editing process for this very short passage. Henshaw's deliberate pastiche approach to assembling her texts, even when they are brief, suggests a patchwork methodology that parallels the graphic design of the page. In fact, her choppy Ohio passages are most legible to readers who are familiar with the traditional "log cabin" pattern for a quilt square.

The map version of Henshaw's "Ohio" is equally interesting as a study in interpretive selectivity. Two aspects of the map stand out. First, it appears that Henshaw may have used conflicting atlases as source images. Second, this map, above all others I have examined, seems to bear traces of a pedagogical practice, perhaps inspired by Willard's teaching style, which otherwise might have been lost to us. I posit that someone, in all likelihood a schoolmistress, read aloud a geography text-book and directed Henshaw and her fellow students to make imaginative placements of voiced elements on the sketched maps before them. After tracing the basic contours of the map of Ohio, Henshaw sought to position forts and internal boundary lines based on descriptive prose she heard read aloud. Evidence of this is borne in the selection and place-ment of elements on the map, but her embedded texts also bear traces of the aural. The city of Cincinnati is spelled "Cincinata." There is a town Henshaw labels as "Nassauville" which every source spells "Masseyville." Many futile attempts to corroborate Henshaw's spelling in text and map archives have led me to conclude that her map of Ohio bears evidence of mishearing. This is perhaps a minor point, but it demonstrates how much we may be able to learn from a close and computer-assisted reading of historical maps.

Whatever Henshaw's cartographic practice may have been, it is clear that it is predicated on selection and interpretation, rather than complete-ness and verisimilitude—and that she was working with text and image in equal measure. In places, it is obvious that she was creating emotional landscapes. Despite her sources, which fill northern Ohio with an over-whelming density of geological features, waterways, settlements, marked historical events, and place names, Henshaw's schoolgirl map contains a solitary, sentimental note gleaned from a reading of history books: "Major Truman killed."

Today, for all of our increasing sophistication in managing, analyzing, and creating maps, our cartographic and GIS tools place us nowhere near the allusive, creative, and generative impulse Henshaw manifested in 1823. Where is the software that will allow contemporary humanists—descendants of Henshaw—to play with maps?

I sense that analysis of the production of historical maps is best done through an experimental performance of similar cartographic processes—in the way that students of bibliography may fold sheets into gatherings in order to understand the construction of a book. The truest humanities GIS exercise, then, may be conducted completely offline, although the Scholars' Lab Neatline project offers an interesting platform for sketching on maps and interrelating them with texts and contexts (Nowviskie et al.).

It is impossible to imagine that the intellectual framework through which humanities scholars approach GIS would ever shed its formative connection to the arts. To that end, we would do well to look closely at the liberating and ludic aspects of constraints-based methodology, validated by wranglers of poetic form throughout history and self-consciously addressed through aleatory and procedural experimentation in twentieth-century art and poetry. This is well-trodden ground, for which our best pathfinders are not critics, but performers and practitioners.

It is no surprise that GIS is often regarded as positivist and mechanistic by humanities scholars. But we have a great opportunity to reform that perception—hence my emphasis in this chapter on processes as much as products of research. What if we did not assume that GISes were merely "analytical or information-presentation tools," but rather that they hold what Jessop calls "reflexive" (44) potential? Operating in a reflective way within the mechanical framework presented by these tools may be as useful as inventing entirely new tools for humanities inquiry. Where they do not function optimally, we ought to use existing GIS tools to reflect on our methods and aims as humanities scholars interested in place and space in the documentary record, and thereby reconsider the construction of our disciplines.

The time has come, however, to build our own versions of these tools—to engage actively with GIS in the realm of interpretive literary and textual studies: from support for complex mapping of print culture production and distribution networks through space and time, to the visualization of highly subjective spatial expression within and about historical and literary documents. We should also be perverting GIS—maybe lying, certainly playing with it—in order to examine not just literary and historical content (although that will be vastly interesting), but also the spatial and typographical features of books. Can we imagine the next generation of spatial analysis tools in support of the visual and aesthetic aspects of book history?

I close this chapter with two questions that inspired the Scholars' Lab Neatline project and continue to drive my spatial humanities research agenda. They pertain to geospatial editing in the two guises in which we understand all textual production and editorial and scholarly work— that is, with representation on the one hand, and generation on the other. First, representation. The question here is how to represent the intertwined cartographic and textual condition that is foregrounded in a project like Henshaw's, but is actually evident in every atlas or map that we find incorporated into a printed or manuscript book. How might we, as scholarly editors, approach all the maps and geospatial data we either have been ignoring or, for decades, been treating like illustrations rather than the embedded geospatial information systems they are?

The question about generation is meant to be both merry and pragmatic, a balance I deem especially important in digital humanities scholarship. First, I wish to know how to create interpretive environments (sets of toys as much as tools) that will allow humanists to play with geographic expression—how, for instance, to incorporate cartographic sketching practices within our hermeneutic tool kit. Finally, I want to know how to make new digital mapping environments so naturally joyful to use that humanities scholars will see clearly that these tools are, indeed, toys.

NOTE

1. This portion of the chapter draws on research previously published in the 2010 issue of *Poetess Archive Journal* as "'Inventing the Map' in the Digital Humanities: A Young Lady's Primer." Additional slides and illustrations slides may be observed in the recording of the keynote presentation at the Canadian Writing Research Collaboratory Conference, Ryerson University, Toronto, October 27, 2011, available at http://www.cwrc.ca/cwrc_news/cwrc-conference-keynote-bethany-noviskie/.

WORKS CITED

Arrowsmith, Aaron, and Samuel Lewis. *General Atlas.* Boston: Thomas and Andrews, 1812.

Brückner, Martin. *The Geographic Revolution in Early America: Maps, Literacy, and National Identity.* Chapel Hill: University of North Carolina Press, 2006.

Carey, Mathew. *Carey's American Pocket Atlas.* Philadelphia: M. Carey, 1805.

Clay, Jenny Strauss. "Mapping the Catalogue of Ships." *Scholars' Lab Blog.* 13 January 2012. http://www.scholarslab.org/announcements/mapping-the-catalogue-of-ships

Drucker, Johanna. *SpecLab: Digital Aesthetics and Projects in Speculative Computing.* Chicago: University of Chicago Press, 2009.

Gregory, Ian, and Paul S. Ell. *Historical GIS: Technologies, Methodologies, and Scholarship.* Cambridge: Cambridge University Press, 2007.

Henshaw, Frances Alsop. "Book of Penmanship Executed at the Middlebury Female Academy." 1823. *Library of David Rumsey.* Pub. List No. 2501.000. http://bit.ly/dmbgHL

Jessop, Martyn. "The Inhibition of Geographical Information in Digital Humanities Scholarship." *Literary and Linguistic Computing* 23 (April 2008): 39–50.

Monmonier, Mark. *How to Lie with Maps.* Chicago: University of Chicago Press, 1996.

Morse, Jedidiah. *Geography Made Easy: Being an Abridgement of the American Universal Geography.* Boston: Thomas and Andrews, 1802.

NINES: Networked Infrastructure for Nineteenth-Century Electronic Scholarship. *Juxta: Collation Software for Scholars.* University of Virginia. http://www.juxtasoftware.org

Nowviskie, Bethany. "'Inventing the Map' in the Digital Humanities: A Young Lady's Primer." *Poetess Archive Journal* 2.1 (2010). http://paj.muohio.edu/paj/index.php/paj/article/viewArticle/11

Nowviskie, Bethany, and Adam Soroka. "*Neatline*: Facilitating Geospatial and Temporal Interpretation of Archival Collections." NEH Level II Start-Up Grant White Paper. http://bit.ly/xnEJdl

Nowviskie, Bethany, David McClure, Wayne Graham, Adam Soroka, Jeremy Boggs, and Eric Rochester. "Geo-Temporal Interpretation of Archival Collections with Neatline." *Literary and Linguistic Computing* 28.4 (2013): 692–99. http://llc.oxfordjournals.org/content/28/4/692.abstract

Renear, Alan, Elli Mylonas, and David Durand. "Refining Our Notion of What Text Really Is: The Problem of Overlapping Hierarchies." 1993. http://www.stg.brown.edu/resources/stg/monographs/ohco.html

Scholars' Lab. *Neatline: Plot Your Course in Space and Time*. University of Virginia Library. http://neatline.org

———. *Spatial Humanities: Institute for Enabling Geospatial Scholarship*. University of Virginia Library. http://spatial.scholarslab.org

Schulten, Susan. "Emma Willard and the Graphic Foundations of American History." *Journal of Historical Geography* 33 (2007): 542–64.

Willard, Emma. Letter to Miss Foster, 5 Nov. 1848. *The Life of Emma Willard*, by John Lord. New York: D. Appleton, 1873.

———. *A Plan for Improving Female Education*. Middlebury: S.W. Copeland, 1819.

Willson, Marcius. "A Critical Review of American Common School Histories: As Embraced in a Report Submitted to the New Jersey Society of Teachers and Friends of Education." *Biblical Repository* (July 1845): 517–39.

Woodbridge, William Channing, and Emma Willard. *Geography for Beginners*. Hartford, CT: Oliver D. Cooke, 1826.

———. *A System of Universal Geography*. Hartford, CT: Oliver D. Cooke, 1827.

EDMONTON PIPELINES

Living and Playing in the Digital City

Heather Zwicker

What is Pipelines?

Edmonton Pipelines is a research cell based at the University of Alberta that is interested in bringing together urban theory, digital technologies, and creative mapping techniques in order to narrate the city of Edmonton. Our goal is to create a series of interactive digital maps of the city of Edmonton to serve as a platform for both our own and other scholars' experimentation and research. While we take the city of Edmonton as our focus and object of study, we are also the founding research group in the Canadian Institute for Research Computing in Arts' (CIRCA) Digital Urbanism Collaboratory. Through this structure, we also hope to connect and collaborate with urban and digital scholars around the world, building a network of humanists who share our interests and concerns.

Pipelines is not a single installation; rather, as the name might suggest, it is a collection of multiple granular projects akin to the plethora of pipelines one might see at an oil refinery. To cite three relevant examples: "Amiskwaciwâskahikan" (the Cree name for Edmonton) will lay bare the city's colonial logic by superimposing Treaty 6 Aboriginal maps over conventional maps of the space we know as Edmonton; "Vertical Suburbia" will search for the scattered signs of an untold material history of the suburbs; and "Past Futures" will look at the Edmontons that never were, superimposing planning maps onto city maps to analyze the differences that emerge.

This approach of capturing overlapping perspectives reflects our belief that a city is not a single construct, but rather a ragged collection of meanings that cross each other, sometimes without ever meeting. Each of the Pipelines projects mobilizes the genre most appropriate to its theme, using the richest digital media suited to the pipeline. Photography, video, narrative, animation, and audio are used to link analysis with representation. Each pipeline is led by an individual researcher connected to a specific team. One of the key philosophies behind our diffuse structure is to allow the concerns and research questions of each pipeline to drive the format of expression. Nonetheless, a majority of our projects will be mapped in some form, and we have selected the HyperCities platform as the prototype for our map-based work.

This chapter is more speculative than descriptive, designed to raise questions about representational possibilities. The question that drives this chapter is whether there are modes of representation that can recreate, digitally, the ludic ways in which we inhabit our twenty-first-century city. In what follows, I address "the city"—in particular, the city of Edmonton—review some existing digital cartographies, and then use a Pipelines case study to raise questions about the affordances and limitations of ludic digitalism.

Why the City? Why this City?

To understand how Pipelines conceptualizes the city of Edmonton, we need to acknowledge four theoretical underpinnings that are related both intricately and contentiously.

First, Pipelines asserts that the city is a place. The distinction between place and space has traditionally rested on the individual, subjective experience of the city. Space is a set of co-ordinates, an area delineated by objectivity alone, whereas place is what happens when this area is experienced by someone who creates memories, who builds his or her own path along with the traces left behind, who questions the layers of meaning and experience in any given location.[1] Space is the Google map on one's smart phone; place is the creative cartography of the Hitotoki projects, which impregnate Google maps with "singular experiences tied to locations."[2]

Second, and at cross purposes with the notion of city as place, we are living less and less inside a city, and more and more inside urbanization itself—that is, inside a material and social space increasingly perceived to be in a constant state of flux—and in regards to which the stakes brought forth by material development—expansion, superposition, destruction, reconstruction—are challenging the formerly strict structural distinctions between centrality and periphery.[3] The reshaping and acceleration of urban life at the onset of the new century offers a renewed context in which to think about the production of knowledge itself, since urbanization's native tongue is not geography but data: demographics, corporate holdings, square footage, and housing values. The notions of flux and circulation endemic to such data permeate and infect our conception of the urban fabric itself.[4]

Third, we are no longer content with simply walking, commuting, or driving in our cities. Many of us are now reflecting on how we accomplish these things while on mobile digital devices and Global Positioning System (GPS)–enabled maps. The space between the digital and the urban is shrinking and moving toward the surface where subjectivity and urban space intersect, specifically the screen on which we are becoming our own characters in a new urban narrative. This urban reality is less "virtual," or disincarnated, than it appeared to be even a decade ago. Pipelines holds that there is a new creativity in the redoubling of one's experience on the screen of a mobile device, even while our belief in the classical, linear, bildungsroman-type narrative is challenged by these unforeseen digital parameters. The mobility of the screen itself has become as important as the mobility of images. Not only is the representation of urban experience being transformed by technology but so is the way we look at ourselves through the city.

Fourth, it appears to us that lesser known Canadian cities recently have become sites of fascinating activity. Entire neighbourhoods spring up from the ground in a matter of weeks; large downtown areas are reconceived and rebranded through ambitious projects. Since the turn of the twenty-first century, Canadian cities like Edmonton, for example, have been made infamous by such spectacle. This is a unique period in the history of urban development. From the perspective of the everyday, individual life, it might very well be an untold experience. As a postwar, mid-sized, car-centred city, Edmonton is at once unique and a representative case study. It is unique in that it is North America's most northern city of over one million inhabitants, but it is also representative of the main type of urban space—based on mobility—that developed after the Second World War. Such cities have been either understudied or dismissed as characterless manifestations of "sprawl." It is precisely this lack of attention that animates this project. This is starting to change, with books by Linda Goyette, Darrin Hagen, and my own beginning to chronicle Edmonton. But it is still possible to pick up a book subtitled *Writing Canadian Cities* and see no mention of Edmonton. Far from a detriment, however, being understoried is a boon to the Pipelines project, as it means the Edmonton city space is still malleable, amenable to a plethora of stories that intersect in complex ways. Any single city location might mean a number of things, and our various pipelines attempt to distribute distinct meanings through semiotically dense urban spaces.

Implication: The Need for New Representational Forms

These four contentiously linked theoretical convictions demonstrate the need for new urban narratives—new narrative forms, in fact. The Pipelines project aims to define the city from the ground up. But the combination of self-reflexive digital mediations, the rapid and disorienting pace of urbanization, the ubiquity of data, and the increasing typicality of urban forms (even walkable European cities are being transformed by housing tracts and big box stores) urges us to ask new questions about a city like Edmonton today. How can we narrate the personal experience of living inside urbanization? What do individual narratives absorb from their physical urban surroundings? What happens to these individual narratives when they incorporate urban data to show how physical surroundings are themselves the result of complex histories yet to be told? What narrative forms can address the experience of relating to our own stories and feelings in a constantly shifting urban space? How is the assertion of place meaningful in the face of geographic information systems' (GIS) blank spatiality, or in the face of multinational corporatization that makes all spaces look and feel the same? Exactly how might a place acquire an aura of authenticity in such a context? Also, how does urbanization exist in the past? What are the visual forms of its memory? And what of all those dreamt-up presents that never were realized, of all those possible futures that never occurred?

Pipelines is an attempt to tell new city stories for our twenty-first-century reality. The project draws on traditional narrative practice—literature, creative non-fiction, close reading, and literary theory, for instance—but it also seeks inspiration in new ways of inhabiting the city. Traditionally, theories of urban culture have suggested three major concepts for inhabiting the city as place (versus space): the flâneur, the everyday, and psychogeography.[5] More recently, however, the city has also emerged as place in the form of a playground for tech-savvy adults engaged in city games like Manhunt, parkour, and geocaching.[6] Manhunt, a massive game of hide-and-go-seek organized online and played by strangers, turns denizens into fellow game players for a few hours on a specified night; when the game ends, the community dissolves back into the urban flow. Parkour uses urban space against the grain, using city structures as a physical and orienteering challenge. And geocaching creates secret communities by hiding small objects in plain sight, unnoticed except by the online community swapping geolocations. These games, specific to cities, engender twenty-first-century urban subjectivities, less individualistic than those of the late nineteenth (flâneur) or twentieth centuries (psychogeography and the everyday), even though the forms of community they produce are fleeting and often accidental.

Like their predecessors, Manhunt, parkour, and geocaching are technologically mediated. As automatic writing is to psychogeography, so is the website to Manhunt; as poetry is to flâneurie, so is the digital map to geocaching.

Digital Cartographies

Of course, there are already many web-based cartographies that take cities as object and inspiration. Hitotoki, mentioned above, offers short place-based narratives from Tokyo, New York, Shanghai, Paris, and Sofia. The site has recently become Twitter-based, but in its "classic" form Hitotoki asserts the importance of place by insisting that even quotidian stories take place somewhere, and imbues that somewhere with significance. In a different vein, sound maps such as London's Caledonian Road project demonstrate new ways of collecting and publicizing popular history (Dein and Panetta).[7] The Cleveland Historical Map similarly spatializes local history. Finally, the mapping projects that Christian Nold has initiated are particularly compelling for the way they map urban intensities (the San Francisco Emotion Map) or their opposites (the Stockport Emotion Map). Nold equips community mappers with an electronic device that measures physical responses and then he sends them into city spaces. After he amasses responses, he can map the city sites that evoke particularly strong physical responses. Nold's work also has evolved into community-based mapping, and, as in the case of Stockport, helps citizens understand how and why the city might fail to elicit intensity. Pipelines hopes to adapt many aspects of projects like these—their community-mindedness, their attention to narrative, their understanding of history "from below," for instance—while mobilizing the city's open data to make sense of this particular city, in the here and now.

Even these superbly thoughtful digital cartographies, however, assume the co-ordinates of latitude and longitude, the truth-telling aspects of mapping. As we know from even basic critiques of cartography, maps hide as much as they reveal. Maps are technologies of mastery that too often participate in the tyranny of the visible, organizing knowledge along unacknowledged co-ordinates—spatial co-ordinates, one might say, instead of place-based knowledge. This tendency is germane to all cartography, but perhaps is especially so for digital technologies, where the flat, disembodied screen underscores the myth of a *terra nullius* filled by the mapper's genius.

The question I pose at this stage of Pipelines' development is whether we might use digital technologies against the grain. How might we represent a meaning-rich place using digital means without assuming unfettered visibility, total mastery, and pure knowability? How can we map a place whose meaning is—as with all lived places—incomplete, dynamic, and subject to power struggles? How can we draw a digital map that recognizes, rather than disavows, its own inadequacy? How can we show something important while drawing attention to the fact that we cannot show everything? A Pipelines case study will serve as a way to begin answering these questions.

Rossdale

The Rossdale Flats, a two-square-kilometre zone geographically central to Edmonton yet topographically as well as symbolically beneath the city core, have staged quintessentially urban contests between private and public, efficiency and commemoration, settlement, commerce, and resource extraction. Rossdale occupies the site of pre–Treaty 6 Aboriginal settlements, the second Fort Edmonton, the inauguration of the Province of Alberta, a burial ground, an ice house, a fair ground, a ball park, and a power plant. In the early twentieth century, it offered working-class housing near the coal seams of the North Saskatchewan River; in the early twenty-first century, it is characterized by expensive vinyl-sided Victorian houses alongside the Capital City Recreation Area. The conflicts of civic, corporate, and environmental interests have circulated in Rossdale. It is the site for powerful past futures: here is where the planetarium was to be built, where baseball would flourish, where power generation would triple, where artist studios and chic cafes would heighten Edmonton's cosmopolitan cachet.

Such a dense city space hosts multiple, contradictory stories. What does it mean to "read" such a densely signifying space? I want a technology that can represent the following. Stand in one spot in the Rossdale Flats to apprehend the complexity of place. If one looks closely at the boreal bush along the bicycle trails, one can discern raspberry canes and apple trees on the riverbanks, domestic remnants of the backyards from houses expropriated in the 1970s to build the "Ribbon of Green," the development of Edmonton's river valley and ravine system. Where one stands and marvels, trying to imagine the vanished cityscape, is a riverbank hollowed by coal extraction: a formative city phenomenon beneath the plane of the visible. Beneath that vision lies another, forcibly made invisible by the false celebration of this city as merely one hundred years old: Aboriginal Rossdale, routinely inhabited for six thousand years. One may be watched by a ring-necked pheasant, red squirrels, a coyote, foxes, and certainly magpies: denizens of the urban river valley. Look uphill, downriver, and one will see the brick brewery, now the residence of Gene Dub, the city's best-loved architect, implicated as well in gentrification; upriver, the brickyard site has become a fitness centre. Running past is the North Saskatchewan River itself, linked to the Saskatchewan Glacier, though heated and treated by the Rossdale power generating station.

Rossdale does not tell a narrative of progress. In fact, it does not tell a narrative at all. Instead, it shows that every urban phenomenon has contestatory values that collide in one moment and diverge in another—it highlights the "flux" and "circulation" of urbanization mentioned earlier. Rossdale tells us that a city is a palimpsest, replete with connotations that concentrate and occlude one another. How to represent this? Our traditional humanist tools—principally, writing—cannot do it well enough. Writing is linear and moves from "here" to "there"; I want a more kaleidoscopic tool. Poetry proffers possibility, but I suspect that digital technology may prove more flexible and adaptable. My hope is that the Rossdale collection in HyperCities will show industrial histories against natural histories, reveal the burial grounds and the traffic circle built over them, demonstrate the power relations and neighbourly relations that together built this place and continue to give it meaning.

What the Rossdale collection will look like is still to be determined, but I want to close by speculating about digitizing ludic tropes for inhabiting the city. With regard to Manhunt, for example, is there something in the way players find and use spaces that do not appear on a map that might allow us to better tell stories? In a sense, Manhunt turns the specificities of GIS in on itself: one might geolocate an individual and still not see her. As I mention above, parkour quite explicitly uses urban space against the grain. Could we imitate parkour's hard-body insistence on taking built environments as a challenge? What if we take the built environment (whether that is urban space or Google Earth imagery) not as a given but as a dare? As for geocaching, it creates secret communities, populating the city with secret caches we cavalierly bypass all the time. Unlike maps, which pretend to tell everything, a map that uses geocaching as its formative metaphor would pretend to tell nothing. But everything is there, under the surface. Urban meaning is precisely that: not inert, but actively formed by adopting a purposeful perspective, by looking carefully at places where others see nothing, following power lines and lost burial grounds to uncover something telling. Nowhere is this truer than in Edmonton, where the one thing most people accept is that there is nothing to see in the city.

AUTHOR'S NOTE

I wish to acknowledge the assistance of colleagues Russell Cobb, Maureen Engel, and Daniel Laforest, as well as Erika Luckert, the student who has worked most closely with me on the Rossdale project.

NOTES

1.   This distinction is hinted at by Edward S. Casey in his 1997 book *The Fate of Place*. But it is most clearly made by Augustin Berque in his 2000 book *Écoumène: Introduction à l'étude des milieux humains*. See also Lucy Lippard, *The Lure of the Local* (1997).
2.   *Hitotoki* is a Japanese word meaning "a moment in time." Hitotoki sites exist for several global cities, including New York, Tokyo, and London. See http://www.hitotoki.org/classic/about for an overview of the project.

3. Saskia Sassen expresses it best when developing her well-known concept of the global city: "Today, there is no longer a simple straightforward relation between centrality and such geographic entities as the downtown and the central business district" (110).

4. On circulation particularly, see Boutros and Straw.

5. For representative approaches to each, see Merlin Coverley, Will Self, and Ralph Steadman, respectively.

6. This is to say nothing about locative games like Parallel Kingdom, Wherigo, Gbanga Familia, or TrailHit, few of which were even in production when I began writing this essay, nor of less ludic locative apps like FourSquare—the point being that urban gaming is a burgeoning field.

7. This map stands in for a growing number of sound maps, to say nothing of the less crafted, more encyclopedic acoustic city maps like those of Toronto (http://www. torontosoundmap.com), Montreal (http://www.montrealsoundmap.com), and New York (http://www.nysoundmap.org).

WORKS CITED

Digital Sources

Cleveland Historical. http://www.clevelandhistorical.org

Dein, Alan, and Francesca Panetta. "Sound Map: The Caledonian Road." *The Guardian* 26 April 2010. http://www.guardian.co.uk/society/interactive/2010/apr/26/caledonian-road-sound-map

Mod, Craig. Hitotoki: Narrative Mapping the World. http://www.hitotoki.org

Montreal Sound Map. http://www.montrealsoundmap.com

New York Sound Map. http://www.nysoundmap.org

Nold, Christian. *Bio Mapping / Emotion Mapping*. 2004–ongoing. http://biomapping.net

Toronto Sound Map. http://www.torontosoundmap.com

Print Sources

Berque, Augustin. *Écoumène: Introduction à l'étude des milieux humains*. Paris: Éditions Belin, 2000.

Boutros, Alexandra, and Will Straw, eds. *Circulation and the City: Essays on Urban Culture*. Montreal and Kingston: McGill-Queen's University Press, 2010.

Bruegmann, Robert. *Sprawl: A Compact History*. Chicago: University of Chicago Press, 2006.

Casey, Edward S. *The Fate of Place: A Philosophical History*. Berkeley: University of California Press, 1998.

Coverley, Merlin. *Psychogeography*. London: Pocket Essentials, 2010.

Edwards, Justin D., and Douglas Ivison. *Downtown Canada: Writing Canadian Cities*. Toronto: University of Toronto Press, 2005.

Goyette, Linda, and Carolina Jakeway Roemmich. *Edmonton In Our Own Words*. Edmonton: University of Alberta Press, 2004.

Hagen, Darrin. *The Edmonton Queen: Not a Riverboat Story.* Edmonton: Slipstream Books, 1997.

Jacobs, Jane. *The Death and Life of Great American Cities.* 1961. New York: Modern Library, 1993.

Lippard, Lucy. *The Lure of the Local: Senses of Place in a Multicentered Society.* New York: New Press, 1997.

Lynch, Kevin. *The Image of the City.* Cambridge, MA: MIT Press, 1960.

Mumford, Lewis. *The Culture of Cities.* 1938. New York: Harcourt Brace, 1981.

Sassen, Saskia. "The Global City: Introducing a Concept and Its History." *Mutations.* Rem Koolhaas, Stefano Boeri, Sanford Kwinter, Nadia Tazi, Hans Ulrich Obrist. Barcelona: ACTAR; Bordeaux: Arc en rêve centre d'architecture, 2001. 104–15.

Self, Will, and Ralph Steadman. *Psychogeography: Disentangling the Modern Conundrum of Psyche and Place.* New York: Bloomsbury, 2007.

Zwicker, Heather, ed. *Edmonton on Location: River City Chronicles.* Edmonton: NeWest Press, 2005.

REPRESENTING CANADIAN
QUEER AUTHORSHIP

Making the Internet a Women's Place

Michelle Schwartz & Constance Crompton

Reflecting on her life, Jane Rule mused that after the 1964 publication of *Desert of the Heart*, English Canada's first literary lesbian novel, she "became, for the media, the only lesbian in Canada" (Martin S8). Rule passed away in 2007, but not before she became a featured activist on the website of the Canadian Lesbian and Gay Archives' National Portrait Collection and one of the few female activists from the Canadian lesbian and gay liberation movement with an entry in *Wikipedia*. Her inclusion in these online spaces meets one of the political goals of the Lesbian and Gay Liberation in Canada (LGLC) project—namely, to increase the online visibility of queer Canadian history.

When we first formulated the LGLC project in December 2010, we envisaged a straightforward online publication of *Lesbian and Gay Liberation in Canada: A Selected Annotated Chronology, 1964–1975*, a groundbreaking work by Donald McLeod, a long-time volunteer at the Canadian Lesbian and Gay Archives and a librarian at the University of Toronto. We planned to augment the digital edition with maps and network graphs that would illustrate the relationships between the events, people, and places that were central to the gay and lesbian liberation movement in Canada. From the outset, our project was tied closely to the Canadian Lesbian and Gay Archives (CLGA), since CLGA material underpins much of McLeod's chronology. And, indeed, our project was guided by the CLGA motto, "keeping our stories alive." The 107 women (including, for instance, author and politician Judy LaMarsh, authors Jackie Manthorne and Marie-Claire Blais, and activists Pat Murphy and Lamar Van Dyke) whose stories are represented in McLeod's book, and in CLGA's collection more broadly, wore many hats; they were and remain writers of fiction and polemic, experts in poetry and politics. Their work as authors has been informed by their activism; their writing has, in turn, shaped the Canadian political and literary landscape, and yet they are underrepresented in high traffic online areas.

Our encoding of the events of the gay and lesbian liberation movement in TEI (the markup language of the Text Encoding Initiative), for addition to the Canadian Writing Research Collaboratory's (CWRC) corpus, is part of our attempt to make the Internet a women's place: one that reflects women's multiple experiences and supports their multiple perspectives. We seek to intervene in the online representation of the women in our data set, with the hope of increasing their visibility to the traditional and citizen scholars who work within CWRC, and to the public at large. Our 2011 inclusion within CWRC has compelled us to look outward, not just at the relationships represented within our material source (McLeod's chronology), but at the social relationships represented and, indeed, *forged*, online. CWRC is a digital space designed to foster interaction among traditional scholars, citizen scholars, and, in the case of our project, perhaps even the living persons represented within our data set.

This chapter introduces our project in the context of the Canadian Lesbian and Gay Archives. First, we introduce our source text, the type of community story we aim to tell, and demonstrate how TEI might help us tell that story. We go on to investigate the difficulties associated with this project: the implications of the current representation of the women in our data set on *Wikipedia*, in the online instantiation of the CLGA's National Portrait Collection (NPC), and on the Internet more generally. Using our project as a case study, we argue that digital scholarship and online activism can be paired in order to spur on the larger discussion about whether Internet behemoths like *Wikipedia* and Google should be the primary gatekeepers of our cultural history.

In addition to reproducing McLeod's text, the LGLC project reconfigures his chronology as a digital resource that will let researchers trace the events of the gay liberation movement aided by maps and timelines; model the shifting identities of the actors within the text; contribute personal reflections about the events in the text; and critically evaluate the relationship between the text and the bibliographic materials that make up its content. Our project is underpinned by material from the Canadian Lesbian and Gay Archives, so we want our project, from the code on up, to be a credit to the organization.

Don McLeod and Lesbian and Gay Liberation in Canada: A Selected Annotated Chronology, 1964–1975

Donald W. McLeod was born in 1957 in Cornwall, Ontario and grew up in Calgary, Alberta. Since receiving his master's degree in library science from the University of Toronto in 1983, he has worked in both publishing and librarianship. He is now the head of book and serial acquisitions for the University of Toronto Libraries, and continues to be involved in the publication of documents on gay and Canadian history. In addition to his writing and editorial work, he has been a volunteer at the Canadian Lesbian and Gay Archives for twenty-five years. He first became involved with the CLGA when he was commissioned by the CLGA and the AIDS Committee of Toronto to work on *Medical, Social, and Political Aspects of the Acquired Immune Deficiency Syndrome (AIDS) Crisis: A Bibliography,* which was published in 1985 (CLGA, "National Portrait Collection").

McLeod began work on the first volume of *Lesbian and Gay Liberation in Canada: A Selected Annotated Chronology* in 1989. The work was inspired by "Victories and Defeats: A Gay and Lesbian Chronology, 1964–1982," which James Fraser compiled and published in the 1982 anthology *Flaunting It!: A Decade of Gay Journalism from* The Body Politic (edited by Ed Jackson and Stan Persky). In the course of his work at the CLGA,

McLeod often consulted Fraser's chronology but was frustrated by its lack of bibliographic citations. McLeod believed that a detailed chronology of gay liberation history *combined* with a bibliography of sources for each entry would be an "authoritative reference guide to the origins and development of lesbians and gay liberation in Canada" (McLeod viii).

From 1989 to 1996, during his free time, McLeod laboured over his chronology. The CLGA served as the base of operations for his research, as the archive possesses the world's largest collection of lesbian and gay periodicals, as well as the records for many of the most influential gay liberation organizations for the period in question. Along with the CLGA, the holdings of two other organizations formed the tripartite backbone of the sources for McLeod's book: the Archives gaies du Québec in Montreal, and the Canadian Women's Movement Archives in Ottawa. McLeod supplemented these collections with materials found in the archives of the University of British Columbia and the New York Public Library, and further augmented them with accounts from his direct correspondence with fifty of the key actors in the events mentioned in his book. These individuals were called upon to correct errors or misconceptions and to offer additional sources of information. Finally, "more than ten of them were asked to examine an earl[y] draft of the project and were able to offer cogent advice" (McLeod ix).

Lesbian and Gay Liberation in Canada: A Selected Annotated Chronology, 1964–1975 was originally published by Homewood Books in 1996 and reissued in 2011. The book consists of a chronology of the first twelve years of the "organized homophile/gay liberation movement in Canada." The chronology begins with the formation of the Vancouver-based Association for Social Knowledge, the country's first large-scale homophile organization. It ends with the founding of the National Gay Rights Coalition/Coalition national pour les droits des homosexuels, the "first truly national coalition of Canadian lesbian and gay groups" (McLeod viii). The book's subtitle—"A Selected Annotated Chronology"— refers to McLeod's primary focus on "self-declared lesbians and gay men and their activities in regard to the forging of lesbian and gay communities and liberation in Canada" (viii). Hence, the book devotes most attention to demonstrations, political actions, lobbying, and legal reforms.

As a secondary and supplementary focus, it lists "artistic and cultural contributions with significant lesbian or gay content," and includes three appendices listing lesbian and gay organizations, periodicals, bars and clubs. Heterosexuals who were instrumental either in supporting or opposing the gay liberation movement are included, and foreign events are noted if they either had a direct impact on the Canadian gay liberation movement or featured the prominent involvement of gay Canadians. McLeod is currently completing a second volume that will span from 1975 to 1981, from the founding of the National Gay Rights Coalition/Coalition national pour les droits des homosexuels to the start of the AIDS crisis.

McLeod's chronology is structured as a series of entries, first by date, then by location. Each entry is followed by a dense bibliography of primary sources. The combination of chronology and bibliography drew us to TEI encoding as a potential methodology to enhance access to McLeod's text. We were not motivated simply to digitize the chronology—in fact, it is available online on LGBT Life with Full Text and as a PDF on T-Space, the University of Toronto's research repository. Rather, we saw potential in Lesbian and Gay Liberation in Canada: A Selected Annotated Chronology, 1964–1975 as both a text and a rich geospatial and temporal database of landmarks in Canadian history.

The Canadian Lesbian and Gay Archives

Originally called the Canadian Gay Liberation Movement Archives, the core of the CLGA's collection consists of the records of The Body Politic (TBP), a gay liberation newspaper published in Toronto between 1971 and 1987. In just over fifteen years, The Body Politic published 135 issues, becoming "the leading journal of gay liberation in all of Canada and—with an eventual third of its circulation outside the country—an internationally respected voice of radical gay thought" (CLGA, "A Chronology of the Archives"). The Body Politic was published by a collective that incorporated in 1975 under the not-for-profit umbrella of Pink Triangle Press. The creation of Pink Triangle Press ensured that "if legal charges were ever laid against TBP, those charges would be brought against the corporation and its officers, leaving most Collective members untouched and able to continue to publish the magazine" (CLGA, "The Collective Years").

By establishing Pink Triangle Press, *The Body Politic* collective placed itself directly into the fray of the gay liberation struggle. Never content with simply reporting the news, the collective sought to reinforce "opposition to state censorship as a form of social control" through the publication of material "about practices seen by some as beyond the bounds of conventional gay rights" (CLGA, "The Collective Years"). Pink Triangle saw this open goading of institutional power as part of its "commitment to a wider struggle for liberation, and [a] refusal to marginalize others out of concern for 'respectability'" (CLGA, "The Collective Years"). By printing cartoons depicting oral sex to articles about fist fucking, the collective provoked the Morality Squad of the Metropolitan Toronto Police to remove issues of *The Body Politic* from newsstands, and the joint Toronto–provincial pornography squad (known as "Operation P") to raid its offices and seize crates of material, including the newspaper's subscription lists (Bébout, *Promiscuous*).

Most notably, following the publication in 1978 of *The Body Politic* article "Men Loving Boys Loving Men," the Pink Triangle Press was charged by the Crown with "possession of obscene material for distribution" and "use of the mails for purpose of transmitting indecent, immoral or scurrilous materials." The ongoing series of trials and appeals lasted until 1982, with the acquittal of the entire collective (Bébout, *Text*). The drama of the trials helped feed the protests over the 1981 Toronto bathhouse raids (CLGA, "The Collective Years"), which, in turn, were backed by extensive coverage in *The Body Politic*, including the famous March 1981 cover that headlined black and white photographs of the police conducting the raids with one word—RAGE—in blood-red capital letters.

In 1973, the CLGA's nascent archivists began soliciting additional material in the pages of *The Body Politic*, and the collection soon expanded beyond the basement of the archive's founder and first champion, *Body Politic* member Ron Dayman. The archives changed its name to the Canadian Gay Archives in 1975, and began gathering material from all over Canada and from beyond the confines of the gay liberation movement. This broadening mandate led to its current name, the Canadian Lesbian and Gay Archives, adopted in 1993.

The CLGA has had a series of homes since its beginning in Dayman's basement at 203 Boulton Avenue in Toronto. The collection has grown from its origins as a personal hobby, out of storage space in the homes of various members of *The Body Politic* collective, to a large-scale research collection in need of workspace for archivists and researchers alike. In 1988, it moved to a 1,000-square-foot space on the second floor of 464 Yonge Street in Toronto. By 1992, the collection had grown so large it demanded a move to the archive's first fully independent space—2,000 square feet at 56 Temperance Street in Toronto (CLGA, "A Chronology of the Archives"). The collection eventually outgrew the space on Temperance Street and the archive moved to yet another location at the corner of Church and Wellesley Streets—the heart of Toronto's historic gay village. In 2009, thanks to the work of former city councilor Kyle Rae and the generosity of the Children's Aid Society of Toronto, the CLGA was able to acquire the Jared D. Sessions House, an Italianate heritage home built in 1858, and located at 34 Isabella Street in Toronto (CLGA, "Doors Open Script"). The house was envisaged as a public showcase for the vast amount of material amassed over the course of almost four decades. For the first time ever, the archive had a dedicated gallery. The gallery's per-manent collection is the CLGA's National Portrait Collection.

The National Portrait Collection was established in 1998, in celebra-tion of the archive's twenty-fifth anniversary. Commissioned works have been added regularly over the years, bringing the total number of por-traits in the collection to seventy. The purpose of the NPC is to honour individuals who have made "significant contributions to the growth of diverse, out and proud lesbian, gay, bisexual and trans (LGBT) communi-ties in Canada. The collection is regularly exhibited...in Toronto as well as at other venues across Canada, in celebration of all LGBT communities" (CLGA, "National Portrait Collection"). The CLGA has made it part of its mandate to continue to expand the National Portrait Collection, "thereby actively engaging in the creation of our own historical record" (CLGA, "National Portrait Collection"). In addition to public exhibitions, the CLGA also maintains a digital display of the NPC on its website. Each inductee's portrait is accompanied by a brief biography in both English and French. Often, these biographies represent the main web presence for NPC inductees, even when they have been central to the lesbian and gay liberation movement in Canada.

The CLGA has always been a volunteer-run, community-based organization. It is an open space, welcoming any member of the community—regardless of age or academic affiliation—who wishes to use its materials. Access is open and usage fees remain minimal. Moreover, volunteers of any skill level are welcomed, trained, and assigned any number of tasks. While similar collections, like the Canadian Women's Movement Archives and the ONE National Gay and Lesbian Archives, have been subsumed by government and university libraries, the CLGA has opted to remain independent. Run by and for the community it serves, it turned down an offer from the Archives of Ontario to take over the curation and storage of a portion of the CLGA's holdings (CLGA, "A Chronology of the Archives").

The CLGA's mandate is to "acquire, preserve, organize, and give public access to information and materials in any medium, by and about lesbians and gays, primarily produced in or concerning Canada" ("About Us"). This expansive mandate, perfectly encapsulated by the CLGA motto "keeping our stories alive," was born out of a need by the LGBT community for the representation they lacked in mainstream society (CLGA, "Collections"). It was born, too, of a desire to preserve archival material that might otherwise disappear. In the twenty years since CLGA added "lesbian" to its name, it has been working to rehabilitate its reputation from an organization concerned only with gay men. We hope to support those efforts by amplifying McLeod's chronology: the addition of personographic and place records will help establish the importance of women's materials at the CLGA and the importance of queer history in online communities like CWRC.

"Keeping Our Stories Alive"

Before outlining TEI's markup utility in teasing out new meanings from the details of McLeod's chronology, we would like to relate the sort of story we hope the LGLC project will bring to the fore. On January 15, 1974, four women took the stage on amateur talent night at the Brunswick Tavern. The Brunswick, an institution in what was then a working-class Toronto neighbourhood that was just starting to cater to students at the nearby University of Toronto, was a rowdy place, a cavernous hall lined with wooden tables and benches, with a plywood stage at one end of the hall. Heather Beyer Elizabeth, Pat Murphy, Adrienne Potts, and Sue Wells got up on the stage and sang "I Enjoy Being a Dyke," their lively send-up of "I Enjoy Being a Girl." The management asked the four women to leave. Although they were surrounded by beer-spitting, catcalling patrons, the women refused to depart (Schwabel). They were arrested and, after hours of verbal harassment by Toronto police officers, were charged with creating a disturbance (Warner 40). The incident galvanized the Toronto gay community, whose defense of the Brunswick Four has been likened to the consciousness-raising that followed the Stonewall riots of June 28, 1969 in New York's Greenwich Village. The Brunswick Four may be a prime example of women's centrality to the gay liberation movement in Canada, but representing the Brunswick Four and their influence through TEI helps dramatize the difficulty of trying to build a reliable and ethically responsible personography of the actors in the movement.

The Lesbian and Gay Liberation in Canada project is not interested solely in recovering gay history; it is also responsive to the very debates that have shaped that history. LGLC's initial personographic encoding has been motivated by the rise in the 1990s of those seeking to recuperate lost lesbian and trans histories. The debates may be familiar. In the 1980s, there was a rush to assert lesbian status for biological females who lived as men (including surgeon James Barry, music hall performer Annie Hindle, and pianist Billy Tipton)—those who previously did not have access to "lesbian" as an identity marker. In the following decade, the trans community rejoined with competing claims that these historical actors were part of trans history. Jack Halberstam draws on the typical characterization of jazz pianist Billy Tipton to summarize the debate: "Tipton, the jazz musician who lived his life as a man and who married a woman, is often represented within lesbian history as a lesbian woman forced to hide her gender in order to advance within her profession, rather than as a transsexual man living within his chosen gender identity" (Halberstam 293). These debates over identities are far from settled. The LGLC project seeks to intervene, not in the interest of taking sides or settling debates, but in re-imagining how encoding can be used to produce a temporally sensitive folksonomic articulation of identity that extends beyond the categories represented by the acronym LGBT.

What is the conscientious encoder to do in the face of such temporal specificity? The particular actors in the LGLC project are far removed from the cultural context that led Tipton to identify as a man in the 1940s and 1950s; however, that many individuals in the LGLC data set share similar stories gives us an opportunity to code for self-identification over time. Encoding practices may offer a new way to comprehend the relationship between gender performance, sexual practice, and the cultural context embedded in identity-naming practices.

If, at the start of the project, we were wary about encoding identity, we are all the more wary today about personographic tagging practices. Rather than impose identity definitions from on high, our aim is to develop a tagging method that would produce temporally specific identity definitions built from collective self-naming. Our personographic encoding, complete with explicit and temporally specific records of self-naming, results not in a dictionary definition of what, for example, the word "dyke" meant in 1974, but rather a list of women whose self-identification produces a definition by example. Our desire is to reconstruct what Eve Kosofsky Sedgwick calls nonce taxonomies, formed through "the making and unmaking...of hundreds of old and new categorical imaginings...for mapping [a particular social] landscape" (23). Interesting in itself, this endeavour will further serve one of the central goals of our project. In order to make sense of our populated, rather than verbal, definitions, users will have to learn about the women in the archive, thereby increasing the general knowledge about women's contributions to gay liberation in Canada.

We have been preoccupied with TEI standards when encoding personographies. For example, the TEI standards that categorize sex may facilitate interoperability,[1] but they simultaneously limit our encoding's expressiveness. Our initial goal—to make women's contributions to the CLGA more visible—was soon mired in our desire to have the contributors and materials speak for themselves. In trying to design a personography-derived definition of "dyke" or "queer," do we risk reproducing labels that actors within the LGLC data set abhorred in the first place? Is a secondhand account of one person's identification enough to include in our markup? We find ourselves combing through the archive, happy to recount instances where women, like the Brunswick Four, stood up, microphones at the ready, to proclaim their identification at a particular moment and place.

A Women's Place on the Web

The stories that we would like our data to tell through prose, maps, and graphs are conspicuous (to us, at least) in their absence from popular knowledge repositories, such as *Wikipedia*. For example, even though she does not have her own *Wikipedia* entry, National Portrait Collection inductee Pat Murphy is mentioned in the *Wikipedia* entry that describes the arrest of the Brunswick Four. Indeed, none of the Brunswick Four women have individual *Wikipedia* entries. Moreover, there is no *Wikipedia* entry for the Community Homophile Association of Toronto (CHAT), one of the first gay liberation organizations in all of Canada, which Murphy founded with George Hislop and others in 1971 (McLeod 56).

It is nearly impossible to find information about Murphy through Google. Google's new customized search results have reduced the serendipity of Google searches, returning results that Google's algorithms suggest for each user based on previous searches. When *we* search for Murphy, her NPC biography is elevated to our first page of Google hits because Google has collected data on our preferred search results. Our frequent visits to the National Portrait Collection through the Google homepage, rather than through direct links, ensure that we are linked to Murphy through Google. These modestly promising returns are wiped out, however, when Google's default personalization is turned off, reducing the number of relevant hits on the first page of a Google search from one to zero. Due to Google's reliance on personalization and "relevance" (determined in large part by the number of links on a page), it is unlikely that users who are not already running Google searches related to the Canadian lesbian and gay liberation movement will ever locate information about Murphy.

It is extremely difficult, even when conducting more traditional online research, to discern the connections between organizations, events, and people, and to piece together women's involvement in Canadian LGBT history. For instance, via correspondence with Lamar Van Dyke (formerly Heather Beyer Elizabeth), one of the Brunswick Four, we learned the reason the four women had been at the Brunswick Tavern on the night of their arrest; Van Dyke, then co-ordinator of A Women's Place, a feminist community centre, sought a rapprochement with Murphy, who had been working primarily with CHAT, an organization perceived by the women's movement as focusing only on gay men's issues. Searches for variations of "A Women's Place" returned no relevant Google hits—even for us—despite the fact that A Women's Place was the original location for what became the Toronto Women's Bookstore, a fixture of the feminist and LGBT communities in Toronto for thirty-nine years (the store closed on November 30, 2012). In the *Wikipedia* entry on the Toronto Women's Bookstore, A Women's Place is referenced in passing as an unnamed women's resource centre located on nearby Dupont Street. TEI will help us draw these very connections between the various events, places, and people in the LGLC data set within the Collaboratory.

Although the scope of our project is currently bound by the years 1964 to 1981, the date at which Don McLeod's chronology ends, we are keenly aware of the dearth of online information about queer trailblazers. Pioneering activists from the LGLC data set and later waves of the lesbian and gay liberation movement do not fare much better in *Wikipedia* than in Google search results. Persimmon Blackbridge, author, mental health activist, and recent National Portrait Collection inductee, only appears on *Wikipedia* in the entry for Kiss and Tell, her Vancouver-based art collective. At the time of writing, Blackbridge's name appears in red on the Kiss and Tell page, which signifies that even though she does not have a dedicated entry in *Wikipedia*, at least one *Wikipedia* editor has suggested that such an entry ought to exist. The Kiss and Tell *Wikipedia* entry is itself an orphan—an article to which no other article links. To read about Kiss and Tell on *Wikipedia* one must have prior knowledge of the collective, which works against the serendipitous knowledge acquisition that makes encyclopedias such wonderful resources. If links are the currency of the Internet in general, and in Google's indexing algorithm and *Wikipedia* more specifically, then the women in the LGLC's data set lack sufficient cultural capital.

Our examples bear out the general trend of the LGLC National Portrait Collection inductees' representation in *Wikipedia*. Of the seventy inductees, forty are without *Wikipedia* entries. Of the thirty inductees that do have entries, nine have been marked as "stubs," the *Wikipedia* term for one- or two-paragraph entries. Of the twenty-eight women in the CLGA's National Portrait Collection, however, only 39 per cent have their own dedicated *Wikipedia* entry, as opposed to the 47 per cent of NPC men who have *Wikipedia* entries. Moreover, half of the women's entries are stubs.

Our findings are consistent with the general trend in *Wikipedia*. Using length as a proxy for quality, Shyong Lam, a computer scientist from the University of Minnesota, has noted that the *Wikipedia* content that attracts male editors is of higher quality than the content that attracts female editors. We are especially interested in the distribution of gendered articles across *Wikipedia*'s seven content areas: Arts, Geography, Health, History, People, Philosophy and Religion, and Science. Women are more likely to contribute to "Arts" and "People" (the areas most relevant to our project) than they are to other content areas, but, due to the relative lack of female *Wikipedia* editors, entries on men in the "Arts" and "People" sections outnumber those on women by a ratio of ten to one.[2] Lam attributes this gap to the culture of *Wikipedia*: women do not have a critical mass in the encyclopedia, and the *Wikipedia* community treats them far less affably than it does men. Just 16 per cent of *Wikipedia* editors are women, and new female editors are more likely than their male counterparts to have their edits reversed. Women's lack of participation in *Wikipedia* has skewed the encyclopedia's content, quality, and, by extension, the visibility of subjects that, due to the enculturated differences between the sexes, are of particular interest to women (including the lesbian focused events, places, and women in the Lesbian and Gay Liberation in Canada data set).

Through our involvement with cwrc, we hope to further expand the network of online connections, drawing on the rich array of materials available under the umbrella of cwrc's Online Research Canada repository. For instance, author Jane Rule played an important role in Canadian gay history, initiating, to McLeod's mind at least, the Canadian lesbian and gay liberation movement with her publication of the lesbian themed novel, *Desert of the Heart* (McLeod 2). In addition to *Lesbian Images*, a study of lesbian writers, and several other novels, Rule also wrote extensively for *The Body Politic*, the Canadian gay liberation newspaper that gave birth to the clga. Her column, "So's Your Grandmother," began in response to the police raid of the offices of the newspaper and archives after the publication of the article "Men Loving Boys Loving Men." To show her support for the organization and her opposition to censorship, she offered to write regularly for the duration of the legal proceedings (Averill).

We need to have a conversation, while the online sphere is still open, as to whether *Wikipedia* and Google ought to be the gatekeepers of our cultural knowledge—a conversation that we can pair with activism (such as that carried out under the aegis of cwrc) and will empower traditional and citizen scholars alike. After all, we now know that Rule was not the only lesbian in Canada in 1964, nor is she the only lesbian on the Internet today. The Lesbian and Gay Liberation in Canada project seeks to represent historical lesbian and gay experience in order to make the Internet truly a digital Women's Place.

NOTES

1. The four values offered as sex attributes are *male, female, unknown,* and *not applicable.*
2. According to Lam, who was using data from 2008, 11.8 per cent of "People" and "Arts" contributors are self-identified women (Lam et al.).

WORKS CITED

Averill, Harold. "Re: Women's Accessions." Email to the authors. 5 March 2011.
Bébout, Rick. *Promiscuous Affections: A Life in the Bar, 1969–2000.* Toronto: n.p., 2003.
———. *Text Crimes: Yet Again...The Issue That Won't Go Away.* Toronto: n.p., 2003.
Canadian Lesbian and Gay Archives (CLGA). "About Us." http://www.clga.ca/about-us
———. "A Chronology of the Archives." http://www.clga.ca
———. "Collections." http://www.clga.ca/collections
———. "Doors Open Script." 30 May 2010: n. pag.
———. "National Portrait Collection/La Collection nationale de portraits." http://www.clga.ca/npc
Fraser, James. "Victories and Defeats: A Gay and Lesbian Chronology, 1969–1982." *Flaunting It!: A Decade of Gay Journalism from* The Body Politic: *An Anthology.* Ed. Ed Jackson and Stan Persky. Toronto: Pink Triangle Press; Vancouver: New Star Books, 1982. 224–43.
Halberstam, J. Jack. "Trangender Butch: Butch/FTM Border Wars and the Masculine Continuum." *GQL: A Journal of Lesbian and Gay Studies* 4.2 (1998): 287–310.
Jackson, Ed, and Stan Persky, eds. *Flaunting It!: A Decade of Gay Journalism from* The Body Politic: *An Anthology.* Toronto: Pink Triangle Press; Vancouver: New Star Books, 1982.
Lam, Shyong, et al. "WP: Clubhouse? An Exploration of *Wikipedia's* Gender Imbalance." *WikiSym 2011: Seventh International Symposium on Wikis and Open Collaboration.* http://dl.acm.org/citation.cfm?doid=2038558.2038560
Martin, Sandra. "B.C. Novelist Wrote a Cult Classic and Became a Lesbian Role Model." *Globe and Mail* 2 November 2007: S8.
McLeod, Donald W. *Lesbian and Gay Liberation in Canada: A Selected Annotated Chronology, 1964–1975.* Toronto: ECW Press/Homewood Books, 1996.
———. *Lesbian and Gay Liberation in Canada: A Selected Annotated Chronology, 1964–1975. LGBT Life with Full Text.* http://www.ebscohost.com/academic/lgbt-life-with-full-text
———. *Lesbian and Gay Liberation in Canada: A Selected Annotated Chronology, 1964–1975. T-Space at the University of Toronto Libraries.* https://tspace.library.utoronto.ca/handle/1807/4397
———. *Lesbian and Gay Liberation in Canada: A Selected Annotated Chronology, 1976–1981.* Toronto: Homewood Books, 2014. *T-Space at the University of Toronto Libraries.* http://lglc.library.utoronto.ca
Pink Triangle Press. "The Collective Years." http://www.pinktrianglepress.com/collective-years
Rule, Jane. *Lesbian Images.* Garden City, NY: Doubleday, 1975.
Schwabel, Fania. "Our Shocking Past: Queer Youth Offer Four Quickie Histories." *Xtra!* 23 September 1999: n. pag.

Sedgwick, Eve Kosofsky. *Epistemology of the Closet*. Berkeley: University of California Press, 1990.

Warner, Tom. *Never Going Back: A History of Queer Activism in Canada*. Toronto: University of Toronto Press, 2002.

PART II

WRITERS AND READERS

Mapping Textual Space

SALOMANIA

Maud Allan, Postcards, and Early Twentieth-Century "Viral" Circulation

Cecily Devereux

This chapter is concerned not with the digital per se or even with digit-al histories (histories of the media of representation and the processes by which those representations are reproduced and circulated), but with attempting to define and to trace the cultural genealogies that can also be seen to undergird the digital. It considers postcards, a technology of com-munication and of the circulation of images that took shape at the end of the nineteenth century, looking in particular at one crucial group in one category of early twentieth-century postcards—those bearing images of erotic dancers. My interest here is even more particular: this chap-ter focuses on postcard images of Canadian-born dancer Maud Allan in studio poses from what was, by 1908, her internationally known dance "The Vision of Salome." Allan's Salome postcards, carrying the image of the dancer around the world and from the space of performance into the space of the home, or the domestic, are a foundational element in what the rhetoric of media representation suggests was a kind of disease: "Salomania," the name for the condition of proliferating performances of Salome in the manner of Maud Allan, was a "condition" that mobilized in the early twentieth century what is now familiar as the rhetoric of the "viral." Maud Allan's Salome postcards, as I hope to demonstrate, are important as both analogous to and precursors for the digital sphere and in particular for the circulation of images of women that represents a crucial circuit for the web as an ideological apparatus and a structure for constituting gender and sexuality. The "digital" is a cultural appara-tus with histories in earlier technologies and practices of representation. By suggesting that postcards' mobilization of images of women as erotic dancers anticipates and establishes a culture of the rapid circulation of images that women undertake to embody through imitation or what we might understand as corporeal mimesis (embodying the image), this chapter works toward an understanding of other "digital" histories.

"The Vision of Salome"

On August 23, 1908, the *New York Times* reported an event that had taken place in London:[1] headlined "Salome Dinner Dance," the article claimed that "one of the great hostesses of the metropolis a few weeks ago issued invitations to twenty or thirty ladies whose names figure in Court and other fashionable lists, to attend a 'Maud Allan' dinner dance, which would be undesecrated by the presence of any man, and at which the guests were bidden to appear in Salome costumes" ("Salome Dinner Dance"). According to the report, "Each of the ladies proceeded to outvie her sisters in providing herself with a costume matching in all details the undress effect of Miss Allan's scanty attire." After dinner, at "the coffee and cigarette stage," some of the women reportedly "demonstrated that they had not only succeeded in matching Miss Allan's costume, but had learned some of her most captivating steps in movements." The event, the article suggested, worked "as convincing proof that the classical dances make for public immorality" and, in particular, as "evidence of the 'insidi-ous effect' Maud Allan, Isadora Duncan, and other American 'classic' dancers are having upon public morals in England" ("Salome Dinner Dance").

By 1908, when this article appeared in the *New York Times*, Maud Allan (1873–1956) was one of the best-known dancers in the world, even, arguably, surpassing her contemporary Isadora Duncan (1877–1927), who had been "before the public," as Allan's mother described her daughter's ambitions, a little longer. Both dancers had risen to fame in the first decade of the twentieth century as creative, "classical," interpretive dancers. It was Allan, however, frequently accused of imitating her younger predecessor in the field, and described in a review in 1925 as "an Isadora Duncan of the music hall" (cited in Cherniavsky, *Maud* 137), who erupted sensationally into the more or less high side of popular culture in Europe with her performance in the self-choreographed "Vision of Salome." Allan's dance, as her biographer Felix Cherniavsky indicates, was first performed publicly in Vienna in 1906 (*Salome* 143). It was, as Cherniavsky also suggests, inspired by Max Reinhardt's 1902 production in Berlin of Oscar Wilde's 1892 dramatic representation of Salome,[2] daughter of Herodias and step-daughter of Herod Antipas at whose request John the Baptist was beheaded following her dance for her step-father.[3] Allan toured briefly and sensationally through Europe, and in March 1908 "The Vision of Salome" opened in London at the Palace Theatre. It would run for eighteen months, with Allan as a main performer among a range of variety shows.[4] By October of 1908, Cherniavsky notes, the Palace Theatre marked the 250th performance of the dance with a gala event and publication of Allan's autobiography, *My Life and Dancing*, a slender volume that was distributed as a souvenir program (*Maud* 8).

Allan's was neither the first nor the only Salome dance of its moment. American-born dancer Loïe Fuller (1862–1928) had staged what Rhonda Garelick describes as a "dance-pantomime version" of *Salome* in 1895 in Paris (5–6), preceding Allan as well as the women who played the part in the first European performances of Wilde's *Salome* from 1896.[5] Richard Strauss's opera *Salome*, like Allan's dance, inspired by Wilde's play, had been performed for the first time in Dresden in 1905, giving rise to growing numbers of women who performed the title role in various locations and who performed the "Dance of the Seven Veils" when the singer could not or would not do so. Dutch dancer Mata Hari (Margaretha Geertruida Zelle) (1876–1917), who debuted her "Oriental" temple dancing in Paris in 1905, had asked to "create" the "Dance of the Seven Veils" for the Paris premiere of Strauss's opera in May 1907 (Tydeman and Price 144). Denied that opportunity, Toni Bentley suggests she nonetheless added the dance to her repertoire.[6] Meanwhile, as Lacy McDearmon notes, Fuller developed a second Salome dance in 1907, "a much more elaborate version, with a specially commissioned score by Florent Schmitt, La Tragédie de Salomé, to a scenario by Robert d'Humières" (88; see also Tydeman and Price 138–39).

Like Wilde's play, Strauss's opera, and Maud Allan's "Vision of Salome," the performances by Fuller and Mata Hari are themselves part of what Udo Kultermann demonstrates was a growing interest in Europe and North America in the representation of the figure of Salome in visual arts, theatre, and music. Kultermann traces the circulation of cultural representations of Salome from around the 1840s through to the 1970s, focusing on the intensification of such representations in the first decade of the twentieth century. Of these many representations, it was arguably Wilde's play that led to the popularizing of Salome's dance: the "Dance of the Seven Veils" was a climactic event in the play and, although not described in the stage directions, figured prominently in the famous illustrations developed by Aubrey Beardsley for the first English edition of 1894. But it was arguably Maud Allan's performance that gave rise to what the New York Times in 1908 called "Salomania."

"Salomania"

"Salomania" was a term used in the wake of Maud Allan's spectacular success in 1908 to describe the "craze" for "the sensational dance" that one writer in the New York Times suggested "flowed over the Continent of Europe [and] is in process of covering our Anglo-Saxon lands" (Pollard). In this and other articles in the New York Times in the summer of 1908, Salomania identified a condition characterized by the proliferation of the image of Salome in cultural representation and by the repeated performance of Salome by women in theatres and music halls. An article in the New York Times on August 16, 1908 ironically addressed "Rumours that

Salomania Will Have a Free Hand This Season." An editorial earlier in the month, on August 3, complained vigorously about the proliferation of "half-dressed women in all the variety theatres...doing the dance of seven veils and joyfully receiving a human head (in papier maché) on a platter" ("The Salome Pestilence"). This editorial likewise looked forward unhappily to a theatrical season dominated by Salome dancers. "We shall have," it ends sadly, "this deplorable dancing creature with us, more or less all Winter": "any chorus girl" might be tempted to perform her own Salome dance and thus add to what is described as a proliferating number of Salomes and to the ubiquity of the dance in the theatrical scene.

This ubiquity is well charted. Cherniavsky notes a number of imitators of Allan's Salome dance, some serious, some parodic, at least one— the well-known "female impersonator" Julian Eltinge—in drag (*Salome* 187–88n21). Kultermann reproduces a page from *Theatre Magazine* in April 1909 showing what are described as "All Sorts and Kinds of Salomes" (Kultermann 204). The eight images on the page include Allan in symbolic first place at the top left: she is described in the article as "the pioneer of the present revival" (Kultermann 132). Allan's followers here include a mix of dancers and singers. There are images of "Folies Bergère" dancer "La Sylphe" (Edith Lambelle Langerfeld, 1883–1968) and vaudevillian Gertrude Hoffmann (1885–1966), identified by Cherniavsky as the dancer who, reportedly sent to watch and imitate Allan in London, brought a copy, or version, of the Salome dance to the United States before Allan could arrive with her own.[7] These Salomes are aligned with the putatively "higher" culture performers who played the roles of Salome in Strauss's opera, represented here by Olive Fremstad (1871–1951) and Mary Garden (1874–1967). Some of these women also comprise what the *New York Times* article of August 16, 1908 reported with mock seriousness as "the 'Salome' Club": "President, Gertrude Hoffmann; Vice President, La Sylphe; Treasurer, Lotta Faust; Secretary, Eva Tanguay" ("The Call of Salome"). Eltinge was identified as an "honorary member."

What is compelling in so much of the media representation of Salomania is its framing in terms of infection and contagion: it is depicted as an "epidemic" and as "pestilence." Indeed, "The Call of Salome" begins with an ironically serious report:

It is announced on good authority that the management [at the New Amsterdam Theatre] has been exceptionally active in guarding against outbreaks of Salomania among members of the company. As soon as any chorus girl shows the very first symptoms of the disease she is at once enveloped in a fur coat— the most efficacious safeguard known against the Salome dance—and hurriedly isolated. ("The Call of Salome")

The representation of Salomania as a disease is also implicit in the account of the "Salome Dinner Dance" with which this chapter began. Although slightly tongue-in-cheek in its portrayal of Salomania as evidence of British morals corrupted by American dance—or Englishness by Americanness—and in its suggestion that danger to "public morals in England" lies partly in the exclusion of men from the dance, the "Salome Dinner Dance" article makes an important point when it implies that the "effect" of Allan "and other American 'classic' dancers" is comprehensible as a kind of infection and Salomania as a culture of imitation—reproduction, replication, proliferation, circulation—that is arguably best understood as "viral."

Defined in the *Oxford English Dictionary* (OED) in a January 2005 "Draft Addition," the contemporary phrase "to go viral" has emerged from the digital sphere. Used chiefly, the OED suggests, in marketing, "going viral" designates or involves "the rapid spread of information (esp. about a product or service) amongst customers by word of mouth, e-mail, etc." "To go viral," it further suggests, is "to propagate in such a manner; to (be) spread widely and rapidly." Website marketing company Volacci adds to this definition in a May 26, 2010 blog on the question "What Does It Mean to 'Go Viral'?" Citing the online definition resource *Answers.com*, Volacci suggests that "*viral* means becoming extremely popular in a very short amount of time. Often for something to be considered viral it needs to make its way into everyday non-internet life" (cited in Volacci SEO Blog). Not only "extremely popular," and a mechanism for marketing, the viral is also arguably implicitly and foundationally—or, at least, rhetorically—constituted as *hazardous*: when the viral moves into "everyday non-internet life," it does so in way that is also simultaneously uncontrollable and undesirable. Indeed, viruses, in the context of the digital, refer to the machine counterpart of infecting agents for human bodies: a computer virus is a "piece of code which is capable of copying itself and typically has a detrimental effect, such as corrupting the system or destroying data" (OED).

Salomania was likewise represented as a "corrupting" agent. The real danger of the "outbreaks" of Salomania in New York theatres, as these articles all suggest, was its potential infection of white and Anglo-Saxon femininity at home. Toni Bentley draws attention to a "lengthy piece" that appeared in the *New York Times Sunday Magazine* in 1908 issuing a "warning about the current threat" (Bentley 68) posed by Salome dancers and expressing concern not only that "this virus could lead [in the other direction]—to North America" (Veteran Diplomat) but into domestic space. "At the present rate," the article suggests,

> it is probable that Salome dances will invade the fashionable drawing rooms of
> New York during the coming Winter, as they have of the London Great World
> during the season which has just come to an end....From the presentation of
> the Salome dance in English homes, and the lionization of the performer as
> an honored and gushed-over guest, to the appearance of some of these femi-
> nine enthusiasts of rank and lineage in the same role, is but a step. (Veteran
> Diplomat)

Like the earlier editorial of August 3, this piece, headlined "Salome in English Homes," uses a vocabulary of contagion and voices explicit concern that "the spectacular, theatrical Salome has invaded our homes" ("The Salome Pestilence"; see also Cherniavsky, *Maud* 70). Salomania can thus be understood as the "craze" not simply for "the sensational dance" ("The Salome Pestilence") in theatres but as a "virus" carrying "pestilence" not only from the Old World to the putative New, and not only from the theatrical to the home, but from the dancer to the "everyday" woman. It was a domestic "epidemic," infecting the bodies of women "of rank and lineage" or, in other words, those white middle-class women called upon across so many late nineteenth- and early twentieth-century discursive registers as "mothers of the race," the women who would do reproductive duty for the Empire and produce the babies that would ensure its growth and continuity at home and throughout colonial spaces.

Although the *New York Times* drew attention to the numbers of proliferating Salomes, drily noting that membership in the "Club...was limited to fifty thousand" ("The Salome Pestilence"), and the *Theatre Magazine* made a similar reference to "all sorts and kinds of Salomes," it is clear that in 1908 there was actually only one "kind" of Salome. All of the women whose photographs the *Theatre Magazine* includes, for instance, can be understood not just to be doing a Salome dance but, like the women at the London dinner dance, to be doing "Maud Allan." Thus, they strike similar poses to Allan and wear versions of the costume that she made famous in her dance.[8] Like the women at the London "Salome Dinner Dance," they can be seen to be imitating Allan, their poses indicating that they too "had learned some of her most captivating steps in movements" and their costumes "matching in all details the undress effect of Miss Allan's scanty attire" ("Salome Dinner Dance"). It is not surprising that what the *New York Times* called "Salomania" in the United States, contemporary critics in London, as Judith Walkowitz has observed, described as the "Maud Allan boom" (344).

The extraordinary success of "The Vision of Salome" and the emergence in 1908 of a culture of imitation that turned not to the many women performing Salome but to Allan in particular raises important questions both about this culture of imitation (what it signifies, where it comes from, what it leads to) and about Allan's Salome (what it did, how it did it, what was at stake in this representation, and why it achieved what other representations did not). In her study of Allan and "The Vision of Salome" in London, Walkowitz suggests that "Allan's performances materialize[d] a new femininity" that, among other things, "facilitated the entry of respectable women into what one turn-of-the-century writer termed the 'Night Side of London': the cosmopolitan spaces of the commercial West End" (346). What is clear, however, is that in doing so Allan's performances not only materialized but also mobilized "a new femininity," literally taking women out of their homes and into "cosmopolitan spaces," and putting into circulation an image of white femininity that was itself complicatedly mobile. This mobility is implicit and foundational in the dance as it staged that mobility: Walkowitz astutely points out how the dancer's movement in "The Vision of Salome" is emphasized by the "visual juxtaposition of a mobile female body and a very immobile, trunkless male head" (352). In another register, the mobile female body is implicit and made spectacular in the fact of the performing woman who has travelled to appear on stage: Allan's presence in front of the audience is evidence of her having come from elsewhere, of not being at home. Although this fact of mobility is implicit in every female performer's appearance on stage, Allan again made it emphatic: her own ambiguous nationality—she was Canadian-born, American by her father's naturalization, trained in Europe, and, increasingly following her success in England in 1908, British-accented, as some interviewers noted, with flashes of Americanism[9]—was a significant part of her staging of the mobile body. It was, arguably, precisely this mobile identity—the travelling woman, the border-crossing body, the woman not at home and out of place—that is significantly remediated in the images of Allan as Salome that circulated in the early twentieth century.

The Salome Postcards

During the first decade of the twentieth century, when Allan was touring Europe and performing in London, images of her in her Salome costume were reproduced on numerous postcards. These cards, manufactured and sold in many countries, and preceding the kinds of controls that would help put the protection of the images in the hands of the artist and/or her managers, are probably too numerous to count. In fact, they are arguably significant in terms of their proliferation rather than their precise numbers, and of their similarities rather than their differences. Even now, postcards remain the dominant record of Allan's performance. A Google image search (April 3, 2012) using the term "Maud Allan" yields "about 347,000 results." Of the first twenty-five images, twenty are certainly postcards; two are possibly postcards; one is a sketch; one is an image of Allan's Salome costume worn by a contemporary model; and one is a postcard of Wilde. Of the twenty postcards with the image of Allan, seventeen are Salome postcards. A Google search (April 3, 2012) using the term "Maud Allan Salome" yields "about 30,900 results." Of the first twenty-four, all but three are postcards. Allan's *Wikipedia* entry is illustrated with a Salome postcard. Postcards with images of Allan outnumber all other Allan objects on the Internet auction site eBay: of the items listed by international sellers on April 17, 2012, seven are Salome postcards, two are newspaper clippings, and one is a print from 1908. The blog *About Postcards* makes the point that original postcard images of Allan "are in considerable demand" and that "those featuring her in her Salome costume" are "some of the most desirable" and can "be priced much higher than other Edwardian stage and actress postcards" ("Maud Allan: The Salome Dancer Postcards"). Most of the eBay postcards are listed between US$3.00 and US$4.00, but higher prices can be found across the Internet.

Given their dominance of the online record of Allan, it is not surprising that postcards represent an important part of her archive or, at least, of the archival record of Allan and her art. Allan's papers and personal effects are concentrated in two locations. The first is Toronto's Dance Collection Danse (DCD), a non-institutional repository of documents and materials related to dance history. In 1996, through a donation from her biographer Felix Cherniavsky, DCD acquired Allan's papers, two of her own handmade Salome costumes, and some other objects. The DCD collection includes several postcards, some of which date from the early twentieth century and some of which are recent reproductions. The second major location of Allan's papers is the Charles E. Young Research Library at University of California, Los Angeles (UCLA). The UCLA Library holds some of Allan's books, photograph albums, some performance ephemera, a "letter book" containing carbon copies of letters written by her manager Angus MacLeod during a tour of India, Asia, and Australasia between 1913 and 1915 with the Cherniavsky Trio, and a postcard album containing cards Allan received and acquired, only some of which reproduce her image; many are records of visits and travel through Europe. Other collections of materials related to Allan (the San Francisco Performing Arts Library, the New York Public Library for the Performing Arts) also include significant numbers of postcards.

The Salome postcards online and in these North American repositories are by and large staged studio stills rather than captured images
of the performance itself: they are images of static poses rather than of
motion. Nonetheless, as Walkowitz has suggested of photographic images
of Allan, they represent the movement of Allan's body that was a fundamental part of her dance—what Walkowitz calls "pose" dancing—and
help to explain the range of responses to "The Vision of Salome" in the
first decade of the twentieth century. Even more compellingly, however,
they serve by their sheer numbers as extant evidence to demonstrate how
much the circulated and static print image actually meant to the rise of
Allan as Salome.[10]

Although Salome postcards dominate the DCD collection, as they do
the other collections, including the online record and eBay listings, the
earliest Allan postcards, which appear to date from 1905 and 1906, are not
Salome cards. The UCLA Library "Postkarten" album, probably acquired
by Allan in Germany, contains a card advertising the 1905–06 season at
the Stadthalle in Berlin with an image of Allan and an announcement
of a "Kunstlerabend" ("Artists' Evening") performance on November
8, 1905. Allan is identified here as Maud Gwendolen Allan, as she was
known in her early years of performance in continental Europe. Another
card, from the same generation, and using the same image, identifies
her as Maudy Gwendolen Allan. This postcard album also contains what
appears to be a very early black and white postcard of Allan as Salome,
before the idiom had been so well established in and through the proliferation of Salome postcards, and before her own name had come to be well
known: the card, with a grainy photograph of Allan in her Salome costume, identifies her as "Miss Allan Maud."

The non-Salome postcards of 1905–06 suggest that the image of Allan
as "Maud Allan" had begun to circulate in the earliest days of her performances.[11] These cards also indicate this medium had an established
work and value in circulating images to advertise an event and to bring
"before the public" the image of a performer, and suggest how this value
would be exploited in the groundswell that would be called the "Maud
Allan boom," if not by Allan or by Allan alone, certainly by many others
in the business of image reproduction. Postcards, as the proliferation of

Allan cards demonstrates, made it possible to capitalize on the image in ways that had not previously been possible. The image could be bought and sold; thus, while its work, as I am suggesting here, is importantly symbolic, the postcard also facilitated the emergence of the image as not simply the representation of the thing but the thing itself—or, as Jean-Luc Nancy suggests, of the image as "a thing that is not the thing [but] distinguishes itself from it" (2). The image on postcards of Allan as Salome may reference the body of Allan dancing, but they are, as images on postcards, things themselves.

Postcards and the Circulation of White Femininity

Postcards, as Lisa Z. Sigel suggests, were not a brand new form of communication at the turn of the nineteenth century (860–61), but they were quite new—about as new in communication at that moment, arguably, as email or texting is now. According to different histories, postcards appeared somewhere between 1865 and 1870 but became a functional medium of international communication, says Esther Milne, only after 1874 (115) when the General Postal Union made it possible to send cards across national borders: prior to this date and to international postage agreements, Milne observes, postcards routinely were returned to their senders. Postcards, notes Sigel, "gained the full authorization of the Congress of the Universal Postal Union" (860) in 1886. Between 1894 and 1919, she indicates, "roughly 140 billion postcards were sent worldwide" (861). In Britain, "over 300 million cards were actually posted... in 1895, over 400 million in 1900, and over 850 million in 1908. The number merely sold was much greater" (Donnachie and Macleod 98). By 1909, when Allan's Salome cards were in wide circulation, "800,000,000 postcards were sold in England alone each year" (Sigel 861).

Although postcard images of Allan circulated widely and were produced in Europe and North America as well as England, I am focusing here on England for two key reasons. First, it was in England that Allan rose to spectacular fame, and where the picture postcard's mobilization of her image can be seen to have had its most telling effect on her celebrity.

Second, the postcard emerged in England as an imperial medium, a form of communication across the space of empire and a means of putting into circulation Anglo-Saxon presence in places outside of England—or, in effect, of affirming what Percival Pollard described in his *New York Times* Salomania article of 1908 as "our Anglo-Saxon lands." The British postcard's imperial function is suggested in accounts of its beginnings. In *The Picture Postcard and Its Origins*, Frank Staff cites a 1900 account of a deliberate decision on the part of the first publishers of "pictorial postcards" to "issue cards of a topical character, that is, having views or portraits of interest at the moment" (89). Thus, according to this record, the "first topical picture postcard [in England] was that illustrating the Nile Expedition of 1897. It bore portraits of [imperial heroes Charles George] Gordon and the since famous Sirdar, Lord Kitchener" (Staff 89). The early turn to imperial events and portraiture suggests that, in England at least, the postcard was functionalized from its first appearance as a medium for carrying information across and about imperial space— that, indeed, it was a form of communication that operated precisely in the context of empire.

According to Staff, and to Julia Gillen and Nigel Hall, when picture postcards were introduced into the United Kingdom in 1894 they typically bore an image on one side and the address on the other, with room around the picture for "a very short message in the margin" (Staff 88; Gillen and Hall 2). By 1900, as Tonie Holt and Valmai Holt note, picture postcards had become a regular form of communication. The Holts cite Margaret Mead, writing in the *Girl's Realm* in 1900: "The Picture Postcard," Mead writes, "is with us. It suits us. It meets our needs" (cover blurb). These needs, Gillen and Hall suggest, can be understood to pertain to "quick, informal and attractive written messages" (2) that could be sent and answered in multiple postal deliveries a day. In January 1902, Gillen and Hall further indicate, the British post office "gave in to popular demand and permitted the use of postcards on which one side was wholly taken up by an image, and the other side had half address and half message" (2). The space for the image, by then, exceeded that of the address and of the message, whose space was stipulated on many cards with statements such as "This space for communication only." If the communication was important, the image was no less a part of the circuit established in the transmission of the postcard from sender to recipient, and was certainly crucial to the rise of postcards as objects themselves.

Postcards developed alongside and in unsurprising tandem with photography. The picture postcard is based, in part, on the earlier medium of the *carte de visite*, itself an evolution of the calling card, with a photograph to identify the visitor. It also follows the emergence of commodity media such as the cabinet card and the cigarette card. The cabinet card emerged as a primary medium for portraits in the 1860s. The cigarette card was popularized in the 1880s as a means of stiffening soft cigarette packages. Both media served as locations not only for personal portraiture to circulate among friends, but for the reproduction specifically of photographic images of women and, in particular, women dancers, actors, and burlesque performers, the latter often photographed wearing tights and closely fitting body suits, or, like the Salome images, in genital-defining, jewelled bra and torso filigree, and semi-transparent skirts. The images on these cards (especially the cigarette cards) are often identical or very close to those reproduced on postcards; hence, the shift from one commodity form to another at the fin de siècle makes sense.

Cigarette cards were mobilized to sell cigarettes; postcards were mobilized as images that were themselves for sale, quickly becoming not only a medium of communication but itself a commodity to collect. Staff traces "the craze for collecting" that developed in Britain (64). The Holts note that in 1900 the *Picture Postcard Magazine* was first published in Britain, described by its editor E.W. Richardson as "the first magazine to combine travel, philately and art through a natural connecting medium, the Picture Postcard" (qtd. in Holt and Holt 37). Not only did postcards emerge as a technology of communication alongside photography, they also emerged in tandem with increased travel—across categories of gender, race, and class. In both instances, postcards are, as Richardson put it in 1900, "a natural connecting medium" (qtd. in Holt and Holt 37) across these registers.

What does it mean to have—and to be known through—an archive in which postcards play such a central role? What does it mean to have risen, as Allan did, to international fame in part through this form of

representation and circulation? On the one hand, the postcards function as representations of Allan's own mobility, their travels replicating
hers and providing a visual record of the movement of white women
such as Allan across national boundaries or, at any rate, out of the home
or domestic space, into public, and, perversely, back again into the
home, but with a different value or "insidious effect." They do work that
is in some ways similar to what Galit Hasan-Rokem has described as
"mark[ing] routes of traveling and migration" (510) while also reproducing
the travel itself. Hasan-Rokem frames these operations in her discussion of the figure of "the wandering Jew" and late nineteenth-century
mobility with the doubled figure of what she terms "Jews as Postcards, or
Postcards as Jews" (505). On the other hand, the postcards of "The Vision
of Salome" also function, like all postcards, as commodities, representing metonymically what is exchanged in the erotic performance. In this
work, they operate to mobilize the image and to monetize it. They are
things to buy that are also representing something that makes people
want to purchase them for circulation. One Salome postcard in the DCD
Maud Allan collection, postmarked December 1908, makes this point
evident in its referencing on the back the image on the front. "How's
this of Maudie?" the sender asks. Walkowitz cites a postcard in the San
Francisco Performing Arts Library that emphasizes not only the value of
the circulating image as spectacle but specifically the collector's interest
in images of Allan: the sender writes of the photograph of Allan in her
"Chopin's Funeral March" costume, "Hope you haven't got this p.c. Are
you still gone on this person?" (362n94). Walkowitz draws attention to
"schoolgirls who exchanged picture postcards of [Allan] and wrote of their
'crush'" (362). As Walkowitz notes, girls could thus observe Allan in performances and then could "try out Allan's movements in the privacy of
their abodes" (362), like the guests at the Salome Dinner Dance, imitating Maud Allan at home.

The postcard archive of Allan does a particular and crucial kind of
work with regard to the image that represents the dancer and the "here"
to which the sender wishes the recipient could also be present. It does
this work across what Milne describes as a "double logic": both the sender
and the image on the card are constituted as being in transit, out of place,

on the move. Milne has suggested compellingly that postcards indicate
and affirm presence, like calling cards "stand[ing] in for the corporeal
presence of their author" (95) and, importantly, for the corporeal presence of the figure represented on the card itself. The calling card, in these
terms, conveys a message akin to "I am here." It is also the case, however,
that the postcard always references and represents what is absent—both
the sender and the object. They "take the place of one's self" when the self
is not actually there. They are, as image, absent (marking, as Nancy suggests, "the absence of the thing" [37]); thus, they function as a space to be
filled in by the woman looking at the image and seeing herself through
its imitation or replication on her own. In this way postcards' "double
logic" is doubled again, and the card, with its message that may say something like the classic "Wish you were here," counters the image that says,
in effect, "You are here." At least, this is what it might be understood to
say to women and girls bringing the image of Allan as Salome home and
"matching" it in the "privacy of their abodes" (Walkowitz 362).

Private and public; static and mobile; an index of presence and of
absence; a record of a place and a record of the sender—postcards have
a complex ambiguity that makes them peculiarly appropriate for circulating the image of women in spectacular and erotic performance and
building an archive of women staging white femininity at the end of the
nineteenth and the beginning of the twentieth centuries. Allan's Salome
postcards constitute what we might regard as an archive of the mobile
subject, representing as they do figures who are not "here," women who
are not at home but on the move and in public. Thus, they not only index
but constitute a growing economy of the image itself as the space and the
"reality" that women inhabit. At once indexical of Allan's own movement
through and across national spaces and of the commerce of exchange
in white female bodies that Allan incorporates foundationally into her
Salome dance, postcards also function as a space where white femininity is staged, representing and standing in for the body that has been
rendered as image. That is, although the travels of the mobile body are
central to Salomania, the "craze," as it developed in 1908, proved to be
not only or even primarily about the infected *body*. What is materialized,
what is in circulation, what is imitated and copied, what is reproduced,

what proliferates, and what "goes viral" is the image of Allan as Salome: indeed, it is the image itself that is a key element in the rise of Salomania as a culture of imitation. "The Vision of Salome" put into circulation an image of mobile, fungible white femininity that lent itself to imitation and generated mimic performance because it was itself foundationally "pose." Allan did not embody but staged white femininity, functionalizing the body itself as image and thus as the space for the performance of racialized gender in what we might best understand as corporeal mimesis, and thus making evident and overt the terms under which white femininity could be understood to circulate at the turn of the century.

The image of Allan as Salome in the first decade of the twentieth century, in its circulation, its work of outlining and affirming ideologies of white femininity, and its own travels in the form of photographs, objects, and especially postcards is central to what Walkowitz suggests is the emergence of a "visual culture where women predominated both as spectacles and increasingly as spectators" (338), where, in effect, women came increasingly to recognize themselves, to see themselves reflected in the performer on stage, and to reflect back to the performer what they had seen, constituting themselves in and as image. This point has particular relevance to the figure of the white erotic dancer who had been emerging into visibility around the Anglo-Saxon empire since the 1860s. Women, as Sara Jeannette Duncan suggests in her 1894 novel *A Daughter of To-Day*, came increasingly by the fin de siècle to recognize that the erotic dancer in particular materialized a version of femininity that was easily recognizable because it was "true"—"truer," indeed, than representations that did *not* eroticize, commoditize, monetize, and circulate white femininity as image in precisely the way it can be seen to operate now. That operation at this time is primarily evident in the digital sphere, but it was also evident in the nineteenth-century circulation of images of women on postcards. The work of the Salome postcards, therefore, is neither simply archival (of the dance and its dancer) nor indexical (of Allan's celebrity or even of her mobility).

The history and the meaning of the digital sphere are not comprehensible only with reference to new technologies and media, but to older, sedimented histories—of the reproduction and circulation of images, of the politics of gendered performance through embodied imitation or the corporeal mimetic, of a circulation that can be understood as viral not only through its rapid spread but through its "invasion" of the spaces of the domestic into which the media can spread and the concomitant "infection" of the bodies that inhabit domestic space. The Salomania of the early twentieth century is, I have undertaken to suggest, an effect of the rapid circulation of images in what was at that time the relatively new technology of postcards and, crucially, the mobilization of images of women that could move from public into domestic space, from body to image. Postcards of erotic dancers and, in particular, Maud Allan's Salome postcards, whose foundational importance to digital image culture is indicated in their reproduction and proliferation in digital media, are records of an earlier moment in the development of that culture; analogous to the digital circulation of images of women, they are also important precursors of that circulation.

NOTES

1. On this "Maud Allan Dinner Dance," see Cherniavsky, *Salome* 176–77 and Bentley 67–69.
2. Originally written in French, the first English edition of Wilde's *Salome* appeared in 1894, published by Elkin Mathews and John Lane in London and by Copeland and Day in Boston. It was translated by Lord Alfred Douglas and illustrated by Aubrey Beardsley.
3. Cherniavsky notes that both Maud Allan and Marcel Rémy, who composed the music for "The Vision of Salome," saw this production in Berlin in 1902 (*Salome* 142). See also Tydeman and Price 140.
4. See Judith Walkowitz on the Palace Theatre, its history from 1893 of presenting "Living Pictures" (348–50), and its identity as a variety theatre (347–48).
5. Tydeman and Price indicate that "the first performance of Wilde's *Salome* was staged by the Théâtre de l'Oeuvre in Paris on 11 February 1896" (25). Lina Munte played the title role. It was not "performed again until 15 November 1902 at the Kleines Theater, Berlin...in a production directed by Friedrich Kayssler and Hans Oberländer under the supervision of the twenty-nine-year-old Max Reinhardt" (Tydeman and Price 31). (Hutcheon and Hutcheon suggest the "German version premiered in 1901 in Breslau" [205].) Cherniavsky notes that both Maud Allan and Marcel Rémy, who composed the music for "The Vision of Salome," "saw this Reinhardt production in Berlin" (*Salome* 142).
6. Mata Hari, Cherniavsky points out, was also appearing in Vienna at the time of Allan's first public performance of "The Vision of Salome" (*Salome* 143).

7. Cherniavsky writes, "In April 1908—within weeks of [Allan's] sensational debut in London—Oscar Hammerstein had sent Gertrude Hoffmann, well known in the United States as a 'mimic' dancer to London, to study Maud Allan's performance at the Palace Theatre. On July 13, 1908, Hoffmann duly opened a six-week season at the Hammerstein Theatre on Broadway featuring a skillful imitation of *The Vision of Salome*. After Labour Day, Hoffmann set out on an ambitious tour that aroused more controversy than acclaim" (*Maud* 69).

8. Tydeman and Price suggest that Allan's costume was "strongly reminiscent of [Charles] Ricketts's design" for a 1906 production in London (140). It is not clear, however, that Allan had seen this production prior to designing and making her costume.

9. See, for instance, an interview in the Chicago *Tribune* on January 23, 1910, in which the interviewer notes that "[a] whole-souled eastern drawl seems all the time trying to break through the shell of an English veneer. Every now and then—when the owner grows excited—it gets out in the open and cavorts around until she grabs it and pushes it back, under its covering of rolled r's and forgotten h's" (qtd. in Cherniavsky, *Salome* 194).

10. It is not necessarily clear that Allan oversaw a campaign of self-promotion through photographs. In fact, there is evidence that Allan herself was not involved in the circulation of postcards, except as model for the images. In a copy of a 1913 letter in the UCLA letter book, for instance, Allan's manager, MacLeod, writes to a company wishing to use her image:

> Miss Allan has no objection to your advertising your cigarettes in the way you propose + can supply you with a block but cannot undertake to distribute your post-cards...I will however give you a list of the places in India Miss Allan will visit & you could forward the matter yourselves. It must be understood that no liability of any kind attaches to this permission + that the wording on the post-card will not be altered without my consent in writing first obtained. (89, 24 November 1913, by MacLeod in *Bombay at the Taj Mahal Hotel*)

Although MacLeod's note indicates that Allan would supply blocks images for printing postcards, which suggests that she had some control of the image if not of its circulation, it also suggests she does not profit by attaching her image to a commodity such as cigarettes, from the circulation of postcards themselves, or, in effect, from others capitalizing on her Salome performance.

11. Christened Ulla Maude Durrant, she adopted the name Maud Allan following the conviction and execution of her brother Theodore Durrant in 1899 for the murder of two women in San Francisco.

Archival Sources

Allan, Maud. Maud Allan Clippings. New York Public Library for the Performing Arts, New York.

———. Maud Allan Collection. Dance Collection Danse Archives, Toronto.

———. Maud Allan Collection. Museum of Performance and Design, San Francisco.

———. Maud Allan Papers. Collection 2038. Department of Special Collections, Charles E. Young Research Library, University of California, Los Angeles.

Secondary Sources

Bentley, Toni. *Sisters of Salome*. New Haven, CT: Yale University Press, 2002.

"The Call of Salome." *New York Times* 16 August 1908.

Cherniavsky, Felix. *The Cherniavsky Trio*. Vancouver: Felix Cherniavsky, 2001.

———. *Maud Allan and Her Art*. Toronto: Dance Collection Danse Press/es, 1998.

———. *The Salome Dancer: The Life and Times of Maud Allan*. Toronto: McClelland and Stewart, 1991.

Donnachie, Ian L., and Innes Macleod. *Victorian and Edwardian Scottish Lowlands from Historic Photographs*. London: B.T. Batsford, 1979.

Dragon, Andrea. "The Salome Dancer: An Eastern Dance Takes Western Roots." PowerPoint presentation. N.d. Salome—People Server at UNCW. Accessed 3 April 2012. http://people.uncw.edu/deagona/raqs/Salomes%20dif.ppt

Garelick, Rhonda K. *Electric Salome: Loie Fuller's Performance of Modernism*. Princeton: Princeton University Press, 2007.

Gillen, Julia, and Nigel Hall. "The Edwardian Postcard: A Revolutionary Moment in Rapid Multimodal Communications." Paper presented at the British Educational Research Association Annual Conference, Manchester, 2–5 September 2009. http://www.lancs.ac.uk/fass/projects/EVIIpc/docs

Hasan-Rokem, Galit. "Jews as Postcards, or Postcards as Jews: Mobility in a Modern Genre." *Jewish Quarterly Review* 99.4 (2009): 505–46.

Holt, Tonie, and Valmai Holt. *Picture Postcards of the Golden Age: A Collector's Guide*. London: MacGibbon and Kee, 1971.

Hutcheon, Linda, and Michael Hutcheon. "Staging the Female Body: Richard Strauss's *Salome*." *Siren Songs: Representations of Gender and Sexuality in Opera*. Ed. Mary Ann Smart. Princeton: Princeton University Press, 2000. 204–21.

James, Russell. "London Olympics 2012." 5 June 2011. *Internet Archive Wayback Machine*. http://web.archive.org/web/20110615041339/http://www.russelljames.co.uk/rjolympics.htm

Kultermann, Udo. "The 'Dance of the Seven Veils': Salome and Erotic Culture around 1900." *Artibus et Historise* 27.53 (2006): 187–215.

"Maud Allan." *Wikipedia*. 8 April 2011. http://en.wikipedia.org/wiki/Maud_Allan

"Maud Allan Costume Restoration." *Dance Collection Danse: The Magazine* 44 (1997): 7. http://www.dcd.ca/general/Resources/44DCDTheMagazine.pdf

"Maud Allan: The Salome Dancer Postcards." *About Postcards: A Reference Resource for Postcard Collectors.* 4 December 2007. http://aboutcards.blogspot.com/2007/12/maud-allan-salome-dancer-postcards.html

McDearmon, Lacy. "Maud Allan: The Public Record." *Dance Chronicle* 2.2 (1978): 85–105.

Milne, Esther. *Letters, Postcards, Email: Technologies of Presence.* New York: Routledge, 2010.

Nancy, Jean-Luc. *The Ground of the Image.* Trans. Jeff Fort. New York: Fordham University Press, 2005.

Pollard, Percival. "The Regnant Wave of the Sensational Dance." *New York Times* 23 August 1908. http://www.nytimes.com 3 April 2012.

"Salome Dinner Dance." *New York Times* 23 August 1908.

"The Salome Pestilence." *New York Times* 3 September 1908.

Sigel, Lisa Z. "Filth in the Wrong People's Hands: Postcards and the Expansion of Pornography in Britain and the Atlantic World, 1880–1914." *Journal of Social History* 33.4 (2000): 859–85.

Staff, Frank. *The Picture Postcard and Its Origins.* London: Lutterworth Press, 1966.

Tydeman, William, and Steven Price. *Wilde: Salome.* Cambridge: Cambridge University Press, 1996.

Veteran Diplomat. "The Spread of Bohemianism in English Society." *New York Times* 16 August 1908.

Volacci SEO Blog. "What Does It Mean to 'Go Viral'?" *Volacci.com.* 26 May 2010. http://www.volacci.com/search-engine-optimization-defining-going-viral

Walkowitz, Judith R. "The 'Vision of Salome': Cosmopolitanism and Erotic Dancing in Central London, 1908–1918." *American Historical Review* 108.2 (2003): 337–76.

TORONTO THE GOOD

IN THE FICTION AND LIFE

OF GRACE IRWIN

Patricia Demers

Stories and theories about the city have created their own crossroads of understanding. Attempts to analyze the importance of the Toronto cityscape from the 1920s to the 1950s in five novels by lifelong Toronto resident Grace Irwin necessitate some acknowledgement of the varied array of registers and metrics reflecting multiple perspectives and changing social practice. A re-entry to early twentieth-century Toronto, before Metro and Greater Toronto Area designations, might be managed by working back from current conceptualizations of urban place and space. Since interdisciplinary urban studies, like its subject, have experienced explosive growth since the 1960s, such a look backward could also help to chart both the divides and some interconnections between then and now.

In the realms of the scalar geographical imagination, Raymond Williams's formula for the city as "the physical embodiment of a decisive modern consciousness" (239) often leads to a series of polarizations—between "core and periphery, metropolis and hinterland, or centre and margin" (McCann and Smith 70). The porosity or openness of the city is an influential matter of debate. For women citizens, in particular, the city as a "cultural artifact" can exclude their participation and also free them "for the first time from their isolation in the private home" (Squier 5). Its forms and structures can "ensure social conformity" or point to the "marginality [of] ghettoization" (Grosz 109). As "spectacle,...spaces for face-to-face contact of amazing richness" (Wilson 158), the city presents both "the challenge of space,...of the full recognition of coeval others," and "the essential openness of place to the beyond" (Massey 216, 217). The intersections of the city, then, can afford opportunities for voice, agency, and experimentation, as well as structures of powerlessness and domination.

Globalization theory has affected contemporary views of human agency, locality, and cultural practices within urban environments. Michael Peter Smith insists on the more precise language of trans-national urbanism; he sees "people's everyday lives [as] sites of criss-crossing communication circuits" constituting "sometimes sepa-rate, sometimes overlapping, and sometimes competing terrains for the contestation, as well as the reproduction, of cultural meanings" (127). For Saskia Sassen, "economic globalization has contributed to a new geography of centrality and marginality" (Sassen 194). In "emergent transnational urban systems," she argues, where "globalities [are] cen-tered in cities," powerlessness can become "a complex condition in the concrete space of cities where multiple groups and projects intersect" (Sassen 194).

Through the experiences and ruminations of her fictional protag-onists, Grace Irwin clothes concepts of place and space, the challenges of openness and modernity, and class-enabled or -restricted occasions for voice or silence, in human encounters with Toronto. Although transnational globality is not a prominent feature of her early and mid-twentieth-century city, Irwin's Toronto embodies both the "iden-tity-endowing" (Ball 185) specificity of place and the liminality of space through which her characters move, question, and discover them-selves. Aware of the fragmentary, isolated, atomistic quality of city life, her perception of Toronto does not draw on the demi-monde scurrility of Christopher Saint George Clark's late nineteenth-century exposé, *Of Toronto the Good: A Social Study.* Cataloguing "unwholesome truths" and familiar with the "shabby tumble-down houses" where "the poor were obliged to live," Clark delighted in poking a finger in the eye of righteousness, asserting the omnipresence of street walkers: "on every street in the city...I have been solicited" (Clark 209, 3, 131). Citing the success of "unprincipled knaves [who] can secure entrance to the best social circles" (Clark 27), yet granting that "Toronto is essentially a city of churches" (147), he derided these institutions' sermons as "the vilest billingsgate" (165), their choirs as "the dumping ground for all the old stagers" (153), their hymns as "Pharisaic twaddle" (154), and clerics, "'fishers of men' who do not pay their debts" (31), as practitioners of "chicanery and infidelity" (164). The Toronto Irwin presents thirty years later and beyond is not simply a backdrop for exposing hypocrisies. A city of parishes and doubt, landmarks and expansion, past and present, it possesses a hermeneutic architecture.

Clergyman Andrew Connington is the central figure of three of Irwin's novels, *Least of All Saints, Andrew Connington*, and *Contend with Horses*, all published by McClelland and Stewart and translated into German. Irwin fashions Connington's 1920s Toronto as an observant, dialogic milieu—"there was nothing peculiar about church attendance in Toronto" (*Least of All Saints* 5)—shot through with a Modernist angst of disbelief. "'No honest man with an intellectual grasp of what it involves,'" maintains Connington's industrialist uncle, "'can accept orthodox Christianity today'" (*Least of All Saints* 24). Andrew Connington himself defends the Blue Law by observing, "I like Sunday in Toronto" and praising "the comparative quiet in the city as...incalculably beneficial in an age of haste and nervous strain" (*Least of All Saints* 218). Despite this tension between attendance and ebbing belief, the Toronto of churches, compendious theological debate at Emmanuel College, and the domestic life of an ejected pastor, who is also a husband, parent, and eventually widower, is not a satirical indictment of clergy; rather, Irwin's Connington novels are a deeply attentive, engaged exploration of the shaping, testing, and expansion of a clerical vocation within the shifting geographies of centre and margin of an altered urban milieu.

The changing Toronto of Irwin's novels is her city as well. Growing up in "a typical middle-class West Toronto Methodist" (Irwin, *Three Lives* 8) milieu, daughter of a schoolteacher mother and an "officer of the law" (20) father, who was a member of Toronto's morality staff, Irwin (1907–2008) majored in classics at the University of Toronto (honours BA and MA in Greek drama and philosophy). Following her retirement as a high school teacher of thirty-nine years, all but one of them at Humberside Collegiate, she became an ordained minister of the Christian Congregational Conference of Ontario at age seventy-three, serving at a church in West Toronto. Today, the Word Guild of Canadian Christian Writing offers the Grace Irwin Award as its top prize.

Announcing that she has "lived in only three permanent homes, all in Toronto's west end, attended one public school, one high school, one university, [with her] teaching career in one school," Irwin's autobiography maintains that "change has flowed, been seen more clearly as change than it would against the confusion of an often altered background" (*Three Lives* ix). The solid positioning and narrative attitude toward this sea of change distinguish and complicate Irwin's Toronto. Her Toronto supplies what Elizabeth Wilson longs for, "spaces for face-to-face contact" (Wilson 158); it fulfills John Clement Ball's criterion as "the constitutive context for the self" (Ball 192). But how does this city of church politics and biblically-fuelled wrangles, recalled childhood picnics and hikes, and close, venerated family ties unbroken until death meet what Doreen Massey articulates as "the full recognition of coeval others" and the responsibilities of "the essential openness of place to the beyond" (216, 217)?

More than a backdrop or a scene-plotting Global Positioning System (GPS), the city of Toronto and, after 1954, Metro Toronto, is the essential social space of five of Irwin's seven novels. Outside this grouping are her acclaimed historical biographies of reformed slave ship captain John Newton, in *Servant of Slaves*, set in the Mendips, Georgian London, and aboard slavers in the Middle Passage; and of the Earl of Shaftesbury, the Ragged School Union founder, in *The Seventh Earl*, set in Victorian London. *Servant of Slaves* was hailed in the *University of Toronto Quarterly* as "the best historical novel of the year" (Watt 466) and subsequently translated into German, while the cover of Eerdman's paperback edition of *The Seventh Earl* posted the praise of Newbery Award–winner

Madeleine L'Engle commending Irwin's portrait "of an extraordinary and many-faceted man, who spoke forcefully and ahead of his time on many issues which still, today, cry out for his vigour and vision."

Irwin sketches a Toronto of specific neighbourhoods, ways of living, and networks of social, economic, and ideological preoccupations throughout her oeuvre—in the three novels spanning Andrew Connington's ministerial career; the character study of a high school Latin teacher, *In Little Place*; and *Compensation*, the romance occurring between Haliburton and Toronto in the early 1920s, which was written when she was an undergraduate and published over seven decades later. Evidence in her autobiography, published when she was seventy-nine, buttresses her depiction of the city of Toronto in these works. Topographic realism, external details of landmarks, and tradition link and illuminate the interior realities perceived and endured by her protagonists. Her city becomes what Pamela Gilbert terms a point of "intersection of narrative and place, time and space" (120). More than postcards of nostalgia, Irwin's blending of locale and disposition comments acutely, often critically, on both. Such commentary could allow her particular social space to function as what Smith calls "a cross-roads or meeting ground for the interplay of diverse localizing practices" (Smith 127).

The novels of the Connington trilogy share a linking design: framed by contrasts, their narratives explore Connington's realization of the breadth and dimensionality of his ministry. In the conversion experience of *Least of All Saints* he transitions from an ambitious preacher attracting great crowds to his services yet lacking faith to a committed, engaged believer. Framed by the death of his first child, a five-day-old infant, and the birth of a healthy son, *Andrew Connington* charts the conflicts of conscience Connington undergoes as a pastor who refuses to trim his principles to accommodate a well-heeled congregation. With the passage of twenty-five years, *Contend with Horses* is framed by the death of his wife in a car accident and his refusal of a wealthy widow's offer of re-marriage; noting tectonic social shifts in his home, church, and city, Connington still considers "rising and fighting another round" (*Contend with Horses* 284).

Neither a romance nor the account of a flâneur, *Least of All Saints* concerns the interplay of the city and human consciousness. Returning veteran, Oxford graduate, former employee of the League of Nations, Connington spends a lot of time walking—in search of himself, his vocation, his faith. Since his success as a preacher masks a lack of true conviction, faith follows vocation. He saunters under the direction of the purposive narrator who has a direct line into his perceptions. Every point of his walking itinerary holds significance for this ruminative seeker—from the Russell Hill Road home he shares with his aunt and uncle, down Avenue Road to Queen's Park, past the new Hart House, to University College, Gate House, Jackson Hall, to Victoria College chapel, to Shorncliffe United Church (the stand-in for Timothy Eaton Memorial Church, perhaps), the prestigious scene of Connington's first appointment as minister, and on to his delayed appearance at a Victoria College con-vocation at Annesley Hall, where he meets the Victoria graduate, Cecily Ridout, who very shortly will become his wife. Each locale is the occasion for learning more about his determination and priggishness. He shocks his nominally observant relations with plans to study theology, expresses his intolerance for "the 'arty' set, a dreary imitation of sets he had seen in England the previous summer" (*Least of All Saints* 87), and uses his knowledge of Greek to convince his Emmanuel College peers wondering about their commitment to, in his words, "give the Bible a fair chance" instead of "the conviction that the authors were fools" (111). He is aware, too, of the power of his intellect to deceive. With "a certain ironic humour" he entertains his uncle by recounting how he repeated the Apostles' Creed "prefacing each clause with Non credo" (28). But he also clarifies his pas-toral ambitions, convincing his uncle that he does not anticipate "years of drudgery in the backwoods"; as he expostulates, "You must think I'm crazy. No, my philanthropic impulse doesn't carry me as far as that, I assure you. It's a city pulpit for me, or nothing. And believe me, I'll get one. Does that convince you of the worldliness of my intentions?" (28).

By far the most resonant occasions are Connington's encounter with the stained glass windows in the Victoria chapel depicting Milton, Newton, Luther, and Wesley and his meeting of Cecily, who stirs this immensely successful orator to realize his lack of faith. Although the

temperate Connington allows his emotions to surface in such ano-
dyne outbursts as "dash it all" (*Least of All Saints* 46), "what the deuce"
(169), and "tell your own blasted crowd to go to blazes" (171), these
instances prompt moments of introspection that unsettle, finally, his
self-assured demeanour. After passing "the arched elms of St. Mary's
Street," beholding "the red roofs of Victoria College against a turquoise
sky," and striding "under the arch of Gate House," Connington experiences the "gloriously rejuvenating sensation about returning to school
in the crisp October air" (40). His brief stopover in the chapel, however,
and examination of the windows, illustrating what Massey later identifies as "the fact of multiplicity within and the essential openness of
place to the beyond" (Massey 217), effectively dislodge Connington's confidence in being "a model theological student" (*Least of All Saints* 40).
When he first examines the windows and their epigraphs, Connington
finds no qualms in aligning himself with them. Milton's "justify[ing]
the ways of God to men...was precisely what he was taking upon himself to do" (42). Newton's "The great ocean of Truth lay all undiscovered
before me" tinges his thoughts "with an inward humility which never
betrayed itself to others" (42). While he admits the need of Luther's fighting words "against an all-powerful hierarchy and a half-hostile, ignorant
world: 'Hier stehe ich; ich kann nicht anders. Gott helf' mir'" and "the
sheer force of his dogged personality" (42), Connington spends most
time with Wesley's "The best of all is God is with us" (43). Battling
momentary disappointment in such "a simple statement for a scholar like
Wesley!," he determines "to find out when the words had been uttered,
to be considered worthy of their position as an epitome of Wesley's message" (43). This very simplicity is what he must discover. Privately shaken,
Connington realizes that "the attitudes of the scientist and the poet-
philosopher might be his, but the affirmations of the two divines met in
his heart only emptiness that could not echo" (43).

As the rising star at Shorncliffe he trades in the Wesley connection,
telling a fawning journalist of an unidentified Toronto daily newspaper
that John Wesley "converted [his] great-great-great grandfather back in
1770 or thereabouts" (*Least of All Saints* 138), yet Connington only confronts his own inadequacy with the help of Cecily. Even before they meet

he overhears her misgivings about this "magnificent preacher": "I can't be sure he means it or feels it himself....I've heard ministers not a quarter so brilliant that I liked much better" (191). His "arrogance seep[ing] from him, like air from a pricked balloon," Connington realizes "he was a failure, whatever the world might think" (278). The narrator ushers us into his self-scrutiny: "He was a spiritual failure because he had ambitions for the well-being of others which he could not realize in himself.... Success in hoodwinking any number of credulous people by sheer force of personality was a pitifully inadequate weight" (279). Ironically, his epiphany takes place removed from Toronto the Good (or, the fashionable), in a "plain white clapboard" (279) church in Haliburton, where he accompanies Cecily's relatives. A small but ardent congregation, a substitute minister "with an extraordinarily spiritual face" (280), the psalmist's invocation to "Be still and know," and the Wesleyan hymn lead Connington to understand—without the puffery of family history— that "Wesley had indeed possessed the secret; and being dead, yet spoke" (282). After his first post-vacation sermon, a Shorncliffe matron candidly criticizes his delivery as "a bit too serious, too intense, too theological, too much old-fashioned stress on the personal. We've got beyond that," she insists. "We must have a wider outlook today. And we must preserve moderation in religion especially. One shouldn't force things on people, you know" (301). Serious theology untrimmed to the corporate tastes of his congregation becomes Connington's hallmark.

Such strength actually leads to his ejection from Shorncliffe in the sequel, *Andrew Connington*, a move precipitated by his denial of communion to a cost-saving executive who fires a long-time employee weeks before his pensionable service would be activated. Significantly, as Connington steels his courage to deny the communion salver, he silently recites Luther's words while realizing and embracing "the pathos, the loneliness, the unthanked nobility of the true reformer, who is always the reluctant reformer" (*Andrew Connington* 145). Set largely in the 1930s as "the depression hit[s]" (28), the narrative details Connington's overriding of management board objections to welcome thirty transients to the basement of Shorncliffe. But this novel is more calibrated around disjunctions and changes—in Connington's marriage, his ministry, and the city

itself. As a couple, the Conningtons enjoy 1930s entertainments, hearing contralto Sigrid Onegin at Massey Hall and seeing Hubert Henry
Davies's *Mollusc* at Hart House. But growing tensions at the church
disrupt their union. Before their separation Cecily warns her husband
against "a melancholy pleasure from being a suffering saint," but it is
only in his subsequent walk in High Park, past the Duke of Devonshire's
Gate, the bob-sled run and the toboggan slides, to the "reflective waters
of Grenadier Pond" that this historic pleasure place prompts the realization that he wants neither "a public hearing" nor "an outright clash" (189,
190). Instead of fighting his ejection, Connington accepts "a suburban
gospel hall" (230) where "an improvised pulpit," "broken panes of glass,"
and a squeaky piano cannot diminish his "deep solemn joy [to be] preach-
ing again" (225). This time, however, the role of the penitent is reversed;
Cecily admits she was wrong in hoping Connington would hold out for
a better church. Another Shorncliffe marriage is on shakier ground.
Connington, "absorbed in admiring contemplation of the neo-classical
details of Eaton's new College Street store," is viewing "the massive tri-
umphal-arch entry with its Minerva head keystone" (34) when a shy
heiress enters the narrative; she is infatuated—imprudently, the reader
is warned—with a callow unbeliever, who is also proven to be a playboy
and a drunk. The marriage, rushed into at the urging of the girl's social-
climbing mother, and the funeral after the bride's honeymoon suicide are
both Connington's solemn duties at Shorncliffe. Along with old verities,
old places are changing, as Toronto expands beyond his childhood memories: "The district west and north of Jane and Bloor...surprise[s] him";
Swansea is no longer "a dusty country road"; Clendenan Hill and Quebec
are not "the end of the line...to hike to the Humber for corn roasts" (59).
These observations lead Connington to conclude that "youngsters won't
have any open land for picnics around the city soon" (59).

Fifteen years separate the publication of *Contend with Horses* from the
earlier two novels, but Connington's life leaps ahead a quarter of a century. The sense of shifting space in this text evokes what Paul Ricoeur
identifies as "the idea of different possible traversals following a multitude of itineraries,...a stratified structure assembled like a pile of sheets
of paper, [getting] away from the idea of the past so assembled as a simple

chronology" (208). With a title borrowed from the answer to Jeremiah's complaint (Jeremiah 12.5) about the wicked prospering, the narrative testifies to Connington's stalwartness. The widowed father of an adult son and daughter, working half-time at his uncle's Connington Glass Company, and devoted to his unfashionable parish, which is no longer officially affiliated with the United Church, he continues to face the postwar critique "about the failure of the Church to appeal to the intellectual" (*Contend with Horses* 69). Called away from a lecture at Victoria College chapel to the emergency ward at St. Joseph's Hospital where he learns of Cecily's death at the outset, to putting down the telephone after having rejected re-marriage at the close, Connington faces a changed city throughout the novel. As the escort and guest of the widowed Beth at the opening night of *King John* at the Stratford Shakespeare Festival, he senses more than "the anguish of Constance and the fearful innocence of Arthur" (108); as sports personalities, politicians, arts patrons, and board of trade chairs greet Beth, he realizes "how completely the social life of Toronto had left him behind" (106). References to his reading are more prominent in this novel; he pores over Charles Hartshorne's process theology and finds relief in a crime novel by Michael Innes (the pseudonym of Oxford professor J.I.M. Stewart). His own book is drubbed in the popular press as "a thinly if skilfully camouflaged re-statement of nineteenth-century dogma," though in Connington's mind "his wit too had eluded or exasperated" (192). Despite vilification and criticism for stormy petrel, his sense of justice and loyalty to principles remains unshaken. When he confronts an attorney who has had a wealthy, childless, and elderly woman—her client for thirty-five years—transferred from her mansion on Park Road to the Whitby Institution and thus hastened her death, Connington's tongue can be sharp and his reprimand searing, to the extent that the lawyer herself succumbs to a heart attack minutes after his departure. Significantly, as he meets this lawyer, Beryl Sexsmith, she calls to mind "Lewis's most dreadful creation, Miss Hardcastle, the Fairy of *That Hideous Strength*" (209). The connection between the direct glance of Sexsmith's opaque blue eyes and Lewis's sadistic head of police at the National Institute for Coordinated Experiments—known for her torture of female prisoners—underlines the lawyer's menace as it reinforces Connington's resolve: "Once this resemblance came home to him, he had no further doubt of the justice, only of the result, of his mission" (209).

Aran Waring, the unmarried high school Latin teacher of *In Little Place*, is as forceful a personality in her spatial and creedal allegiances as Connington and as much a reflection of their creator. With a protagonist who opts for living "fully and excitingly in a fairly circumscribed area" (*In Little Place* 214), Irwin's title, from the prologue to *Henry V*, praises the imaginary force of the theatre in which a single zero or "the wooden O" (line 13) of the stage may multiply a number or "attest in little place a million" (line 16). Her evocation of this little place conveys the synecdochic importance of Waring's life and decisions, so rooted in and loyal to her family background and milieu, occupying the same house for over fifty years and retracing the route between home and school four times a day, so much at odds with casual affections or liaisons. The mirrored glance onto Irwin's own life is revealing and intentionally refracted at the same time. As Waring's own narrator, Irwin indulges in self-deprecatory humour about the prospect of Waring's writing an autobiography "when she had two books already written concerning which no publisher had shared her enthusiasm" (*In Little Place* 16). In fact, the first two Connington novels had been successful enough for McClelland and Stewart to enter into an agreement for a German translation. Linked to the half-concealed desire to write and be published is Irwin's explanation to herself and her readers, and through the autobiographical stand-in of Waring, her single, unattached, independent state. During a University of Toronto reception at the Royal Ontario Museum, as guests wander from the Chinese galleries to the refreshment table, forty-five-year-old, self-possessed but "manless" (10) Waring surveys the scene, longing to "remove her frozen expression of animation" and struggling with "her Methodist conscience between what she wanted and what was, she felt, expected of her" (8). Waring acknowledges that she herself is an exhibit, a curiosity, as awkward in this gathering as she would be in a Harlequin romance, yet Irwin ensures that her protagonist's rational position resonates with a joint conviction: "Why did people not realize that an incurable tendency to be guided by the head did not indicate lack of heart; that an instinctive prescience concerning the passing and dissipation of unguided emotion by no means quelled the violence of the emotion itself?" (14).

With the novel's mixture of first- and third-person narration, Waring and Irwin revisit childhood, positioning individuals within segments of a metropolis changed radically by the 1950s. Irwin's developed yet exuberant Methodist conscience recreates a past presided over by a revered though melancholic father and a warmly hospitable, necessarily frugal mother. Hers was a Toronto of picnics, hikes, and amusement parks. Whether for Sunday afternoon walks or family picnics, High Park, "Howard's blessed legacy" (*In Little Place* 73), was a favourite, lore-filled destination. She charts their hiking routes to the Humber River with cartographic detail, her precision indicating repetition and immense fondness. From her vantage point in contemporary "Metropolitan Toronto," Waring recasts "a largely motorless Toronto" where her mother's "urge for outdoor life" and her father's need to be near the city resulted in memorable and unique family camping experiences: "Ashbridge's Bay, or central Rosedale, or the top of Scarboro Bluffs in two outmoded streetcars, purchased as a bargain by my father instead of tents, afforded then more primitive camping life than is now permitted by the effeminacies of existence in Muskoka or Haliburton" (79).

Waring's climactic moment is her tour-de-force performance as a panelist on a Canadian Broadcasting Corporation (CBC) television talk show, *Everybody's Agora*, in a live telecast devoted to the superior preparations of contemporary education. The event supplies another occasion for Irwin's ventriloquizing through Waring, who proves to be as dedicated a reader of C.S. Lewis as Connington. After having been "transformed by the heavy pancake make-up into a sort of wax-works replica," Waring considers the studio preparation, debating with herself about a sense of belonging and acceptance:

> Another aspect of the phenomenon C.S. Lewis had discussed in *The Inner Ring*! How every group, every profession, had its circle, those who had arrived, those who knew the ropes, those who talked, and in some cases invented, its special language or jargon. And on their own ground at least, they were the priests and priestesses who could admit or exclude the uninitiate. (*In Little Place* 155)

Waring proves how well she knows the work of former Massey Commissioner Hilda Neatby in her polemical indictment of education, *So Little for the Mind*, which happened to be a best-selling imprint for Clarke, Irwin, the publishing firm Irwin's brother co-founded. Taking up the cudgels for scholarly standards, she advocates education as a privilege, a lowered school-leaving age, competition, memory work, "the infinite power of words and their discovery" (*In Little Place* 164), and students, "who are capable of so much more than we are expecting of them by our slackness" (185). Though the panelists patronize Waring for "her ivory tower of Greek and philosophy—natural enough dwelling for a teacher of dead languages" (166)—and for "'pontificat[ing] concerning the upbringing of children, being...the only unmarried person in [the] group" (185), she wins the applause of her teaching colleagues at Rivercrest Collegiate the next day and declines an offer to teach classics in translation at an American college, declaring that she is "Canadian" and would consider acceptance to "be running away" (210, 214).

While Connington and Waring are fashioned, in fact, indelibly imprinted, by a changing city, Irwin's first though last-published novel, *Compensation*, deals most explicitly with the contrasts between city and country, metropolis and hinterland. Promising student and only surviving child Iris Dale leaves her parents' home in 1920s Haliburton to complete high school in Toronto. The "unfashionable remoteness" of the community she has known, with its "intermarriage," "lack of mental stimulus," and "odd-jobbing" (*Compensation* 84) is replaced by colours and crowds, the "hub-of-the-universe attraction" of the old Union Station, "the high vaulted roof, the candy and fruit stalls flanking the arcade, the fat red pillars and carved gallery in the rotundas," and "the crowds of people thronging Yonge Street" (76). Stores are closed on Saturday afternoons, but from her aunt's boarding house Dale can see "flags hanging from shop windows on Yonge Street and...hear the clanging rush of passing streetcars" (78). Thanks to the benign paternalism of the Logans, a bourgeois Toronto family who, much like the Irwins, discovered in Haliburton an ideal location for their summer home, Dale enjoys a D'Oyly Carte company performance at the Royal Alexandra Theatre and Hart House Theatre "with its magically lighted underground auditorium" (100). The sudden death of her father, her return to Haliburton, and the proposal of a local "unlovely and unheroic male" (49) prompt her internal debate about compensation, her attempt to weigh the tough opportunities of the city against the stultified ease of a country life: "She was still essentially country-bred....But of what use was all the beauty of a country if, sinking into mental decadence, she should come to accept it casually, unastonished?" (191). Rejecting the local's offer of marriage, Dale opts to face her future "bravely and doubtless find in it some compensations" (191). That she comes back to Toronto to work "in the Canadian branch of an English publishing house" (262) and accepts the love of a forestry cartographer (yes, a godly University of Toronto man) braids the best of all Irwin's worlds: united creedal and intellectual loyalties, in both city location and country retreat.

In considering Irwin's five Toronto novels, it is easy to itemize what is missing as historical and cultural landmarks: the eruption of Yonge Street for the subway line, the battles over the first leg of the Gardiner Expressway connecting downtown to the suburbs in the west, the opening of York University, the growth of racial diversity and visible minority neighbourhoods, the poetry reading scene at the Bohemian Embassy. Attitudinally there is little lament about the rise of carefree, conspicuous consumption or the sprawl of subdivisions like the "gilt-edged suburban labyrinth" (Young 13) from which Phyllis Brett Young's heroine in *The Torontonians* dreams of escape. For today's reader many topographical references also highlight what has changed: department stores have disappeared; the CBC has a new gleaming location on Front Street West; and the Royal Ontario Museum now literally juts onto Bloor Street. What Irwin captures, I suggest, is a Toronto few of her millions of residents would recognize today. The modern consciousness of her Torontonian protagonists has a distinctive theological and apologetic cast. Within the confessional debates and church interiors of her novels there is limited recognition of coeval others. Communication circuits involve a range of ethical and pedagogical topics. Rather than simply reifying her work as glimpses of a past, it is worth considering how they amplify and thicken our understanding of boom and growth. Moreover, rather than positioning Irwin as the baseline against which to measure the urban consciousness of Young, Gwendolyn MacEwen, or Margaret Atwood, it might be time to adjust and re-apply the criteria of the interplay of diversity and the multiplicity and openness of place to resuscitate awareness of the career of this independent, strong-minded individual of great, unswerving conviction. If interest exists in what Ricoeur labelled a horizon of expectations, which "tends toward the breaking open of perspectives" (209), then perhaps the understudied hermeneutic architecture of Irwin's Toronto the Good warrants exploration.

WORKS CITED

Ball, John Clement. "Duelling and Dwelling in Toronto and London: Transnational Urbanism in Catherine Bush's *The Rules of Engagement.*" *Downtown Canada: Writing Canadian Cities.* Ed. Justin Edwards and Douglas Ivison. Toronto: University of Toronto Press, 2005. 183–96.
Clark, C.S. *Of Toronto the Good: A Social Study.* Montreal: Toronto Publishing Company, 1898.
Gilbert, Pamela K. "Sex and the City: English Studies and the Spatial Turn." *The Spatial Turn: Interdisciplinary Perspectives.* Ed. Barney Warf and Santa Arias. New York: Routledge, 2009. 102–21.
Grosz, Elizabeth. *Space, Time, and Perversion: Essays on the Politics of Bodies.* New York: Routledge, 1995.
Irwin, Grace. *Andrew Connington.* Toronto: McClelland and Stewart, 1954.
———. *Compensation.* Belleville, ON: Epic Press, 2003.
———. *Contend with Horses.* Toronto: McClelland and Stewart, 1969.
———. *In Little Place.* Grand Rapids, MI: W.B. Eerdmans Publishing Company, 1959.
———. *Least of All Saints.* Toronto: McClelland and Stewart, 1952.
———. *The Seventh Earl: A Dramatized Biography.* Grand Rapids, MI: William B. Eerdmans Publishing Company, 1976.
———. *Three Lives in Mine.* Toronto: Irwin Publishing, 1986.
Massey, Doreen. *World City.* Cambridge: Polity Press, 2007.
McCann, Larry D., and Peter J. Smith. "Canada Becomes Urban: Cities and Urbanization in Historical Perspective." *Canadian Cities in Transition.* Ed. Trudi Bunting and Pierre Filion. Toronto: Oxford University Press, 1991. 59–99.
Neatby, Hilda. *So Little for the Mind: An Indictment of Canadian Education.* Toronto: Clarke, Irwin, 1953.
Ricoeur, Paul. *Time and Narrative.* Vol. 3. Trans. Kathleen Blamey and David Pellauer. Chicago: University of Chicago Press, 1985.
Sassen, Saskia. *Cities in a World Economy.* 3rd ed. Thousand Oaks, CA: Pine Forge Press, Sage Publications, 2006.
Shakespeare, William. *Henry V.* Ed. David Bevington. 6th ed. New York: Pearson Longman, 2009.

Smith, Michael Peter. *Transnational Urbanism: Locating Globalization*. Malden, MA: Blackwell, 2001.

Squier, Susan Merrill, ed. Introduction. *Women Writers and the City: Essays in Feminist Literary Criticism*. Knoxville: University of Tennessee Press, 1984. 3–10.

Watt, F.W. "Fiction." *University of Toronto Quarterly* 30.4 (1960–61): 401–16.

Williams, Raymond. *The Country and the City*. London: Chatto and Windus, 1973.

Wilson, Elizabeth. *The Sphinx in the City: Urban Life, the Control of Disorder, and Women*. London: Virago Press, 1991.

Young, Phyllis Brett. *The Torontonians*. Intro. by Nathalie Cooke and Suzanne Morton. Montreal and Kingston: McGill-Queen's University Press, 2007.

« WHERE ARE YOU FROM? »

La ville et l'écriture migrante
dans l'autofiction de Marguerite Andersen

Kathleen Kellett

Dans *Le figuier sur le toit*, la narratrice, une vieille dame du nom de Marguerite, est incitée à la veille de ses quatre-vingt-quatre ans à se remémorer les détails de sa vie, aiguillonnée par cette question désobligeante que les Canadiens anglais tiennent à poser aux immigrants dès qu'ils décèlent les moindres traces d'accent : « *Where are you from?* » (29). La question la plonge dans les souvenirs de son enfance à Berlin d'avant et d'après l'arrivée au pouvoir du régime nazi qui entraîne la persécution puis le génocide des Juifs ainsi que l'exécution des homosexuels, des malades mentaux, des Roms et des infirmes. La recherche mémorielle du paradis perdu, celui de l'espace-temps de l'enfance berlinoise innocente, est une thématique qui traverse l'ensemble de l'œuvre autofictionnelle d'Andersen : le profond sentiment de culpabilité d'avoir vécu sous le régime nazi obsède Marguerite tout au long de sa vie, la poursuivant de Berlin à Toronto.

Née en 1924, auteure et éditrice franco-ontarienne, Marguerite Andersen est venue à l'écriture de fiction à l'âge de cinquante-trois ans, mariant cette nouvelle carrière à celle de professeure de littérature française. Elle fait son entrée sur la scène littéraire en 1982 avec *De mémoire de femme*, « récit en partie autobiographique » pour lequel elle reçoit le Prix du Journal de Montréal. Grande admiratrice de Simone de Beauvoir et de ses œuvres autobiographiques, Andersen récidive en littérature intime avec la prose poétique *Bleu sur blanc* en 2000, avec la fiction documentaire *Parallèles* en 2004 et avec le roman *Le figuier sur le toit*, pour lequel elle reçoit le Prix Trillium en 2008. Dans l'avant-propos de *La vie devant elles*, paru en 2011, Andersen se présente comme « écrivaine à tendance autofictionnelle » mais précise que, dans cet ouvrage, elle construit plutôt « trois récits biofictionnels » à partir de la vie de ses six petites-filles (7). Dans ces autofictions, le « pacte autobiographique » (Lejeune) est scellé par le nom propre — parfois, il est vrai, de façon indirecte. Ainsi, dans *Bleu sur blanc*, *Parallèles*, *Le figuier sur le toit* et *La vie devant elles*, la protagoniste s'appelle Marguerite; dans *De mémoire de femme*, comme le remarque Lucie Hotte, le nom d'Anne Grimm établit de façon ludique un lien entre les frères allemands, conteurs renommés, et l'auteur danois Hans Christian Andersen, qui porte le même nom que l'écrivaine (Hotte 11). Tous ces romans retravaillent le passé historique comme le passé personnel de l'auteure, évoquant sous des perspectives diverses la vie mouvementée d'Andersen sur trois continents[1] : elle fuit Berlin en 1945 pour s'installer successivement à Londres, à Tunis, à Montréal, à Addis-Abeba et enfin à Toronto, au gré de ses amours et de sa carrière universitaire.

Chaque ville représente une nouvelle étape dans sa vie. Berlin, ville qui inspire culpabilité et honte à Andersen, est également le lieu privilégié de son père, Theodor Werner Bohner, fils d'un missionnaire luthérien, ancien député au *Landtag*, romancier, biographe et essayiste, qui constitue à la fois un rival et une source d'inspiration. Londres est le lieu d'une évasion désespérée à la fin de la guerre pour sa famille, qui possède des passeports britanniques grâce à la naissance du père au Ghana. Marguerite perd sa citoyenneté allemande en se mariant à un soldat français qu'elle accompagne à Tunis : « J'avais rencontré un Français, jeune officier, j'allais l'épouser... L'amour? Au fond, je m'échappais, personne déplacée parmi tant d'autres » (*Bleu sur blanc* 17). Divorcée, elle s'évade à Montréal, où elle poursuit une carrière universitaire exigeante et mène une vie privée déchirante. Paris, ville-lumière et lieu de congé sabbatique, lui offre brièvement le temps et le loisir pour la création littéraire. C'est pourtant Toronto qu'Andersen présente comme le lieu privilégié non seulement de l'écriture mais aussi de la convivialité d'une communauté artistique, ville où elle participe au débuts de la Société des écrivain(e)s de Toronto ainsi que de l'Association des auteures et des auteurs de l'Ontario français. De Berlin à Toronto, Andersen entreprend la quête difficile de se réconcilier avec une enfance vécue sous le régime nazi ainsi qu'avec le père écrivain et le paradis perdu de l'enfance, représenté dans l'œuvre comme le triangle sacré *Vater, Mutter, Kind* (père, mère, enfant).

Une enfance berlinoise : l'enfant et le père écrivain

Bien qu'Andersen soit née à Magdebourg, petite ville proche de Berlin, c'est Berlin, où elle emménage avec sa famille à l'âge de quatre ans, qui incarne surtout le lieu de son enfance. D'ailleurs, dans *Parallèles*, la narratrice a Berlin comme lieu de naissance (19). Ses parents y côtoient des intellectuels, des artistes et des scientifiques. On pourrait même dire qu'elle vient au monde par l'intermédiaire de l'écriture de son père, Theo, lui-même auteur à tendance autofictionnelle. Celui-ci raconte la naissance de sa fille dans son roman *Das Licht und sein Schatten* (La lumière et son ombre) publié en 1937[2]. Que la protagoniste et sa sœur Emma s'identifient toutes deux à ce nouveau-né souligne le caractère équivoque de l'écriture autofictionnelle (*Mémoire* 40). Le titre du roman est tiré d'un proverbe japonais : « La femme est l'ombre / L'homme est la lumière. / Une femme a beaucoup de malheur / Un homme a beaucoup de bonheur » (*Mémoire* 43). Dans la version du père, la mère est déçue d'avoir eu une fille plutôt qu'un garçon, implorant le père de regarder de plus près pour bien vérifier le sexe de l'enfant, alors que le père n'en est pas trop inquiet, semble-t-il. Cette scène cruciale, Andersen la reprend dans plus d'une version « revue et corrigée par l'intéressée » (*Mémoire* 41; voir aussi *Parallèles* 40-41). Dans l'une de ces versions, racontée du point de vue de la mère, Martha, c'est plutôt le père qui aurait voulu avoir un fils : « Qui avait été déçu par la naissance de leur troisième fille? Qui, au fond, avait peur des femmes? » (*Mémoire* 100). Au moyen de la réécriture, l'écrivaine affronte son père, à la fois modèle, source d'émulation et rival. À partir du récit paternel, qui repose sur une perspective essentialiste de l'homme et de la femme, elle construit un récit du premier jardin, du paradis réconfortant à l'intérieur de la cellule familiale, espèce de fusion pré-œdipienne à trois : « Dans la douleur, dans le sang, dans l'euphorie de la vie nouvelle, il y a entre nous trois quelques instants d'une intimité parfaite. Mon père, ma mère et moi. *Vater, Mutter, Kind.* Voilà mon début, mon origine, mon éden » (*Mémoire* 42). Ce paradis fantasmé est celui du bonheur enfantin et innocent, qui ignore les conflits et les infidélités des parents dans la vie mondaine de Berlin. Lorsque le père exige de la mère la vente de la maison d'été de Ahrensoop, territoire du grand-père et du beau-frère antisémites, Marguerite se sent expulsée du paradis : « Il fallait que quelqu'un me chasse de mon paradis, Theo, le dieu de mon enfance, était prédestiné à ce rôle rien que par son nom » (*Figuier* 105). L'impact du régime nazi et de la guerre fera plus tard de la figure paternelle un dieu déchu.

La perte de l'innocence enfantine fait écho à la destruction de la société berlinoise des années 1920, celle d'avant le régime hitlérien, celle d'une métropole culturelle et intellectuelle qui ne connaît pas encore le feu du Reichstag ni celui de la *Kristallnacht* (Nuit de cristal), ne connaît pas non plus la brutalité du nazisme, bien que les germes de l'antisémitisme y soient déjà bien enracinés. C'est à Berlin que le grand-père maternel, Reinhold Seeberg, recteur de la Freidrich-Wilhelms-Universität, enseigne et rédige des livres de théologie qui font encore autorité dans ce domaine. Il est également l'auteur du *Seeberg-Adresse*, « document de nature pangermaniste et militariste » signé en 1915 par 1 347 intellectuels berlinois, dont 352 professeurs d'université (*Figuier* 142). Même s'il refuse de signer le document de son beau-père, Theodor Bohner, professeur lui-même, n'endosse pas non plus le contre-manifeste signé entre autres par Max Planck et Albert Einstein (*Figuier* 142). En 1928, lorsque Theodor Bohner, qui a reçu une promotion au ministère de l'Éducation, s'installe à Berlin avec sa famille, il s'agit d'une « ville de quatre millions d'habitants, dont 170 000 Juifs, et 50 000 Russes parmi 150 000 étrangers, ville en compétition intellectuelle et artistique avec Paris » (*Figuier* 154). La fin abrupte de l'innocence est soulignée par le récit d'une excursion spéciale au cours duquel son père emmène Marguerite au Reichstag, où elle rencontre certaines relations de son père, dont « un M. Einstein ayant décidément besoin de se faire couper les cheveux » (*Figuier* 73). Son père lui fait remarquer la beauté du style Haute Renaissance italienne du bâtiment créé par l'architecte célèbre M. Wallot : « Peu importe d'ailleurs, bientôt le Reichstag sera détruit par les flammes » (*Figuier* 75).

C'est à Berlin que son père, Theo, qui s'oppose à Hitler et aux idées antisémites de son propre beau-père, est démis de ses fonctions et passe la guerre, avec sa femme et ses trois filles, ayant dû quitter leur logement opulent du centre-ville pour un quartier beaucoup plus modeste de la périphérie. Pour subvenir aux besoins de sa famille, Theo vit de sa plume en composant des romans, des biographies et des études de légendes, tout en craignant d'être frappé du *Schreibverbot* (*Figuier* 197), l'interdiction d'écrire : « Exclu de toute vie publique, Theo vit une émigration intérieure » (*Figuier* 197). Étudiante à Berlin, la narratrice est obligée de se joindre au mouvement de jeunesse hitlérienne pour pouvoir continuer d'aller au lycée. L'enseignement pro-nazi est contesté par la famille Bohner : dans une scène racontée dans *Parallèles* ainsi que dans *Le figuier sur le toit*, la mère s'emporte contre Marguerite, la giflant lorsque celle-ci arrive à la maison avec un drapeau portant la croix gammée. La jeune fille n'est pas à l'abri de la propagande hitlérienne, qui lui inspire un roman familial reposant sur le récit édénique du *Vater, Mutter, Kind*, mais revu : « Marguerite rêvait parfois, le soir, dans son lit, que le *Führer* était son vrai père... Que Theo n'était rien en comparaison de cet homme important, le plus important du pays » (*Figuier* 219). Vers la fin de la guerre, alors que les autres membres de la famille s'enfuient en Autriche, le père reste à Berlin pour soutenir ses amis, qui planifient l'attentat manqué contre Hitler du 20 juillet 1944, et parmi eux Julius Leber. Ce Berlin de l'époque de la guerre ne suscite que de la culpabilité, ce que la narratrice exprime ainsi dans *Parallèles* :

La mère arrêtée brièvement, en 1942, pour avoir écouté Radio-Londres. Une nuit au poste, puis relâchée moyennant la somme de 500 marks. Le père démis de ses fonctions en 1933, mais jamais vraiment poursuivi. Son ami Julius Leber pendu à Plotzensee. Lui, un rouage trop insignifiant dans le mouvement, même pas arrêté. (218)

Après la guerre, pour s'évader d'un pays en ruines, la narratrice se marie à un officier français, originaire de Tunis, qui lui donne deux fils et l'emprisonne dans un mariage malheureux et oppressif. Dans *Parallèles*, la narratrice confie au lecteur ce sentiment de honte qui motive sa fuite de la langue et de la culture allemandes : « je me suis jetée dans un autre milieu, une autre langue. Ai caché mes origines. Pour ne pas être accusée des horreurs commises. Et sans y avoir participé, je m'en sens coupable, encore et toujours » (220). Berlin reste donc un espace narratif marqué par l'ambivalence : l'écriture du père est symbole de la richesse culturelle du Berlin d'antan, mais aussi symbole d'impuissance, pauvre substitut de l'action héroïque. Pour retrouver le bonheur fantasmé de la cellule familiale, la narratrice entretiendra des liaisons amoureuses condamnées à lui apporter de l'angoisse.

Tunis, un paysage de beauté, de pauvreté et de douleur

Entre Berlin et Toronto, entre ces deux espaces urbains et leurs institutions littéraires, cinq villes figurent comme espaces intermédiaires : Londres, Tunis, Montréal, Addis-Abeba et Paris. Ville réelle mais aussi espace-temps construit par l'auteure, Tunis apparaît sous deux jours différents. Dans *Bleu sur blanc*, où Marguerite choisit de ne pas parler « des amours floués » (7), « Tunis la Blanche » est un oasis de beauté après le déchirement d'une jeunesse vécue sous la guerre : « Nous tous / chassés / au loin / exilés / parfois un coup d'œil rapide sur les / paradis perdus / l'enfance / puis la Tunisie / paradis terrestre / clair et simple / bleu sur blanc » (9). Dans *De mémoire de femme* et *Le figuier sur le toit*, par contre, le discours mémoriel dresse un portrait plus sombre de cette ville. Soumise au contrôle de son mari franco-tunisien et de sa mère, qui détestent les Allemands, désignés de l'épithète méprisant de « boches », la narratrice est plongée dans un monde de pauvreté :

> Tout ce que je voyais de la fenêtre de ma chambre, c'était le quartier des ouvriers italiens, de petites maisons misérables qu'on n'avait pas repeintes depuis le début de la guerre. Et c'est resté ainsi dans ma mémoire, telle une banale photo. Encore aujourd'hui, c'est toujours cette image qui me vient à l'esprit quand je me mets à penser à Tunis. (*Figuier* 127)

De mémoire de femme met en relief les dimensions scatologiques de cette pauvreté : tous les jours, la narratrice se plaint de devoir nettoyer la fosse d'aisance afin d'éviter les débordements : « fossoyeuse d'excréments, voilà ma pauvreté » (269). La protagoniste reconnaît volontiers la beauté du paysage, en citant Albert Camus, le grand écrivain d'Oran : « Cependant, et Camus le dit bien, il est plus facile, ou bien moins terrible, d'être pauvre en Afrique du Nord que de l'être ailleurs » (269). L'image récurrente, loin d'être poétique, est celle des tripes qu'elle achète bon marché et qu'elle doit laver à longueur de journée pour en faire quelque chose de mangeable : « Fallait-il avoir faim! » (*Mémoire* 189), comme le dit son fils! Cette tentative de s'évader de son passé allemand aboutit à un échec. La narratrice autodiégétique doit partir en abandonnant pour un temps ses deux fils, qui sont obligés par la famille franco-tunisienne à renier leur langue natale et leurs origines pour devenir résolument français. Elle regrette d'avoir choisi le mariage plutôt que le sort de mère célibataire : « je payais cher mon erreur d'épouser Pierre au lieu de trouver le courage d'élever seule mon enfant, quitte à le priver de son père, à violer finalement l'image sacrée de *Vater, Mutter, Kind* » (*Mémoire* 270). Le père, lui-même « personne déplacée » (*Bleu sur blanc* 75) après l'indépendance de la Tunisie en 1955, relâche son emprise sur ses fils, qui passent un certain temps à Berlin avec leur famille allemande. L'émigration à Montréal fournit à Marguerite l'occasion de refaire sa vie, même si elle doit se contenter pour un temps de laisser l'un de ses fils avec son père.

Montréal, espace urbain dysphorique

Dans l'ensemble de l'œuvre autofictionnelle, Montréal, où Marguerite s'installe en 1958, se présente comme un endroit excessivement pieux et nationaliste. La scène de « l'arrivée en ville », l'intrusion potentiellement subversive de l'étranger dans l'espace urbain dont parle Simon Harel dans *Le Voleur de parcours* (43), coïncide avec l'arrivée au Canada. Dans *Parallèles*, Marguerite, la narratrice autodiégétique, est agressée verbalement par un officier, qui la traite de « voleuse de job » car elle est embauchée comme professeur par la Commission des écoles protestantes de Montréal alors que sa sœur à lui, enseignante également, mais francophone, n'a pas accès aux postes du conseil scolaire protestant : « 'Nous n'avons pas besoin de professeurs au Canada, nous avons besoin de femmes de ménage', me lance-t-il » (151). Cet accès de nationalisme étroit n'est pas de bon augure pour la nouvelle arrivante. Lorsqu'elle commence ses études à l'Université de Montréal, elle est ébahie par la vision du professeur qui se met à genoux en prière avant de commencer son cours. De même, elle est scandalisée par l'idée d'une bibliothèque universitaire où on ne peut pas lire les livres à l'Index à moins d'avoir la permission de son directeur de conscience : « Je suis heureuse de ne pas avoir, de n'avoir jamais eu, de directeur de conscience » (*Parallèles* 67). Elle parle peu de la Révolution tranquille, qu'elle a pourtant vécue, sauf pour remettre en question l'Acte des mesures de guerre lors de la Crise d'octobre (*Mémoire* 82). Elle ne s'attarde pas non plus sur son activisme dans l'association des professeurs. Montréal est surtout le lieu de la culpabilité au féminin : dans *De mémoire de femme*, Andersen fait le portrait de la mère gagne-pain et de la femme amoureuse qui néglige son fils aîné et sa vieille mère infirme pour se dévouer à un mari difficile et à une carrière exigeante. Du point de vue du fils aîné, narrateur à son tour, Montréal est un espace dysphorique associé au souterrain. Il est relégué au sous-sol pour faire place à l'amant possessif de sa mère, un homme d'origine danoise qui deviendra son beau-père. On envoie le fils en pensionnat pendant la semaine dans une école anglaise de banlieue, près des raffineries de pétrole, et il s'agit pour lui carrément d'une descente en enfer : « Je ne vois pas que ces flammes sont celles de l'enfer, que le pasteur qui gère le pensionnat est l'ange des ténèbres » (*Mémoire* 301). Dans *De mémoire de femme* et *Parallèles*, Montréal est associée moins à l'écriture créatrice qu'à l'écriture alimentaire : la femme exilée s'occupe de la rédaction de dissertations et de la correction de travaux d'étudiants, travail qu'elle effectue non seulement pour son propre compte mais aussi pour celui de son nouveau mari, fainéant.

Les défaillances de ce mariage ne disparaissent pas au cours du séjour d'enseignement de la narratrice et de son mari à Addis-Abeba, même si c'est là qu'elle a le bonheur de donner naissance à sa fille. Sa tentative de retrouver le paradis douillet de *Vater, Mutter, Kind* échoue encore. Marguerite et sa famille sont chassées du pays par les puces éthiopiennes, qui se délectent de la peau tendre du mari. Celui-ci est loin d'incarner la vision idéalisée de la figure paternelle. Le bonheur reviendra plus tard sous une configuration familiale moins traditionnelle qui exclut le père.

Il est à noter que dans *La vie devant elles*, composé des récits biofictionnels de ses petits-enfants, Andersen construit une vision plus valorisante de Montréal. Le fils de Marguerite se souvient de ses études universitaires et de la rencontre avec sa femme polonaise, Zosia, avec qui il crée lui-même une cellule familiale *Vater, Mutter, Kind*, quitte à se présenter comme français en taisant ses origines allemandes auprès de ses enfants et de ses amis. Montréal se présente sous un autre jour encore dans le récit de la petite-fille Claire, qui quitte Ottawa pour étudier à l'Université McGill. En tant que Franco-Ontarienne, elle perçoit Montréal plutôt comme une métropole culturelle en ébullition : « Mais Claire choisit d'étudier à McGill, comme tant de jeunes Franco-Ontariens ambitieux, à Montréal, comme le fera plus tard sa sœur Ariane. La grande ville, les deux langues, la culture, les arts aux courants multiples l'attirent » (*Vie devant elles* 198). Montréal, après avoir été le lieu d'exil douloureux d'une « personne déplacée » s'évadant de son passé berlinois, finit par incarner chez Andersen la métropole à prééminence artistique, surtout selon la perspective de ses petits-enfants nés au Canada.

Paris, ville-lumière, métropole culturelle

S'installer à Paris en congé sabbatique pendant un an pour écrire, quel rêve pour l'ex-Berlinoise! Nous avons vu que le Berlin des années 1920, « ville en compétition intellectuelle et artistique avec Paris », se mesurait à l'aune de la ville-lumière (*Figuier* 154). Les traces des géants littéraires se retrouvent partout. Ainsi, l'appartement loué pour l'année rappelle à la narratrice Balzac : « L'escalier sent la cire d'abeille, un écriteau en émail rappelle aux usagers de s'essuyer les pieds, s.v.p., je ne serais pas surprise de voir surgir Mme Vauquer dans ce décor balzacien » (*Mémoire* 20). Le cadre parisien ne se présente cependant pas uniquement comme lieu de pèlerinage littéraire. La narratrice autodiégétique de *De mémoire de femme*, Anne Grimm, s'installe en banlieue, à Bourg-la-Reine, dont le centre commercial évoque pour elle les lieux familiers de l'espace montréalais : « L'endroit m'a rappelé le Canada. S'il n'y avait pas eu le drapeau tricolore flottant sur le parking, je me serais crue à la place Alexis-Nihon, à Montréal » (231). Il s'agit d'un Paris moderne, où elle peut même ressasser les souvenirs de Tunis en fréquentant le hammam du quartier. Le point culminant de cette autofiction est le retour au Canada, lorsque la protagoniste participe à une table ronde composée des femmes qui l'ont influencée, ce que Julie Tennier définit comme « lieu féminin collectif utopique » (65) et qu'elle compare au *Dinner Party* de Judy Chicago et au *Pique-nique sur l'Acropole* de l'auteure québécoise féministe Louky Bersianik (68). La table ronde constitue une affirmation féministe de solidarité, une image du désir d'Andersen de remplacer l'idéal du triangle *Vater, Mutter, Kind* afin de retrouver une autonomie créatrice appuyée par un milieu artistique convivial.

Toronto, lieu de réconciliation avec le père écrivain

Toronto, quoiqu'absente de l'ouvrage *De mémoire de femme*, est la ville associée à l'écriture créatrice dans *Parallèles* comme dans *Le figuier sur le toit*. C'est à Toronto que la narratrice Marguerite finit par assumer son identité d'écrivaine et joue un rôle dans l'établissement d'institutions littéraires franco-ontariennes. C'est à Toronto également qu'elle se réconcilie avec l'écrivain rival, le père. Si le père représente l'autorité quant à « l'allemand » et que l'anglais appartient à la sœur aînée (*Mémoire* 32), quelle langue faut-il choisir pour écrire? Paradoxalement, dans cette ville à prédominance anglophone, Marguerite choisit d'écrire en français, langue qu'elle considère comme maternelle puisque c'est sa mère qui l'a amenée à l'étudier chez une dame belge au cœur brisé : « Le français reste néanmoins la langue de mon choix. Grâce au séjour de Mlle Gralier à Berlin, il est ma langue maternelle. C'est toi, ma mère, qui m'as dotée de cette langue que je choisis aujourd'hui pour m'exprimer » (*Mémoire* 32). D'ailleurs, comme le remarque François Paré dans une étude sur les nouvelles d'Andersen, on retrouve chez cette auteure un « refus de la ville anglophone » (825), une tendance à transformer Toronto en un espace « où la plupart des habitants portent des noms et des prénoms français et fréquentent des lieux appartenant clairement à la communauté francophone » (825). Dans *Parallèles*, la narratrice choisit de raconter sa vie et celle de son amie Lucienne Lacasse-Lovsted, toutes deux membres fondatrices de la Société des écrivain(e)s de Toronto, association décrite comme un « cercle de famille, regroupement de tribu » (178). Toutes les institutions francophones de Toronto sont mises à l'honneur. Par exemple, lorsque Lucienne quitte Montréal et arrive à Toronto, elle est accueillie par une Anglaise qui l'envoie à l'église Sacré-Cœur, à l'angle des rues Sherbourne et Carlton. Pour Lucienne, « migrant[e] de l'intérieur » (Harel 30), Toronto représente un havre après sa vie au Québec, qui apparaît comme soumis aux valeurs patriarcales de l'Église catholique de l'époque. À travers la vie de Lucienne, Andersen esquisse en effet le portrait d'une Église oppressive qui condamne les femmes aux grossesses fréquentes, ce qui épuise des femmes comme la mère de Lucienne, qui meurt dans un asile après un épisode de dépression post-partum. L'Église catholique parraine alors l'Institut des équipières sociales, dont Lucienne avait fait partie à Ottawa et à Montréal et qui impose aux pénitentes de marcher avec des fèves dans les souliers « pour s'empêcher de courir après le plaisir » (*Parallèles* 135). Même si Lucienne choisit d'élever ses enfants en anglais à Toronto pour leur éviter d'être des « *second class citizen* » (*Parallèles* 200), elle-même parvient à vivre en français. Elle passe la fin de sa vie à Place Saint-Laurent, une résidence francophone pour personnes âgées. D'ailleurs, Lucienne n'est pas la seule membre de la Société des écrivain(e)s de Toronto à figurer dans cette « fiction-documentaire » : Marguerite mentionne également, entre autres, « Cécile » (Cloutier), « Mireille » (Déjarlais-Heynneman) et « Lélia » (Young)[3] (*Parallèles* 212).

Pour Andersen, Toronto constitue donc un milieu privilégié de convivialité artistique. Dans *Parallèles*, la narratrice Marguerite fait l'éloge des institutions culturelles francophones, par exemple du Prix Trillium en langue française, créé en 1994 (pour ceux qui ne peuvent participer pleinement à la version anglophone, créée en 1988), ou de l'Association des auteures et des auteurs de l'Ontario français, dont Marguerite Andersen a été présidente de 2000 à 2004. Elle parle également de son travail en tant qu'éditrice de la revue franco-ontarienne *Virages* consacrée à la nouvelle. C'est par cette célébration des institutions littéraires franco-torontoises dont elle fait partie que Marguerite finit par rejoindre le père d'une façon positive. Elle décrit dans *Le figuier sur le toit* la boîte d'archives personnelles marquée « Famille » qu'elle a transportée jusqu'à Toronto et dans laquelle elle conserve les documents de la société d'écrivains allemands dont son père avait été président avant le régime nazi. Écrivaine torontoise, elle retrouve alors un point de contact positif avec le père, écrivain berlinois :

> La coïncidence est remarquable : Berlin, un écrivain, une association professionnelle — Toronto, une écrivaine, des associations professionnelles. Tel père, telle fille! Des époques différentes, mais les mêmes objectifs : liberté d'expression, droit d'auteur, revenu acceptable, habitations à loyer modéré, paiement pour le prêt public, subventions gouvernementales. (*Figuier* 171)

Grâce à cette figure idéalisée, elle crée une forme de complicité avec son père : « Au fond, se dit la vieille dame, heureuse de tous ces parallèles qu'elle découvre entre son père et elle-même, s'il était encore là, on travaillerait ensemble » (*Figuier* 172). Le discours mémoriel réunit donc père et fille, Berlin et Toronto, une littérature allemande renommée et une littérature franco-ontarienne en émergence. Le monde de la convivialité artistique finit par l'emporter sur l'ancien idéal de la famille nucléaire.

La ville multiculturelle et le figuier déterré

Toronto, tout en renvoyant, pour Andersen, au Berlin du père écrivain comme site urbain de l'institution littéraire, se démarque par un *zeitgeist* qui contraste avec les idéaux de pureté ethnique et culturelle prônés par le grand-père Seeberg à Berlin avant la Seconde Guerre mondiale. Dans cette optique, Toronto incarnerait la réussite de la politique canadienne de multiculturalisme, dont l'idéologie demeure d'ailleurs fortement critiquée de nos jours. On pourrait dès lors se poser la question : est-ce qu'Andersen tombe dans le piège de ce que Daniel Coleman appelle la « civilité blanche » (« *white civility* », 32-33) au Canada, cette tendance à se faire valoir en se vantant de sa tolérance envers les dépossédés et les marginalisés?

Le figuier sur le toit, dont le cadre principal est la ville de Toronto, véhicule en fait un message quelque peu paradoxal. Il s'agit, comme nous l'avons vu, d'une réponse à la sempiternelle question des origines posée par un grand nombre de Canadiens, « *Where are you from?* ». À l'instar de l'auteur anglo-allemand W.G. Sebald, entre autres, Andersen entreprend alors de révéler l'antisémitisme du grand-père Seeberg et de ses pairs, les atrocités de l'Holocauste et la culpabilité des Allemands témoins de toutes les brutalités imposées par le régime nazi ainsi que les effets dévastateurs de la guerre (*Figuier* 196). Pour souligner le sérieux de son projet, l'auteure recourt à la mémoire savante en ajoutant l'annexe « Dates et faits importants, et mesures législatives du régime nazi » (*Figuier* 257-58). La vieille dame témoigne de la persécution des Juifs (de la perte de leurs droits jusqu'au génocide), de la persécution des amis homosexuels de ses parents à Berlin, des efforts de sa mère de protéger sa tante toxicomane (que les autorités pouvaient faire disparaître en tant que malade mentale). Elle conclut cette autofiction en affirmant : « Après tout, les réponses aux *Where are you from*, mes enfants et les leurs n'en

ont pas vraiment besoin » (*Figuier* 255). Au contraire de Marguerite, ce
ne sont pas des « personnes déplacées ». Ils sont bien chez eux, jouissant
d'une vie privilégiée dans une ville pluraliste et multilingue. Bien que
les enfants de la narratrice et ses petits-enfants choisissent de vivre
en français, la plupart d'entre eux parlent plus de deux langues : leurs
partenaires proviennent de pays proches ou lointains : « nous sommes un
ragoût, un couscous », dit-elle ; « La tolérance est ce qui caractérise notre
pays, disent-ils » (*Figuier* 251).

Il ne faut cependant pas oublier que la ville est une structure narrative
construite par l'auteure, un espace-temps à forte teneur symbolique.
Ainsi, dans *La vie devant elles*, on retrouve une attitude plus critique
envers le pays d'accueil, lorsqu'Ariane, petite-fille de Marguerite, fait
du camping en Ontario avec son mari togolais et leurs deux enfants et
qu'ils sont confrontés à cette occasion au profilage racial, un policier les
arrêtant sans motif valable. Si Toronto apparaît dans *Le figuier sur le toit*
comme un lieu de tolérance et de paix, c'est pour souligner le contraste
avec un Berlin soumis aux affres de la guerre. C'est peut-être aussi pour
rappeler que le Berlin d'avant la guerre apparaissait, lui aussi, comme un
milieu ouvert à la diversité et à l'épanouissement culturel et artistique.
Témoigner des atrocités de guerre, c'est également une façon de rappeler
les dangers de la suffisance et de l'orgueil.

L'image éponyme du *Figuier sur le toit* souligne l'ambiguïté subversive
de la présence de l'écrivaine migrante à Toronto. La vieille dame parle
de cet arbre exotique qu'elle avait essayé de cultiver et dont elle avait
osé espérer un seul fruit, malgré le climat inclément de Toronto. Une
histoire conventionnelle d'intégration réussie aurait pu aboutir à une
célébration de cet arbre, qui parvient à produire un fruit en dépit des
obstacles. Cependant, par mégarde, par négligence, Marguerite laisse
mourir l'arbre. Elle se résout à le déraciner et à le jeter, malgré la
résistance tenace de l'arbre mort. À la suggestion qu'on lui fait qu'elle
pourrait prendre un autre figuier pour remplacer celui-ci, la vieille dame
répond vivement : « Pas question. Je ne veux pas assassiner d'autres
figuiers après avoir tant aimé celui-ci » (250). Dans ce roman mémoriel
aux accents édéniques, le figuier rappelle l'histoire de l'arbre du bien
et du mal au paradis, où Adam et Ève goûtent le fruit interdit au prix

de leur expulsion. Le couple originel saisit alors des feuilles de figuier pour cacher leur nudité, dont ils ont honte. Perte de l'innocence, perte de l'illusion d'un monde sous le contrôle parfait de Dieu le père. On se souvient aussi de l'histoire du figuier maudit du Nouveau Testament : Jésus, déçu de ne pas avoir trouvé de figues hors saison, condamne le figuier à ne plus jamais porter de fruit (Mathieu 21, *Sainte Bible* 18-22). Que le figuier de Marguerite soit condamné au déterrement brutal n'est donc pas étonnant. Déterrer le figuier mort sans fruit implique ici renoncer au rêve irréalisable d'un paradis perdu, celui d'une famille traditionnelle, à la figure paternelle autoritaire mais rassurante.

L'écrivaine a finalement réussi, en regardant en face son passé et en affrontant l'angoisse liée à ses souvenirs du régime nazi, à s'adonner à la création littéraire et à jouir de la convivialité d'une communauté artistique. À Toronto, où elle demeure fortement impliquée dans l'émergence d'institutions littéraires franco-ontariennes, Andersen réussit à régler ses comptes avec le père berlinois, à lui rendre hommage en tant qu'écrivain tout en acceptant ses faiblesses en tant qu'être humain. Elle a pu y affronter avec lucidité, grâce à l'écriture mémorielle, son passé empreint de culpabilité. Le figuier mort rappelle ce passé honteux, examiné et présenté au lecteur en guise de témoignage. Déterrer l'arbre est un geste de libération personnelle.

C'est ce sentiment de libération qui prédomine dans les récits biofictionnels qui composent *La vie devant elles*, où la réconciliation avec le père ainsi qu'avec le passé berlinois se fait à travers les voyages des petites-filles de Marguerite. Lorsque la vieille dame fait un séjour à Berlin avec sa petite-fille Isa, elle brise le silence sur le passé. Elle lui révèle que son père (le fils de Marguerite), qui a toujours caché ses origines allemandes, a passé une partie de sa jeunesse dans la ville. Elles se délectent de la richesse culturelle du Berlin restauré, de ses musées d'art et de ses magasins. Ensemble, elles visitent le Musée du Judaïsme, elles traversent l'axe de l'Holocauste, l'axe de l'exil et celui de la continuité. L'espace mémoriel révèle les actes honteux du régime nazi et offre en retour une possibilité de guérison. Ariane, autre petite-fille de Marguerite, en voyage en Afrique pour établir un programme d'aide auprès des femmes du Ghana, complète quant à elle le processus de réconciliation avec le passé en retrouvant le pays de naissance de son arrière-grand-père Theo, et elle donne à son fils le nom africain de son aïeul, Kwabla.

Conclusion : « No, where are you really from? »

Dans la scène finale du *Figuier sur le toit*, c'est la fête de la vieille dame et elle craint de déranger ses enfants et ses petits-enfants si elle boit un peu trop et se met à parler de tout ce que les autres veulent taire. En bons Canadiens polis, ils n'aiment pas en effet trop discuter de ce qui pourrait déranger. La fête sera parfaite, selon l'écrivaine, « à condition peut-être qu'elle garde ses idées farfelues pour elle-même... À condition aussi de ne pas révéler la lointaine tare de l'arrière-grand-père balte » (255). Or c'est justement le fait de déranger l'ordre, de briser le silence bienséant, qui confère à ces autofictions leur caractère subversif. Pour qu'on n'oublie jamais la capacité humaine pour l'atrocité, il s'agit plutôt d'espérer que l'écrivaine ne deviendra jamais sage!

NOTES

1. À partir de ces autofictions, Andersen crée ce que Régine Robin appelle un « roman mémoriel » : « Nous parlerons analogiquement de roman mémoriel par lequel un individu, un groupe ou une société pense son passé en le modifiant, le déplaçant, le déformant, s'inventant des souvenirs, un passé glorieux, des ancêtres, des filiations, des généalogies, ou, au contraire, luttant pour l'exactitude factuelle, pour la restitution de l'événement ou sa résurrection » (Robin, 48).
2. Pour satisfaire aux exigences de ce que Robin appelle la mémoire savante, Andersen inclut en annexe dans *Le figuier sur le toit* la bibliographie des œuvres de son père.
3. Voir à ce propos Young (206-07), qui décrit ainsi l'évolution du groupe littéraire : d'abord le Regroupement des écrivains de Toronto, ensuite la Société des écrivains canadiens de Toronto et enfin la Société des écrivain(e)s de Toronto.

BIBLIOGRAPHIE

Andersen, Marguerite. « Autobiography: Tightrope Across the Search for Understanding ». *Institut Simone de Beauvoir Institute Review/Revue* 18-19 (2000): 113-28.

————. *Bleu sur blanc*. Sudbury, ON: Prise de parole, 2000.

————. *De mémoire de femme*. Montréal: Quinze, 1982. Nouvelle édition revue et corrigée, BCF, Ottawa: L'Interligne, 2002.

————. *Le figuier sur le toit*. Ottawa: L'Interligne, 2008.

————. *Parallèles*. Sudbury, ON: Prise de parole, 2004.

————. *La vie devant elles*. Sudbury, ON: Prise de parole, 2011.

Coleman, Patrick. « From Canadian Trance to TransCanada: White Civility to Wry Civility in the Canlit Project ». *Trans.Can.Lit: Resituating the Study of Canadian Literature.* Dir. Smaro Kamboureli et Roy Miki. Waterloo, ON: Wilfrid Laurier University Press, 2007. 25-44.

Harel, Simon. *Le voleur de parcours: Identité et cosmopolitisme dans la littérature québécoise contemporaine*. Montréal: XYZ, 1999.

Hotte, Lucie. « Préface : L'écriture et la vie ». *De mémoire de femme*. Marguerite Andersen. Édition revue et corrigée, BCF. Ottawa: L'Interligne, 2002. 7-12.

Lejeune, Philippe. *Le pacte autobiographique*. Paris: Seuil, 1975.

Paré, François. « Souveraineté et détournement du regard dans les nouvelles de Marguerite Andersen ». *University of Toronto Quarterly* 68.4 (automne 1999): 823-34.

Robin, Régine. *Le roman mémoriel : de l'histoire à l'écriture du hors-lieu*. Montréal: Le Préambule, 1989.

La Sainte Bible. Traduite d'après les textes originaux hébreu et grec par Louis Segond. Édition revue avec références. Paris: La Société biblique, 1972.

Tennier, Julie. « Marguerite Andersen et le moi en l'absence de l'autre : *De mémoire de femme* ». *Voix plurielles* 9.1 (2012): 58-68.

Young, Lélia. « Poésie franco-ontarienne: Un aperçu ». *Perspectives sur la littérature franco-ontarienne*. Dir. Ali Reguigui et Hédi Bouraoui. Édition revue et augmentée. Sudbury, ON: Prise de parole, 2007. 205-33.

LANGUAGES AS SPACES, TRANSLATION AS PLAY

Moving (through) Languages

Lori Saint-Martin

Women, space, place, play: the story of my life. My life is, my life in language and languages. Everything I have ever done comes down to this. This chapter—so different from what I usually do as an academic—is dedicated to my little sister, Cari, who died of breast cancer in May 2010. It has a prelude and five parts. The first speaks to my beginnings in language and in languages. I go on to deal with interpretation, translation, writing, and self-translation, all aspects of my being in language. There is also an interlude involving, of all things, the Brontë sisters, and a non-conclusion with two heads. This piece was originally an intimate and personal keynote address and, though it is not a transcription, I have chosen to retain some signs of the immediacy, of connection, as well as the trace of the voice behind the words that now take written form.

Prelude: Who Do You Think You Are?

On this topic I have only fragments to offer. Or rather, I have chosen the fragment as a way to generate openness and multiple meanings. Spaces in, spaces between: "that's how the light gets in," Leonard Cohen says. Fragments of a life in and through languages.

Languages belong to specific spaces but can be carried anywhere by speaking bodies through travel, immigration, exile. A language is also a space. A space to inhabit, a space to create. It can be a cage, a palace, a garden, a runway. Or a metaphorical space, a part of the self. If you have enough languages, you can become whole. Or, more probably, give up the illusion of wholeness and enjoy all the pieces.

Passages, movement between, within, among languages, are what I spend my life creating. I grew up with only one language, English, but that was never enough. To me, a good day is a day when English, French, and Spanish cross in my reading, writing, emails, and conversations. Back, forth, within, into, from. Going where the other dwells.

"Who do you think you are?" is what my mother angrily asked whenever she sensed my desire for something else, for somewhere else. About my future, this is what my mother said: You'd better think of something else you can do with your life, nobody will ever pay you to read those books. Luckily, though brilliant and intuitively able to see into many worlds, my mother was wrong about that little thing.

My life is not the life a woman of my social class was meant to live. I worked in a hospital laundry when I was an undergraduate and it was hell (but less so for me than for the immigrant and untrained women who had nowhere else to go). Who do you think you are? means: you're not anywhere near as good as you think you are. It means: stop thinking you deserve more. It also means—and this I understood only much later—come back to me, my sweet baby, I see you moving away from me and I can't stand the thought of losing you. My mother and I later reconciled, though that is not my topic here.

So, who *do* I think I am? If I define myself alone—and not as a companion, mother, daughter—I would say: I think I am a woman, first of all. I think I am a traveller, a writer, and a translator. I am a professor of literature and that is central but I will say little about that here. The most important thing to say about me, here and now, is that I am a person with two native languages. One I acquired from birth, in the usual way. The other I learned much later, from the ages of, say, ten to twenty. I have published all my books, including my fiction, in French, my "second language," officially. But I have never seen it that way. To me it was the language I was meant to speak.

I have now spent more than half my life in Quebec, including my years as a PHD student at Laval University. I have been living in Montreal since 1991, a city that "thinks and suffers in two languages," as Gabrielle Roy once wrote (307). Despite the presence of dozens of other world languages, as in any large cosmopolitan city, Montreal is one of the few truly bilingual cities in this world. Paris, Toronto, or Buenos Aires are crisscrossed by other languages, but there is one lingua franca, one standard, one common space. In Montreal, the simplest public transaction begins with a hesitation: English or French? How should I address this person in front of me who has not yet spoken a word? Where do we meet, how do we meet? Language can be fraught with tension in my city. It is a source of division, suspicion, and endless polemics. For many, bilingualism has, historically, been a sign of weakness—the colonized learn the language of the colonizer, but not the other way around. The vast majority of Canadian English-French bilinguals are native speakers of French, for political reasons that are not pleasant to think about. On the other hand, my children have scores of friends who, like them, are totally comfortable in both languages and entirely non-polemical about them.

My own life is nothing if not this play of languages across spaces and within my own body. A story of voices. Voice is the thread, the key.

I. Language and Names: You Are Not Who You Think

My name is not my father's name.

My life is not my mother's life.

I grew up in a working-class family in a grey factory town (more on that shortly) and I was very young—nine or ten, no older—when I discovered I needed to be somewhere else in order to survive. That was a secret I shared with my two best friends, who came from Korea and Guyana and could not believe they had landed there either. Nobody in my family had a passport or had flown on an airplane, nobody had travelled beyond our town and the small scattering of nearby places where everyone we knew lived. They had heard of other countries but had no use for them, no thirst for them.

Both my grandmothers spoke only German, or rather Pennsylvania Dutch, when they started kindergarten. But German was not passed on to my parents—it was shameful during the First World War and beyond. The city that I come from was initially called Berlin, but in 1916 the name was changed to Kitchener as a sign of loyalty to the British Empire. Now Lord Kitchener was a wonderful person, a British field marshal, a proconsul, a military man who won fame for his imperial campaigns. Lord Kitchener was in Egypt. Lord Kitchener was in the Sudan. Lord Kitchener was in India. Lord Kitchener was in South Africa during the Boer Wars. He practised a scorched earth policy, where the army destroys everything in its path as it moves through a territory. He was also famous for herding people—children, pregnant women, the elderly—into concentration camps. The ideal man to name a city after, as one can see.

But how do you end up in exile in the city where you and your parents and the past six or seven generations were born? How do you become a person whose hometown was never home? Why is what they happily take for granted dust and ashes to you, and why do you choke on the air in your parents' house? All I know is that when I was nine or ten, I made a list of places I wanted to go. You have to remember I had never been anywhere and nobody had even told me there was anywhere else to be. And this was the list: Downtown. The cemetery. Paris. So a little excitement—downtown—some peace and quiet—the cemetery—and the world itself. Paris was shorthand for a place where real life unfolds. I was going and I was never coming back.

Other than "Who do you think you are?," "You're different" was the other chorus I heard from teachers, from classmates, from boys who would have liked me more if I had been more the same but didn't mind fooling around with me in the back seat of their cars anyway. I dressed wrong (black, red, flamboyant), I talked wrong (used words I had read in books, probably mispronouncing half of them), I had "big ideas" (this was the only reference ever made to ideas, a thing much frowned upon), but I wasn't *trying* to be different. I spoke English with an accent, even before learning to speak anything else. In simultaneous interpretation, this is called the gap, the "décalage"; you lag a half-sentence behind the speaker. It was like watching someone dance and imitating their steps, I was always off beat, moving the wrong way. My mother said: wipe that look off your face, Missy, who do you think you are? Why do you always have to be different? But I wasn't trying. That was the thing. It was more like a birth defect or a hole inside that nobody else had. Or maybe an extra limb? Something freakish in any case.

When I speak English today I can sometimes hear my mother's voice running under mine, particularly when I am scolding my children. When I speak French I don't sound like anyone I know. (That is probably the whole point.) Sometimes that's lonely. Sometimes it's freedom itself. The first day of our very first French class, in grade six, I was a drowning person suddenly discovering this thing called a raft. Love at first sight? This was love at first sound. Another language was an outstretched hand, it was a parachute, a highway to take me away. There was another way of saying things, and that meant there was another way of being. And that meant there was somewhere else, and I could be someone else, somewhere else. It was, at last, a confirmation of that vague and painful longing I had been feeling, my very own problem with no name. So I worked hard at languages: I was good, I was the best, my life depended on it. And later, at university, I travelled at last to Paris, and then I moved to Montreal, my double city, my home to the extent I will ever have one, the city where my books have been written and my children were born.

II. Interpretation

I have worked off and on for years as a simultaneous interpreter. You may have seen the booth in the back of the room at a conference or worn the headset to hear that other voice in your ear. The true story of how I became an interpreter is not particularly interesting. What may be more interesting is my fictional version of how it happened, which bloomed in a short story I wrote a while ago. Here it is:

> They began with neutral things: tell Daddy dinner's ready. I turn to him: papa, c'est servi. Dis à ta mère que mes chemises doivent aller chez le teinturier. Mommy, Daddy says his shirts...Later it became: Dis à ta mère qu'elle est une grosse vache. Mommy, Daddy says you're a big cow. Tell your father I'm leaving. Papa, maman dit qu'elle s'en va. I ran back and forth between them, translating what they understood perfectly, stretching for the right word, the perfect phrase, happy that they were still talking, even though it was only through me, even though I conveyed only words of hate. If I worked hard enough, they would never stop talking to each other, and one day the tone would change. Those were my beginnings as a simultaneous interpreter: I was the relay, the safety net that kept them from the void.

In fact, this story is a complete fabrication. As a child, I spoke only one language and would have been incapable of switching in that way (my children could, that was my gift to them). Nor did my unilingual and happily married parents need or want that kind of mediation. But this story, for me, although invented, has the ring of truth. The little girl makes language "pass" across borders, she makes connections, she averts disaster. Is this how I glue the two halves of myself together? When I work as an interpreter, I am happy: both sides of me are united, I am fully there, always in transit from one to the other.

I love the speed and the danger of it. I love the immediacy of making the connection happen among people who do not share a language. I love the entry into so many different worlds where the speakers discuss their affairs as if they were alone. I love the lack of a safety net, the fact that the speaker moves on and you have to follow, no matter what. I find, though, that interpreters, although very interesting and congenial people, are too pragmatic about languages. They see them as tool kits, as means to an end, as little lexicons they prepare for each conference. They speak of "having" English or Spanish or Arabic as a working language, whereas I believe that if anything, language "has" us. Still, I love the movement between and among languages, and interpretation is an extreme form of that. Listening to words in one language and, with that half-sentence lag, spinning them into another. "How can you talk and listen at the same time?" is the question always asked by people who stop by our booth to say thank you. There is a switch on our console to change channels when you change languages, so that the listener does not receive the wrong one. Not so easy to flip that switch in your head. But that's what being an interpreter is. "Double A" in interpreter-speak means "two native languages," and I am proud to say I have a double A. Je suis la femme à deux têtes. I am the two-headed woman.

iii. Translation

Summer 2012 marked the anniversary of my twenty years as a literary translator. This is work I always do with my husband, Paul Gagné, and we have published over eighty translations of English-Canadian literature into French. Note the nice irony of translating into my "non-native" language! I also recently translated three books from Spanish to French, another leap of faith and something that I hope to pursue.

Literary translation is about recreating the music, finding the voice. Languages are spaces and translation is travelling between and among them. Translation is play of the most joyous and serious kind.

Translation is also a meeting with the other. In my case, because I work with another translator who happens to be my husband, I am directly faced with him as other; his knowledge and mine, his words and mine. He is an intimate other who is there with me from the beginning. And although he is my other, we ultimately speak as one.

But you don't have to work with another translator to be faced with multiple others within the act of translation. In fact, otherness is everywhere; perhaps there is no such thing as sameness, though we convince ourselves for various reasons that there is. When our son was learning to talk, I remember teaching him: this is your hand. And this? he asked. Oh, that's your other hand. He holds up one, then the other: my hand, my other hand. My other hand, my hand. It took him a long time to realize that if you start with the right hand, the "other hand" is the left, and vice versa. Otherness is a shifting property, and nothing makes that clearer than translation. The other text, the other words, the other that is language, the other in your "own" language, which you can never truly own. There are ways in which it will bend and others in which it will not, at least not without violence. Meeting the other text means confronting everything you know and do not know about "your" language and the "other" language. Both are yours, neither is yours. One hand, the other hand: which one is really the other again?

If you speak more than one language well, you are more than one person. As you translate, those other parts of you and of your languages are thrown into relief. You are another as you write, no longer yourself; the language changes and something about you slowly shifts shape. And this changing, this shifting, is the point of the journey, which has no end point: these multiple others are changing and they are changing you.

And, finally, a metaphor: translation is a tightrope dance. You are high above the ground, and there is no net. You are standing on this tightrope, swaying slightly, but always pushing on. The original is the ground, the anchor, the footing you need. And yet you cannot cling to it, it is not a safety net; it will not catch you if you fall, it is indifferent to your possible failure and will not be changed or moved by it. You must also be far above it, on that tightrope, walking on a path uncharted in your language, looking backwards and forwards at once, hovering there. But you cannot creep along on little cautious steps, no matter how thin the wire, how high. You have to move, dance, invent, sway in the breeze you have just created. One foot on the wire, one foot in the air, you float or fall.

IV. Writing

I am also a writer of fiction. I have published three books of short and short short stories and a novel, *Les portes closes* (2013). It might not surprise you to learn that it involves two characters speaking in two very different voices (although only one language).

Again, it's all about the music, the voice. I work out loud very often. I close my eyes so I can hear better. That makes no sense; it makes perfect sense.

I write as a woman and a feminist though my creative writing has no message. When I sit down to write, I forget everything I know and follow the voice where it leads me. I write with my whole life, as we all do. It is all autobiographical, even when it did not happen to me; it is all fiction, even when I experienced it myself.

I write in French, and this in itself is surprising but consistent. And I rewrite constantly, obsessively. I hate semicolons—that is my confession for today, with apologies to fans of that particular punctuation mark—and love the way a comma provides air and light and space for interpretation. I once wrote a story called "Une femme, seule." The comma, here, is everything. "A woman, alone," is a very different proposition than "a woman alone," I'm sure you can hear that. Or in another story, "Mon père, la nuit," "My father, at night," the comma is the most important element of the title; I like what the comma does, how it separates without separating and makes a kind of hinge that shows just what the father does to the daughter at night.

But instead of talking about writing I will suggest an interlude: a short piece about the Brontë sisters.

Interlude: A Side Trip to Haworth

A train, a bus, another bus and I was at Haworth, the home of the Brontë sisters, loves of my life since *Jane Eyre* at fourteen. Seven novels among them and all dead before they were forty.

From their bedroom window, they could see the cemetery with its large flat stones, the oldest blurred green with moss. They had spent hours on end deciphering the inscriptions, the dead sorrows, dreaming stories of mothers dying with their last-born, of children taken minutes after their first breath or days before their first steps. Death was woven in among the days. And behind the cemetery, the church, the tall grey tower, the promise of eternal life. They dreamed of another love, a different immortality.

They had a spare and stubborn faith but it was nowhere near enough. They burnt and wrote, at night pacing around the scratched and ink-stained table. They read aloud, frowned, crossed out, reflected, began again. Anne sought a reason to hope in the long, plain, oddly stirring Sunday hymns. Emily propped up her German grammar and murmured declensions as she kneaded the week's bread. Charlotte, the only one to cross the seas, loved a married man she would never see again. She thought she would die. And then she began to write.

I think of women's lives at that time, the constraints in space and play, the inner dissidence. Charlotte Brontë needed a chaperone to travel to London and meet her publisher. I somehow knew their straitened circumstances and their smooth grave faces, the narrow stillness that had driven them inwards, the virtue like floorboards scrubbed pale, the pride they could never reveal, prayers and scripture, the plunge in and down. Writing saved them from other forms of despair: a lover, an asylum, the river. Only Charlotte succumbed to marriage, that other leap of faith or of despair.

God and their father wore a single face on Sunday mornings when a voice thundered from the pulpit. Thighs pressed tightly together, they shivered but held their faces blank. They all died young, like their mother. I stayed with them until night fell and the last visitors were banished from their house.

In their rooms, at night, did they touch themselves into sleep? Did they see a face or a page, a pot of ink, a boat, a wave? Darkness fell, light rose, the stars dove towards them and the tide rose and filled the room so that their beds began to float. They opened their eyes. They held out their hands. Mouths awry with iron and glory, they said yes. They said yes.

v. Self-Translation

I have said that I write fiction in French. Recently, I have been translating it, if I can call it that, into English. But in fact, I think I cannot call it
that. Such freedom, such terror! Returning to some of these old pieces
is like meeting with another version of myself. And, through the filter of
another language, with another writing aesthetic. Purely through intu-
ition, I feel there are things I cannot say in English or at least have to say
very differently; subtly or not, the tone changes. And sometimes it's not
subtle at all.

Below are three excerpts from one of four brief prose poems that
make up a series entitled "Four Fruits." They appear in the final poem,
which describes the forbidden fruit as a mangosteen. Here is the first
excerpt:

> Paris était pour elle nouveau, et les voyages, et l'amour.
>
> Paris was new to her then, although she would later visit dozens of times,
> without him.

Obviously, by any standards, this is a terrible translation, and any professional translator who ever dared to attempt such a thing would be fired or
shot down in flames immediately. That is the beauty of self-translation;
you can do anything you like. We could certainly discuss whether this
translation is good or bad, if it works or doesn't work, but that is another
issue. Rather, let me tell you a bit about how I translate and what happens
once it is done.

In this passage, the English version is less lyrical, less sentimental, less beautifully balanced; the cadence in French is like poetry (the
commas with "et les voyages, et l'amour"). In English, the equivalent
("and travel, and love") does not sound like poetry to my ear. In fact, I take
a definite turn towards narrative instead of lyricism. Another difference
is that the English version is more optimistic (we learn sooner that she
survived the affair with the married man and kept visiting Paris anyway)
but also speaks from a different space and time, many years later (the

French tells how she feels in the present). The English is less immediate and more elegiac; "she" is less lost, more experienced, and more of a survivor. But I am saying all this from another space, the space of a literary critic, looking at it from outside, at the effect it produces; when recreating, I don't think of it that way, I just follow the words where they take me, on blind faith.

Here is a second excerpt:

> Elle était si jeune qu'elle croyait encore aller de voyage en voyage, de fruit en fruit, si jeune qu'elle était sûre de toujours voyager en compagnie du même homme, qui n'allait pourtant jamais quitter sa femme.

> She was so young she still thought she would travel again and again with the same man, this man she confused with fate.

George Steiner says that translation is essentially inflationist, but the above English version takes a radically anti-inflationist turn. You might wonder if anything remains on the page by the time I'm done! Again, this is a terrible translation. Here we have a rather shocking erasure: the going "from fruit to fruit." That was just wrong, it could not survive the passage into English. So there is real loss here, there is mourning. Self-translation is about loss, or maybe it's about getting rid of things and finding something else instead. And also the loss, I hope, can be offset at some other point—in translation theory this is referred to as "compensation." The final change, from "the man who would never leave his wife" to "this man she confused with fate," is a major shift. I like this vague version, this image of her as confused (which refers back to the first passage and tells us, but at a different point in the text, about how lost she was then), this idea of fate not being where we thought it was: what we thought counted did not, and vice versa. That difference in perspective corresponds, I think, not only to the differences between English and French but to the gap between the woman I was when I wrote the piece, years ago, and the woman I am now. I wonder what would happen if I translated it back into French again?

Here is a final excerpt:

Dix ans ont passé et pourtant elle voit la chambre, le lit défait, l'amour et le fruit. Elle sourit, confiante, jeune, comme si elle n'avait qu'à tendre la main pour qu'y tombent un à un tous les fruits du monde.

Ten years have passed and yet she sees the room, the open bed, the open fruit. She smiles, confident still and young, as if she had only to reach out her hands to have drop into them, one by one, all the fruits in the world.

The final sentence is more literally translated, but it is worth noting that, although the inversion of the verb and subject is a bit more of a stretch in English than it is in French, I decided to keep it. It is a sign of linguistic otherness, a slightly dissonant structure. The piece had to end with the mention of the fruit, which is the overall title and the thread that runs through the series of four poems. Here is something interesting: the word "love" has again done a disappearing act; is English really more puritanical, or is it just me? That upbringing I so longed to escape and which is still in my narrative voice? Things come back, life is full of cycles. I can accept that now, though earlier in my life it would not have been a joking matter. I like the parallel, which is added, with the word "open": the "open bed" and the "open fruit." In the middle of the piece is a lyrical description of the mangosteen, the bright red inside the brownish shell, and the bright white flesh inside. It is a metaphor of bodies, of desire. I think this parallel with the open bed and the open fruit offsets some of the loss of lyricism in the previous excerpt. I like the word "open" in this context and what it suggests about that confused, lost but vital young girl biting into the forbidden fruit—not an apple, not a pomegranate, but a mangosteen, losing the Eden of that particular passion but surviving to return to Paris over and over again and make it her own private garden. Is all that in the piece? Maybe not for an outside reader, though it is for me. And that is what I think I tried to put into those words.

To sum up: self-translation confronts me with my past as an author and with my linguistic split. But it also allows me to put them back together again. There are some things I would no longer say, years later— this piece is at least fifteen years old—and others I would say instead, and others I would still say, but differently (but of course if you say it differently you are no longer saying the same thing anyway). Languages are spaces and self-translation is a radical form of travel. I see the changes made as intrinsic to the languages I was writing in and into and suggest they be read not as discrepancies or mistakes but as signs of linguistic difference (although we could certainly discuss other choices that could have been made). Just as I feel both my languages to be my first or strongest and equally essential, I consider both versions of the prose poem originals.

VI. By Way of a Non-Conclusion: The Two-Headed Woman in Buenos Aires

Since my sister died—though she, like my parents, was unilingual and uninterested in travel, uninterested really in any of the things that interest me—I have been more restless, less serene. In 2011, a few months after her death, I decided to return to Spanish, a language I spoke very well, once upon a time. I spent a few hours with a private tutor in Montreal and then flew to Buenos Aires.

Such a fall from grace, to give up perfect fluency in two languages only to stammer and grope for words, to fail at the most elementary encounters (foreigners are awkward, foreigners are stupid!). But such freedom, once I gave up shame and shyness to accept and embrace mistakes. Every storefront has a new word, every exchange is a new world, a bookstore is a thousand highways. I have come so far, but the road (and that is the beauty of the thing) is endless.

Languages as spaces, languages as play. I don't believe in purity; I believe in bastard forms and border crossings. I want both, I want all three, I want it all. The marks and markers of gender, of space, of language. Work is play and I love my work. Who do you think you are? Who? Who? Moving through spaces and languages is my life. *That's* who I think I am. That's who I am. This, for me, is what happiness looks like. Take a good look. This is what a very happy two-, almost three-headed woman looks like.

Four Fruits/Quatre fruits *(final poem in the series)*
Lori Saint-Martin

Ils se sont retrouvés à Paris, dans un petit hôtel de la rue Madame. Elle était jeune et elle aimait les livres, lui était vieux et il aimait l'écouter. Alors elle a parlé, elle lui a parlé de Gertrude Stein et de Colette, de la guerre et du salon de la rue de Fleurus, tout près.

Il arrivait d'un voyage d'affaires en Asie, elle de Montréal où ils habitaient tous deux. Paris était pour elle nouveau, et les voyages, et l'amour. D'Asie il lui a rapporté des mangoustans. Goûte, dit-il, tu vas voir.

La chair est d'une vive blancheur, lovée dans une écorce rouge violent. Elle goûte le sucre et l'eau fraîche, le lointain et la source. La jeune femme ne connaissait ni le nom, ni le fruit. Elle était si jeune qu'elle croyait encore aller de voyage en voyage, de fruit en fruit, si jeune qu'elle était sûre de toujours voyager en compagnie du même homme, qui n'allait pourtant jamais quitter sa femme.

Dix ans ont passé, elle n'a jamais rien goûté d'aussi bon. Elle ne s'y attend guère. Dix ans ont passé et pourtant elle voit la chambre, le lit défait, l'amour et le fruit. Elle sourit, confiante, jeune, comme si elle n'avait qu'à tendre la main pour qu'y tombent un à un tous les fruits du monde.

He was waiting for her in Paris, in a small hotel on rue Madame. She was young and loved books, he was old and loved listening to her. So she talked and talked, she told him about Gertrude Stein and Colette, about the war and the salon on rue de Fleurus, close by.

He was returning from a business trip to Asia, she arrived from Montreal where they both lived. Paris was new to her then, though she would later visit dozens of times, without him. From Thailand he brought her mangosteens. Taste this, he said, you'll see.

The flesh was a clear, intense white cradled in a deep red skin. It tasted of calm and of sweet water, of distance, of a hidden spring. She had never seen the fruit nor heard the name. She was so young she still thought she would travel again and again with the same man, this man she confused with fate.

Ten years have passed, and she has never tasted anything so good since. Nor has she ever expected to. Ten years have passed and yet she sees the room, the open bed, the open fruit. She smiles, confident still and young, as if she had only to reach out her hands to have drop into them, one by one, all the fruits in the world.

WORK CITED

Roy, Gabrielle. *Alexandre Chenevert*. Montréal: Éditions Beauchemin, 1954.

L'ESPACE ENSORCELÉ

Les enfants du sabbat *d'Anne Hébert*

Stéphanie Walsh Matthews

Mais quelle lecture invraisemblable! Une nonne démoniaque, permise de passer entre les murailles du temps, invincible à l'exorcisme... Ces rites religieux récités à perfection... Le couvent... Cette cabane... Hélas, ma chère Stéphanie, j'ai honte d'en avoir tiré tant de plaisir. Tu diras à Anne Hébert qu'elle m'a envahie comme un rêve.

—Extrait d'une lettre de ma grand-mère après
qu'elle ait lu *Les enfants du sabbat*

Tel un rêve trop réel, pendant lequel la raison n'interrompt point l'invraisemblable, la structure habituelle des objets est renversée dans un ordre tout de même plausible et, de ce fait, les paroles inconséquentes d'un personnage fabuleux forment un verdict sur le siècle. Le réalisme magique enchante tant il nous désenchante d'un monde fictif cruel et malade. Comme l'exprime son appellation, le réalisme magique oppose des extrêmes qu'il finit par marier, dans un syllogisme irréalisable, dans la complicité des paradoxes.

Au-delà des contextes de production auxquels il est couramment rattaché, le réalisme magique peut imprégner certains romans qui n'ont pourtant pas été étudiés sous l'angle de ce genre populaire. Ainsi, l'espace québécois est un contexte de production réaliste magique idéal du fait de ses fables, de ses superstitions nombreuses et de ses saisons contrastées favorisant le chant et le conte, espace où s'épousent la dure réalité d'une terre et les sentiments d'exil et d'appartenance, où le mysticisme d'un pays rêvé hante les songes et où la culpabilité religieuse domine la mémoire et occupe l'esprit du Canadien français. Cet espace se reflète dans la production littéraire québécoise qui, à son tour, joue avec les crises et les passions de la culture et de l'histoire. Ne suffit-il pas de lire les romans d'après la Révolution tranquille au Québec pour en remarquer la qualité unique, pour ne pas dire subversive, ironique, politique et radicalement empreinte de son contexte social?

Je voudrais montrer ici que le roman d'Anne Hébert *Les enfants du sabbat* appartient lui aussi à cette veine, ce qui peut d'emblée surprendre. Pourtant, avec ce texte, écrit et publié bien avant que le réalisme magique ne devienne le genre préféré des littéraires comme des non-littéraires, avant même l'ascension vertigineuse des Isabel Allende, Angela Carter, Gabriel García Márquez, Toni Morrison, Ben Okri, Salman Rushdie et bien d'autres, Anne Hébert a en fait façonné un récit troublant dont les caractéristiques répondent parfaitement aux critères du genre[1].

En résumé, *Les enfants du sabbat* raconte l'histoire d'une jeune religieuse, Sœur Julie, qui vit au couvent du Précieux-Sang, récit qui banalise à la fois la raison d'être du pouvoir surnaturel et qui subvertit toutes les notions associées à la structure sociale du conservatisme religieux et étatique du Québec. Le roman met de plus en scène les secrets infernaux de la vie rurale et raconte que la jeune nonne est une sorcière possédée par le diable. Dans ce texte, « l'ordre du monde est renversé » : Julie hante et terrorise ses consœurs et la mère supérieure et elle enchante et stupéfie l'aumônier et le docteur. Envahie par sa culpabilité, elle est capable de visions et de voyages extraordinaires : elle retourne dans son passé et revit les abus de ses parents lors des sabbats dans cette vieille cabane de la Montagne de B... Enfant pauvre, violée par son père (qui est en réalité le diable), abandonnée par son frère, pour qui l'amour est incestueux, et sous l'emprise d'une mère qui lui a transmis en héritage ses dons de sorcière et qui, même de la tombe, imprègne la vie de la jeune nonne de ses sacrilèges, sœur Julie finira par donner naissance au bébé diable dans le grenier du couvent. Écrit dans un style féroce où s'entremêlent ironie, parodie, grotesque, horreur et amour, ce roman constitue un modèle du genre et met en relief l'importance du lien au social, marqueur caractéristique du réalisme magique. Il est ainsi impossible d'ignorer que les zones cloîtrées du couvent sont le reflet de l'espace lugubre et violent de la cabane de la Montagne de B...

Si l'on peut s'étonner de l'ajout d'Hébert à la liste des auteurs réalistes magiques, on ne peut guère l'être de l'incursion du genre dans la littérature québécoise. Et, si le Québec est un espace propice à l'émergence du genre, c'est notamment parce que le surnaturel est fortement présent dans sa culture et sa tradition littéraire. Plusieurs critiques québécois ont ainsi constaté que le surnaturel accompagne et traverse la littérature québécoise, ce qu'illustrent les nombreuses anthologies et œuvres critiques sur le sujet[2]. Cet héritage, bien ancré dans les contes fabuleux de la Chasse Galerie, offre des antécédents réalistes magiques qui sont déjà visibles dans la fiction du 19e siècle, dans le folklore et les légendes du pays, ce qui a contribué à instaurer une identité littéraire distincte de celle de la France. La littérature dite contemporaine, c'est-à-dire celle d'après la Révolution tranquille, est fortement marquée par cet héritage.

Outre l'utilisation du surnaturel (qui renvoie à la mythologie et aux traditions folkloriques), la littérature québécoise emploie divers éléments du réel qui reviennent tel un *leitmotiv* : le joual et la religion dominent ainsi depuis longtemps dans de nombreux textes contemporains. Le réalisme est volontairement brisé par l'incursion d'éléments surnaturels lorsque, selon le sociocritique québécois André Bourassa, la littérature québécoise veut exprimer un désir de transformation de la réalité et se débarrasser ainsi de cette réalité. Par l'entremise du surnaturel et des références au traditionnel, le roman est donc un reflet de son contexte de production.

La littérature contemporaine québécoise est dominée par l'inclusion de l'improbable et de l'extraordinaire dans la fiction car elle est héritière d'une culture traditionnelle dans laquelle les superstitions, l'oralité, les croyances religieuses et les fantasmes sont révélateurs d'une situation sociale. Que le Québec se soit épris des grands auteurs latino-américains peut paraître alors moins surprenant.

Si le réalisme magique semble présenter une lacune dans ce contexte littéraire, c'est sans doute attribuable au fait que, malgré son important lectorat, il n'ait toujours pas fait l'objet d'une définition suffisamment lumineuse pour s'appliquer à des œuvres issues de contextes habituellement non associés à ce genre.

Selon diverses définitions, le genre réaliste magique se manifeste dans un roman par l'entremise d'une structure spécifique incluant les codes paradoxaux du réel (code construit selon les paramètres établis du roman réaliste) et du magique (dont les événements sont de l'ordre du surnaturel, de l'extraordinaire, se distinguant ainsi des événements de la réalité hors texte). À l'orée du réalisme magique existe ainsi toujours un lien spécifique entre l'espace de production auquel fait appel le texte et le texte lui-même. Outre cette relation intrinsèque entre espace et texte, le genre réaliste magique implique que coexistent ces deux codes, et donc que leur antinomie soit résolue. Selon Amaryll Beatrice Chanady, c'est par l'instance narrative que ces deux codes antinomiques sont résolus, puisque l'effet réaliste n'est pas brisé par l'incursion d'événements extraordinaires. Au contraire, ce sont parfois les éléments réalistes qui créent un effet de merveilleux, transformant alors le naturel en extraordinaire.

Cette attraction entre des pôles contraires peut-elle servir à révéler des particularités de la réalité hors texte, en mettant en valeur des attributs de l'espace de production? Les théoriciens travaillent sur cette question depuis la parution des textes fondateurs sur la nature du genre réaliste magique, sur ce qui illumine la relation entre texte et contexte. En particulier, depuis la parution de *Magical Realism and the Fantastic: Resolved Versus Unresolved Antinomy*, l'ouvrage fondamental de Chanady, s'ils se sont donné pour tâche de décrire, d'énumérer et de critiquer ce genre insaisissable dans des lancées purement théoriques, ils n'ont pas pour autant abandonné la réflexion sur le lien primordial entre l'espace responsable (et sa culture) et sa capacité à générer le genre. Charles Scheel conclut ainsi que c'est ce désir de considérer le genre (ou mode, ou « label ») comme un effet culturel qui empêche l'érection d'une définition des techniques narratives du réalisme magique[3]. Il est vrai que la juxtaposition de diverses appellations, définitions et utilisations du réalisme magique a contribué à empêcher que se dégage une vision claire et constante de ce genre. De nombreuses publications, surtout entre 1995 et 2005, ont rassemblé des écrits sur le réalisme magique afin d'en dégager la nature[4] mais, selon moi, ces ouvrages ont davantage contribué à entretenir la confusion dans l'usage du terme et des notions qui lui sont associées.

Pour ma part, je considère le réalisme magique comme un genre littéraire au sens où le définit Tzvetan Todorov. Et si je me sers de Todorov comme référence pour une définition générique, c'est qu'on lui attribue l'une des définitions les plus solides du fantastique, genre connexe et similaire au réalisme magique[5]. Si l'on excepte les critiques et débats taxinomiques, les lecteurs du genre acceptent un roman réaliste magique selon des critères inhérents au texte fantastique, sans les distinguer nécessairement[6]. Le genre fantastique a été, lui aussi, fortement relié à son contexte de production, tant il éclaire les situations sociales[7]. De plus, le jeu qui, dans le fantastique, oppose le doute du lecteur à celui du narrateur est révélateur de l'espace contextuel auquel il se réfère. Enfin, le fantastique est sans conteste populaire, comme l'est le réalisme magique.

Afin de sortir du labyrinthe taxinomique, je propose la définition suivante. Premièrement, le réalisme magique romanesque est *a priori* abordé par une voix narrative qui ne distingue pas les événements dits réels des surnaturels. Ou, plus exactement, c'est *au moyen* de la narration que les événements surnaturels sont banalisés et que les aspects réalistes du roman sont organisés afin de les rendre bizarres. Deuxièmement, l'alliage de codes opposés fait appel à une écriture souvent critique, ironique et parodique. Troisièmement, offrant un style qui engage à tout sans rien promettre, plusieurs œuvres réalistes magiques n'offrent rien en guise de moralité explicite — il est plutôt question de remise en cause perpétuelle. J'ajouterai pour terminer que la trame narrative réaliste magique joue avec son contexte de production et qu'en jouant avec l'espace narratif elle subvertit en retour l'espace socioculturel hors texte.

Pour résumer, c'est dans l'espace narratif que se mêlent et s'inversent les deux codes et que naît le réalisme magique. Au-delà de cette structure narrative particulière, dont les subversions sont nombreuses, les thèmes réalistes magiques produisent des effets de perturbation et de questionnement. Si nous concevons aujourd'hui le réalisme magique comme un genre dominant la « *world literature* » et la critique postcoloniale, c'est parce qu'il menace le paradigme dominant avec un couteau à la gorge. Les romans de Allende, de Carter, de García Márquez, de Morrison, de Okri et de Rushdie illustrent bien ce phénomène — voire en sont emblématiques — pointant avec force des lieux mouvementés et subversifs dont les histoires refoulées doivent remonter à la surface.

La parution du roman d'Hébert en 1975 s'insère à un moment propice de l'histoire québécoise ainsi dans une période pertinente de son évolution littéraire, une période étayée par le désir de se débarrasser des valeurs et traditions d'antan. La sociocritique Marie-Hélène Lemieux explique que cette rupture s'accomplit avec la Révolution tranquille car elle se fabrique selon « les réformes politiques, économiques, sociales et culturelles réalisées entre 1960 et 1966 par le gouvernement libéral de Jean Lesage » (97). Selon Lemieux, la société québécoise passe d'une société dite traditionnelle (c'est-à-dire rurale et catholique) à une société dite moderne. Ce mouvement vers le laïque et l'urbain est le résultat d'une revendication sociale s'opposant à l'époque précédente. S'éloignant de la « Grande Noirceur » du gouvernement de Maurice Duplessis, la période 1950-1980 sera caractérisée par ses pluralités, ses contestations et ses changements en faveur de la nouveauté (Lemieux 97).

Je voudrais compléter cette présentation du contexte en rappelant ce que Pierre Nepveu définit comme l'idéologie de la révolte. Selon lui, le « rapport au réel tend à s'établir dans un contexte de lois, de normes, d'idéologies à *subvertir* » (Nepveu 212). J'ajouterai que, depuis 1960, l'écriture au Québec, comme le souligne Jozef Kwaterko, « s'est constituée en un espace de tensions, de jeu ouvert de langage, donnant prise à une réévaluation particulièrement dynamique du rapport au réel, au présent et au passé collectif » (12).

Soutenue par ce cadre sociocritique et à l'aide des théories sur le réalisme magique soulignant le lien fort entre les thèmes et les structures subversives du genre et le contexte hors texte, je voudrais démontrer que Julie constitue, en tant que nonne-sorcière, un dispositif générique, symbolique et critique d'un contexte dépassant amplement le cadre d'un couvent ensorcelé à Québec en 1940. Et, surtout, que l'analyse sémiotique des structures inversées révèle l'existence d'un paradoxe typique du genre réaliste magique. Cela permet d'associer pour la première fois ce discours à la littérature québécoise contemporaine.

Dans le roman sont décrites la vie rurale des années 1930 et la vie au couvent des années 1940. S'opposent ainsi deux décennies, toutes deux antérieures aux années de la Révolution tranquille, mais, si l'on s'appuie sur les écrits de Bourassa, Lemieux et Nepveu, l'air du temps s'y fait toutefois sentir. Dès le titre, nous sommes renvoyés à la fois à la révolte et au surnaturel, l'évocation du sabbat annonçant déjà une antinomie (le sabbat renvoyant à la fois à une célébration de la sorcellerie et à une tradition ancrée dans le religieux). Outre cette « ambivalence »[8], le roman typifie l'inclusion du surnaturel dans des espaces empreints d'effets réalistes.

Ces effets, que l'on peut indéniablement rattacher au style réaliste magique, ouvrent la voie à la subversion sociale. D'abord, le roman a pour sujet privilégié une sorcière qui est également nonne. Julie est réellement sorcière, personnage surnaturel capable d'actes surnaturels[9]. Elle participe néanmoins à la vie du couvent, où elle est Sœur Julie de la Trinité. Ces faits ne sont ni métaphoriques, ni allégoriques. Ce ne sont pas seulement des éléments surnaturels qui sont associés à Julie : elle est un personnage dont les éléments réalistes sont également indéniables. Et, conformément à la définition du genre, le conflit des deux codes antinomiques (le réel et le surnaturel) est résolu grâce à la voix narrative. Afin de rapprocher ces deux codes, l'instance narrative utilise un effet de banalisation, renvoyant un élément surnaturel ou extraordinaire au réel, le réduisant ainsi à un acte ordinaire. Afin d'illustrer cet effet de banalisation, voici un extrait de la nouvelle « Un monsieur très vieux avec des ailes immenses » de l'auteur symbolique du genre, Gabriel García Márquez : « C'est un ange, leur dit-elle. Il venait sûrement pour le petit, mais le pauvre est si âgé que la pluie l'a flanqué par terre » (10-11). Ce court extrait illustre bien l'effet banalisant de la narration : le fait que l'homme aux ailes soit un ange n'importe que peu, c'est plutôt le fait que la pluie, trop forte, l'ait flanqué par terre qui prime. Le mot « flanqué » illustre bien quant à lui ce que les théoriciens du genre réaliste magique entendent par « jeux de langage », l'expression réduisant et banalisant l'ange[10].

Ce qui est, de plus, typique du genre, les événements magiques s'expliquent grâce à une logique traditionnelle, superstitieuse ou de nature mythique. La magie peut être étonnante sans toutefois être considérée comme impossible à l'aune des croyances du contexte socioculturel. Ainsi, dans *Les enfants du sabbat,* on parle de possession et d'exorcisme (éléments significatifs du catholicisme), qui sont des préceptes religieux inscrits dans le réel de l'époque. En cela, ils ne relèvent pas du royaume de l'impossible. En particulier, pour les religieuses du couvent, le diable constitue une véritable menace. Comme le magique dans le réalisme magique, le diable n'est ni métaphorique, ni allégorique. Le roman place de ce fait sur un seul niveau tous les éléments du surnaturel, peu importe qu'ils soient sacrilèges ou sacrés. En réduisant la distance entre ces antipodes, on ouvre la voie à une critique, qui s'y faufile. Le sabbat illustre ce principe : le diable, une métamorphose du père de Julie, viole la jeune fille, et la description du viol est tout à fait ancrée dans le réel. L'acte *horribilis* est ponctué de latin (toujours en italique dans le texte), le « *ite missa est* » provenant de voix désincarnées. Après l'acte sanglant et brutal, Sœur Julie se dévoile à son père, ayant été témoin du viol de sa jeune forme. C'est au tour de la nonne de pouvoir faire subir un acte terrible à son père. Elle choisit plutôt de lui demander son aide. Son agresseur, son père, devra dès lors la servir. L'espace temporel de cet accord est 1930. Toutefois, c'est en 1940 qu'une nonne du couvent, sœur Gemma, va être victime des tours de la sorcière Julie et de son père le diable. Ce passage illustre un nivellement pluridimensionnel qui résout de multiples antinomies sémantiques, typographiques, temporelles et spatiales. Pourrait-on dire alors que le Québec d'antan et le nouveau Québec sont mêlés dans ce brouillage thématique, temporel et spatial? Les rapprochements affutés dans ce roman sont ceux entre viol et rituels religieux, joual et latin, l'instruit et l'ignorant, la violence et l'amour[11].

Que faire de ces « ambivalences »? Afin d'éviter que tout ne devienne possible, le roman réaliste magique est assujetti à de nombreuses lois qui structurent à la fois le réel et le magique. Le récit réaliste magique expose ainsi, par la conjonction d'actes surnaturels et réels, diverses réalités sous-jacentes du contexte de production littéraire.

Dans *Les enfants du sabbat*, il n'y a ainsi rien d'aléatoire. Les pouvoirs de Julie suivent une logique magique interne. Le lecteur accepte bien cet ordre et intègre ces éléments, présentés comme normaux, dans sa perception du réel hors texte, c'est-à-dire du *réel* réel. Dans le récit, la sorcellerie est ainsi léguée à Julie par Philomène (sa mère sorcière). Que Julie soit sorcière n'est pas problématique puisque « (tout le monde sait que la sorcellerie est héréditaire) » (108), comme nous le rappelle le texte en employant une formule qui banalise cet effet généalogique en plaçant entre parenthèses la remarque qui vise à souligner la nature évidente de la sorcellerie. La généalogie est présente dans le code du réel du roman par le truchement d'événements surnaturels. La sorcellerie est introduite de façon « nonchalante » (tel l'ange aux ailes immenses de Marquez) à l'aide de remarques triviales. Dans *Les enfants du sabbat* s'entremêlent alors histoire, biologie et sorcellerie. Je voudrais surtout souligner ici la référence à l'histoire québécoise à l'aide de personnages non fictionnels, comme Barbe Hallé, sorcière et figure historique québécoise qui, dans le récit fictionnel, serait l'ancêtre de Julie. L'histoire générale de la sorcellerie est également présente, de façon paratextuelle, grâce à un inventaire d'études véritables sur la sorcellerie inclus en fin d'ouvrage[12]. Comme nous l'avons vu, le réalisme magique est un genre qui permet souvent une interprétation d'aspects thématiques et idéologiques typiques du contexte culturel de l'œuvre. L'étude de la sorcellerie au Québec révèle ainsi le lien entre ce genre et un aspect fondamental du contexte socioculturel. En regroupant une pluralité de thèmes (religion, pauvreté, sorcellerie et ignorance), le réalisme magique produit ici une vision critique du contexte social. Grâce à ces thèmes, certaines valeurs traditionnelles ainsi que certains éléments négligés ou oubliés dans le contexte contemporain sont mis en évidence et contestés.

Afin de réaliser une analyse des procédés sociocritiques du genre, il faut engendrer *a priori* une première analyse de la construction des personnages et des objets auxquels ils sont associés. Au-delà de la nature du genre, par essence contradictoire, Sœur Julie, la nonne-sorcière, est symbolique d'une ambivalence enrichie par un réseau éclaté et dispersé dans le roman sur plusieurs plans et niveaux narratifs. J'emprunte le terme « ambivalence » à Mikhail Bakhtine, dont la contribution sur le carnavalesque et le grotesque a largement concouru à la riche production d'approches sémiotiques du genre réaliste magique. Comme l'explique Janet Paterson, le concept bakhtinien d'ambivalence renvoie à « l'union de sens contraires » (62). Quant à moi, j'entends par là que les intervertissements et les contradictions dévoilent le système d'inversions qui gouverne le texte. De nombreux objets (des tasses, des statuettes, des couteaux, des habits de nonne) — et pas seulement Julie — sont à la fois religieux et démoniaques. L'objet est ainsi mis en action dans la structure paradoxale du genre et il devient magique car il a été inséré dans un espace également paradoxal, celui du réel du texte (qui est paradoxal du fait que ce code dépend du réel hors texte tout en se posant définitivement comme de la fiction). C'est donc l'inversion spatiale qui modifie l'appartenance au code. Ainsi scindé par l'antinomie, l'objet (comme le réalisme magique) renvoie à la fois à l'ambivalence et à l'inversion. Nous avons vu que, dès son titre, *Les enfants du sabbat* inspire une analyse portant sur les contrastes et les contradictions. Ainsi, comme l'explique Janet Paterson, « la *cabane* des sorciers s'oppose et se juxtapose au *couvent* des dames du Précieux-Sang et à la cellule de Sœur Julie, effectuant ainsi par un transcodage sémantique le passage entre deux espaces et deux signes » (61). Je voudrais souligner toutefois que, dans *Les enfants du sabbat*, la magie n'est pas formellement liée à la cabane des sorciers. C'est au contraire dans le couvent des nonnes du Précieux-Sang que le surnaturel abonde. Comme Julie, l'objet devient magique lorsqu'il transgresse les bornes du passé de la Montagne de B... pour se caser dans le couvent.

Pour mener une critique sociale tout en évitant la censure ou la contestation, les récits réalistes magiques sont souvent empreints d'un ton ironique, à la fois humoristique et critique. Cela permet au personnage de la sorcière de ne pas être confiné à un rôle grotesque ou fantasmagorique. Julie, outre le fait qu'elle offre une complexité polarisée par ses rôles complexes, peut inciter, par l'entremise des jeux présents dans la voix narrative, à de multiples réverbérations critiques. Il n'est donc pas surprenant que de nombreux critiques d'Hébert aient attribué à cette auteure des étiquettes du type « ironique », « satirique », « parodique » ou même « comique ». Ces caractéristiques sont en réalité attribuables au genre, et ce roman en est riche. Voici par exemple comment Julie la sorcière a exercé sa volonté sur la pauvre sœur économe. Elle lui a expliqué où trouver les cigarettes que le docteur a laissées. Voici comment s'enchaînent les événements et comment survient le déclin de la bonne sœur économe :

> La sœur économe a très rapidement appris à fumer. Dès cet instant, sa vie a été changée [...] Dans un brouillard bleu qui la fait tousser, la sœur économe traite des affaires du couvent avec une dextérité et une assurance jamais encore atteintes [et] elle empoigne le téléphone, une cigarette au coin de la bouche, les yeux tout plissés par la fumée. D'une voix de basse russe, elle fait des affaires [...] Ils vendent, à perte, actions, obligations et propriétés, achètent très cher des savanes dans des régions perdues [...] Fureur. Désespoir. La sœur économe est aussitôt destituée de ses fonctions et enfermée dans le grenier [...] La sœur économe hurle derrière la porte qu'elle est un homme d'affaires. (139-40)

Il est clair ici que, malgré la présence de thèmes et d'éléments violents et toxiques, le roman d'Hébert (comme ceux de plusieurs autres romanciers réalistes magiques) incite au rire en offrant un commentaire cinglant. La critique, masquée par le parodique et l'ironique, est possible : Sœur Julie, sorcière qui incarne le diable dans un couvent, subvertit ainsi l'ordre et les idées généralement admises.

Que ce renversement des idées généralement admises constitue un élément central du roman a été bien étudié. Ellen W. Munley, dans son article sur l'emploi de la métaphore dans *Les enfants du sabbat*, explique ainsi que Julie, comme sorcière, incarne et réincarne le diable, représentant alors « les inversions de l'ordre civil établi et de la religion catholique au Québec. Elle est possédée par les forces néfastes et est prisonnière des murs du couvent et de la cabane des sorciers »[13]. De nature subversive, la contestation s'insère à plusieurs niveaux du texte et va au-delà de la critique religieuse. Surtout, comme le constate Munley, elle prend des formes sanguinaires, violentes et scandaleuses (entre autres le viol de Julie, la naissance du bébé diable, les examens et les stigmates de Julie et l'épisode de sœur Gemma qui mange, couverte de sang animal, de la viande crue dans sa chambre).

Dans les multiples structures du roman (thématique, diégétique et typographique), nous constatons que les codes antinomiques s'enchevêtrent pour former un réseau signifiant. Il existe ainsi, dans *Les enfants du sabbat*, un profond désir de libération et de transformation. De plus, c'est son statut d'enfermée, qu'elle partage avec les sœurs du Précieux-Sang et avec son frère Joseph, que Julie réfute lorsqu'elle se sauve par la fenêtre. Dès le début du roman, les lieux claustrophobes, l'habit de la nonne, l'emprise de la cabane ou du couvent et les thématiques de possession et d'enfermement signalent le cloisonnement. Or il faut, comme l'affirme Julie, « se débarrasser de la cabane de son enfance [...] être délivrée du couple sacré qui présidait à la destinée de la cabane » (7). Plusieurs critiques ont mis en lumière ce désir d'être libéré d'une situation opprimante comme constituant un thème privilégié du réalisme magique, et ce thème est bien présent dans la critique québécoise. Un genre qui subvertit les idées généralement admises, qui renverse les structures dominantes et qui donne la voix aux marginalisés est loin d'être étranger au contexte de production littéraire québécois. Ainsi, le texte relève d'un contexte considérablement marqué par la tradition et la religion et, comme le note Denis Bouchard, « ces jeux sont féroces pour [les] Québécois accoutumés à des épopées des Laurentides et du Saint-Laurent. Des rétrospectives dénichant l'inceste et tout un catalogue de vices honteux peuvent en fin de compte se rapporter à nos expériences, inédites à cause d'un manque de courage héréditaire, refoulées à cause de notre culpabilité » (173).

Ce roman, quoiqu'imprégné d'un désir de libération, demeure cependant prisonnier du paradoxe car la libération ne mène pas à l'oraison. Les choix de Julie semblent étonnants car ils ne visent pas l'amélioration ou la morale. Respectant en cela la structure subversive du genre, voici comment Julie espère dépasser ses limites héréditaires : « Je triompherai là où Philomène a échoué. Je coucherai avec mon fils. Telle est la loi antique [...] Je serai mère et grande mère, maîtresse et sorcière [...] J'oublierai ce couvent de si pauvres magies, toute l'Église souffreteuse et mon frère Joseph qui m'a trahie » (174). Ce n'est donc pas la raison qui prime sur l'ordre du monde maléfique. C'est, au contraire, dans ce monde inversé, Julie qui exerce son pouvoir de transformation et de libération. Elle se libère de la cabane pour la dépasser. Comme le note André Gaulin, elle constitue une figure féminine similaire aux autres figures féminines des romans d'Anne Hébert, qui « revendiquent chacune à leur manière un statut social, dans la révolte, dans le refus, luttent toutes du dedans contre un dehors aliénant » (77). Par cette confrontation des codes, Julie s'engage dans une libération qui donne naissance au réalisme magique, permettant ainsi de « [réveiller] les désirs cachés et les passions réprimées » (English et Viswanathan 115). Comme la logique du réalisme magique est interne, il est fort probable qu'elle ne propose aucune solution et, si solution il y a, rarement celle-ci sera-t-elle positive. Ce sont plutôt les renversements qui sont typiques, et qui illustrent bien les propos de Neil Bishop au sujet des thèmes de libération et d'enfermement : « le thème de la clôture spatiale, avec la signification fortement négative d'emprisonnement physique et psychologique qui s'y rattache, se renforce lors de la transgression des plus forts interdits, ce qui suggère ce que peut avoir d'illusoire, comme moyen de libération, ce recours à la sorcellerie » (57).

Le réalisme magique ne se veut définitivement pas un genre moralisateur, « rose » et simplet. Au contraire sont présentes dans ces récits des subversions qui laissent au lecteur un arrière-goût plutôt amer et toxique. Comme le remarque Anne Fonteneau, Sœur Julie dépasse bien les bornes du social acceptées et tolérées, mais ce n'est pas pour autant pour qu'elle est assujettie à des sensibilités plus modernes[14]. Par sa nature antinomique, Julie, dans la misère de son monde, personnage grotesque à la fois victime et bourreau, est troublante et ensorcelante. Anne Fonteneau explique aussi que Julie est initiée par sa « mère, mais que son intronisation ne se produit qu'après le viol du père. Un viol qui se répètera et duquel Julie prendra plaisir. » (183) Faut-il dorénavant comprendre que la libération et la signifiance féminine demeurent dans les limites du rapport au père, à l'agresseur, à une sexualité soumise? Le genre réaliste magique ne résout jamais l'ambivalence des personnages. Au contraire, dans l'espace thématique du réalisme magique, un personnage ambivalent est à la source de tout un réseau d'énigmes à résoudre.

Par l'entremise des renversements caractéristiques du genre réaliste magique, le pouvoir de se voir et de se dire annonce et reflète en même temps son contexte de production. Ainsi, Julie se voit et se dit, s'enchante et se désenchante. Elle peut dépasser ses limites. Écrire dans une veine réaliste magique, c'est se mettre au diapason de cette volonté libératrice, se pencher sur les structures qui forment un lien entre l'envisageable et l'impossible. Le récit se trace dans l'équilibre du contraste et du paradoxe. Dans cet espace, tout est à la fois possible et contestable.

NOTES

1. Pour une analyse approfondie de cette question, voir Walsh Matthews (2011).
2. Surtout la recherche dans le genre du fantastique et son apport au contexte culturel québécois.
3. Dans sa communication « Le réalisme magique : mode narratif de la fiction ou label culturel? », Scheel décrit le problème culturaliste du réalisme magique. Selon lui, le réalisme magique a été assujetti à une étude culturelle brouillant la recherche à son propos en tant que mode narratif de la fiction. S'il est vrai que le réalisme magique

mérite une définition technique, comme je l'explique, il reflète néanmoins son contexte culturel, ce qui constitue un lien intéressant.

4. Je fais essentiellement référence aux textes de Amaryll Beatrice Chanady, de Wendy B. Faris, de Katherine Roussos, de Charles Scheel et de Lois P. Zamora.

5. Chanady s'en est tenue aux propos de Todorov afin d'expliquer son emploi du terme « mode » comme concept générique du réalisme magique. Dans ma thèse de doctorat, j'utilise la notion de genre à la lumière de l'ouvrage critique sur le fantastique dans la littérature québécoise de Michel Lord (*La logique de l'impossible*, 1995).

6. Dès la parution de textes critiques sur ce genre, on a attribué au réalisme magique un ensemble de caractéristiques indéniablement propices à souligner un style particulier, en particulier la présence du surnaturel dans une trame narrative réelle et la critique sociale. Toutefois, en raison de la popularité de certains auteurs, certains liens fondamentaux entre l'exotisme d'un lieu et la magie du texte ont embrouillé la notion générique. Il a fallu préciser la distinction entre réalisme merveilleux et réalisme magique et également faire le tri entre réalisme magique et surréel, baroque et néo-fantastique.

7. Notamment *Le récit fantastique* d'Irène Bessière (1974).

8. Le mot « ambivalence » renvoie ici à l'acception de Bakhtine comme « union de sens contraires », comme nous le détaillerons plus loin.

9. Dans le même ordre d'idées, le rôle de sorcière dans le réalisme magique en littérature caribéenne est discuté dans Walsh Matthews (2012).

10. Dans son analyse des techniques narratives réalistes magiques, Charles Scheel se sert du même passage afin de démontrer que, dès le début, le récit pose des problèmes de lecture, notamment du fait de l'introduction *in media res* et de la « nonchalance » (136-37).

11. Le discours direct de Julie, de Adélard et de Philomène, ainsi que celui des prostituées du roman, est marqué par le joual, langue courante québécoise. Dans plusieurs passages du roman, le joual et le latin sont entremêlés, tout comme le sont la messe et le sabbat.

12. En fin de roman, on trouve une courte bibliographie qui énumère dans la rubrique « Ouvrages consultés » les ouvrages suivants : *Magistrats et sorciers en France au* XVIIIᵉ *siècle, La sorcellerie au Québec du* XVIIIᵉ *siècle, Les dossiers secrets de la sorcellerie et de la magie noire, Les sorcières et leur monde, La sorcellerie, La sorcière* et *Les sorcières*. Je tiens surtout à souligner que tous ces ouvrages venaient d'être réédités (entre 1966 et 1973) au moment de l'écriture des *Enfants du sabbat*.

13. « *the inversion of Québec's established civil order and Catholic religion. Possessed by dark forces between the emprisoning* [sic] *walls of the convent and the rustic walls of the cabin that houses the Satanic rites* » (Munley 57).

14. Anne Fonteneau, dans sa thèse de doctorat *Le féminin et le sacré dans l'œuvre en prose d'Anne Hébert*, explique que les personnages féminins vivent un malaise lorsque la structure établie et les croyances institutionnalisées sont incapables de combler leur vie.

Allende, Isabel. *The House of the Spirits*. Trad. Magda Bogin. New York: Bantam, 1986. (traduction de *La casa de los espíritus*, 1982)

Bakhtine, Mikhail. *Rabelais and his World*. Trad. Hélène Iswolsky. Bloomington: Indiana University Press, 1984.

Bessière, Irène. *Le récit fantastique*. Paris: Larousse, 1974.

Bishop, Neil. « *Les enfants du sabbat* et la problématique de la libération chez Anne Hébert ». *The Art and Genius of Anne Hébert: Essays on Her Works*. Dir. Janis L. Pallister. Cranbury, NJ: Rosemont Publishing, 2001. 54-74.

Bouchard, Denis. *Une lecture d'Anne Hébert : La recherche d'une mythologie*. Montréal: Hurtubise HMH, 1977.

Bourassa, André. *Surréalisme et littérature québécoise*. Montréal: L'Étincelle, 1977.

Carter, Angela. *Nights at the Circus*. London: Vintage, 1994. (1e édition 1984)

Chanady, Amaryll Beatrice. *Magical Realism and the Fantastic: Resolved Versus Unresolved Antinomy*. New York: Garland Publishing, 1985.

English, Judith et Jacqueline Viswanathan. « Les deux dames du Précieux-Sang : à propos des *Enfants du sabbat* d'Anne Hébert ». *Présence francophone* 22 (1981): 111-19.

Faris, Wendy B. *Ordinary Enchantments: Magical Realism and the Remystification of Narrative*. Nashville: Vanderbilt University Press, 2004.

Fonteneau, Anne. *Le féminin et le sacré dans l'œuvre en prose d'Anne Hébert*. Thèse de doctorat, Université Laval, 2001.

García Márquez, Gabriel. *Cent ans de solitude*. Trad. Carmen et Claude Durand. Paris: Seuil, 1968. (traduction de *Cien años de soledad*, 1967)

———. « Un monsieur très vieux avec des ailes immenses ». *L'Incroyable et triste histoire de la candide Erendira et de sa diabolique grand-mère*. Trad. Claude Couffon. Paris: Grasset et Fasquelle, 1977. 10-11.

Gaulin, André. « Lecture politique d'Anne Hébert, point de vue d'une protagoniste ». *Centre d'études québécoises* 92 (1994): 77-82.

Hébert, Anne. *Les enfants du sabbat*. Montréal: Boréal, 1995. (1e édition 1975)

Kwaterko, Jozef. *Le roman québécois et ses (inter)discours*. Québec: Nota Bene, 1998.

Lemieux, Marie-Hélène. « Pour une sociocritique du roman *Kamouraska* d'Anne Hébert ». *Voix et images* 28.3 (2003): 95-113.

Lord, Michel. *La logique de l'impossible*. Québec: Nuit Blanche Éditeur, 1995.

Munley, Ellen W. « Spatial Metaphors in Anne Hébert's *Les enfants du sabbat:* Within and beyond the Confines of the Convent, the Cabin, and the Quotidian ». *Dolphin* 20 (1991): 55-66.

Nepveu, Pierre. *L'écologie du réel. Mort et naissance de la littérature québécoise contemporaine*. Paris: Seuil, 1988.

Okri, Ben. *The Famished Road*. London: Vintage, 1992.

Paterson, Janet. « Parodie et sorcellerie ». *Études littéraires* 19.1 (1986): 59-66.

Roussos, Katherine. *Décoloniser l'imaginaire: Le réalisme magique chez Maryse Condé, Sylvie Germain et Marie Ndiaye*. Paris: L'Harmattan, 2007.

Rushdie, Salman. *Midnight's Children*. London: Picador, 1982.

Scheel, Charles W. « Le réalisme magique: mode narratif de la fiction ou label culturaliste? » *Études culturelles, anthropologie culturelle et comparatisme*. Vol. 2. Dir. Didier Souiller, Antonio Dominguez Leiva, Sébastien Hubier et

Philippe Chardin. Actes du 35ᵉ congrès de la s F L G C (Société française de littérature générale et comparée). Dijon: Éditions du Murmure, 2010. 211-22.

———. *Réalisme magique et réalisme merveilleux : Des théories aux poétiques*. Paris: L'Harmattan, 2005.

Todorov, Tzvetan. *Introduction à la littérature fantastique*. Paris: Seuil, 1970.

Viau, Robert (dir.). *La création littéraire dans le contexte de l'exiguïté*. Québec: M N H, 2000.

Walsh Matthews, Stéphanie. *Le réalisme magique dans la littérature contemporaine québécoise*. Thèse de doctorat, Université de Toronto, 2011.

———. « Les vérités ensorcelantes: les sorcières dans la littérature francophone au féminin ». *MaComère* 13.1-2 (2012): 82-97.

Weisgerber, Jean (dir.). *Le réalisme magique. Roman. Peinture. Cinéma*. Lausanne: L'Âge d'homme, 1987.

Zamora, Lois P. et Wendy B. Faris (dir.). *Magical Realism: Theory, History, Community*. Durham, NC: Duke University Press, 1995.

LIEU HUMAIN / LIEU PERSONNE

CHEZ DEUX ÉCRIVAINES

CANADO-VIETNAMIENNES,

THUONG VUONG-RIDDICK ET KIM THÚY

Mireille Mai Truong

À mon père, Trương bưu Khánh

Introduction

Kim Thúy (Saigon 1968), écrivaine francophone d'origine vietnamienne,
a été lauréate du Prix littéraire du gouverneur général 2010 pour son
premier roman, *Ru* (2009). Thuong Vuong-Riddick (Hanoi 1940) est
l'auteure d'un recueil de poésie bilingue, *Two Shores / Deux rives* (1995),
ainsi que de mémoires, *The Evergreen Country* (2007). Toutes les deux
s'exprimant dans leur deuxième ou troisième langue, c'est la façon
dont les langues d'origine transparaissent dans les comparaisons et les
métaphores qu'elles utilisent qui nous intéressera ici.

Dans des études antérieures menées sur la romancière vietnamienne
Duong Thu Huong[1], deux particularités de la traduction en français de
son œuvre ont attiré mon attention. En premier lieu, la traduction en
français des métaphores et des comparaisons employées par l'auteure
de langue vietnamienne dans un de ses romans (*Itinéraire d'enfance*)

effaçait leurs références locales en les francisant et en les banalisant : par exemple, au lieu de traduire littéralement certaines descriptions, ce qui aurait eu pour avantage de fournir du même coup des indications sur la faune ou la flore locales, le traducteur s'était livré à une simplification du cadre tropical, quelquefois même à la censure ou à l'effacement de ce qui pourrait peut-être choquer le lecteur francophone. Voici quelques exemples de ces phénomènes. Dans la version vietnamienne d'*Itinéraire d'enfance*[2], les bras et les jambes du petit pêcheur à la nasse sont « maigres et rabougris *comme les sarbacanes en cuivre utilisées pour la chasse aux oiseaux* » alors que dans la version française, « ses membres sont si maigres, *on dirait des baguettes* » (Duong 27).

Une « vendeuse d'enfants » dans la version vietnamienne devient une simple « sorcière » dans la version française. De la même façon, dans la version française, on « se brosse les dents » et on « se lave le visage » au lieu de « se laver les dents avec les doigts et le visage en se servant de ses mains » dans la version vietnamienne.

En deuxième lieu, certains phénomènes subtils liés aux différentes façons dont les Vietnamiens s'interpellent ont été entièrement perdus, eux aussi, dans la traduction. Ainsi, il est presque impossible en vietnamien de ne pas établir, dès le premier contact entre deux personnes, une situation hiérarchisée, semblable au vouvoiement français mais beaucoup plus compliquée. Chacun se positionne dans une situation de respect par rapport à l'autre, de reconnaissance d'ancienneté, de pouvoir et de genre féminin ou masculin. Chacun est plus jeune ou plus âgé (jeune frère ou sœur/grand frère ou grande sœur; grand-père ou grand-mère *éloignés* — donc maternels — ou paternels, etc). Il y a une scène dans le roman de Duong Thu Huong où deux petites copines réussissent à ne pas instituer entre elles de hiérarchie en rejetant toutes les formules d'appellation habituelles qui n'admettent pas d'égalité, et en se transformant en lieux respectifs, semblables, peut-être, au « hé, là-bas » français, où le pronom personnel est remplacé par un démonstratif spatial : « lieu-ci » (*đây* = je) ou « lieu-là » (*đấy* ou *đó* = tu).

Dans son analyse des démonstratifs spatiaux utilisés comme pronoms personnels « je » et « tu », le linguiste Nguyễn Phú Phong discute des oppositions je/tu : *đây* (lieu-ci = je) et *đấy* ou *đó* (lieu-là = tu)[3] et indique

que leur emploi « est spécifique au vietnamien » et que par rapport aux langues européennes personnelles (subjectives) et égocentriques, le vietnamien figure au nombre des langues « *loco*centriques » (Nguyễn 168; c'est nous qui soulignons). « L'importance du type de repérage à fondement lococentrique en vietnamien, précise le linguiste, n'est plus à démontrer : l'homme, c'est-à-dire le lieu humain, et le lieu tout court, c'est-à-dire le lieu spatial, se confondent souvent en un signifiant » (Nguyễn 175). J'ajouterai en passant que le mot « écrivain » en vietnamien est « nhà văn », ce qui signifie « maison de la littérature », confirmant la possibilité en vietnamien d'une assimilation conceptuelle de la personne à un lieu.

Les questions que nous allons nous poser à présent au sujet des œuvres de deux Canado-Vietnamiennes qui écrivent dans leur langue seconde ou cinquième sont les suivantes. Que reste-t-il de leur culture d'origine maintenant qu'elles s'expriment dans la ou les langues postcoloniales de leur vie d'immigrées? L'effacement effectué par le traducteur et que j'ai décrit ci-dessus se fait-il *de lui-même* dans leur écriture? Comment les écrivaines en situation de diaspora, mais décrivant leurs communautés d'origine, gèrent-elles les cas très particuliers des appellations vietnamiennes quand elles écrivent en français, en anglais ou dans les deux langues de leur nouvelle vie?

Thuong Vuong-Riddick, The Evergreen Country: A Memoir of Vietnam

Comme son nom l'indique, *The Evergreen Country: A Memoir of Vietnam* est un récit autobiographique, en anglais, de l'auteure Thuong Vuong-Riddick, dont le nom lui-même indique l'hybridité. Le prénom — Thuong — postposé en vietnamien, se retrouve en première position canadienne, et le nom d'épouse — Riddick — est rattaché par un trait d'union au nom de famille Vuong, à la québécoise. Par ailleurs, Vuong est la forme vietnamisée du patronyme chinois Wang (Vuong-Riddick 2007, 10). Vuong-Riddick passa ses vingt-cinq premières années au Vietnam, principalement à Hanoi et à Saigon, puis quitta ce pays pour la France afin d'y poursuivre des études supérieures. Par des chemins détournés, elle se retrouva au Canada, à Montréal, où elle enseigna la littérature francophone à l'Université McGill, puis finit par s'établir en Colombie-Britannique où elle enseigna pendant plusieurs années à l'Université de Victoria avant de déménager à Vancouver. Elle n'est pas vietnamienne « pure laine » non plus, mais, comme le laissait prévoir son nom Vuong, issue d'une famille chinoise, elle-même établie depuis trois générations à Hanoi au Nord Vietnam. Sa langue maternelle est le foukinois (fujianese), vite suivie du vietnamien de la vie locale de son enfance, du mandarin appris en langue seconde à l'école élémentaire, puis du français à l'école catholique et de l'anglais, langue soi-disant « seconde » mais en réalité sa cinquième langue.

Ce qu'il y a d'absolument stupéfiant dans l'écriture anglaise de Vuong-Riddick est qu'elle est pratiquement dépourvue de comparaisons ou de métaphores, ce qui ne peut s'expliquer entièrement par le fait qu'il s'agit d'un récit autobiographique, de *mémoires*, et non d'une autofiction à la manière de l'auteure française Marguerite Duras, par exemple, puisque sa poésie bilingue — *Two Shores / Deux rives* — présente la même nudité.

Dans *The Evergreen Country*, Vuong-Riddick elle-même reconnaît le caractère austère de son écriture et se livre, à l'occasion, à un genre d'autoanalyse diégétique, à une autopsie de sa propre écriture « dépouillée ». Même du temps où elle était à l'école et qu'elle écrivait, son style, dit-elle, n'était pas sophistiqué : « My style was not sophisticated, but my sincerity and simplicity of tone made my writing stand out » (Vuong-Riddick 2007, 71). Même certains passages descriptifs présentent un caractère presque « objectif », comme si la personne observant se contentait de nous communiquer juste assez d'éléments perceptuels — quelques « sense-data » russelliens de base — pour que nous puissions nous former par nous-mêmes une image de la scène, à la manière pointilliste, sans que la propre perception du peintre n'intervienne :

Early on summer mornings, my elder sister and brother and I rode bicycles, stopping first at the East Gate where our grandparents lived, close to the Lake of the West, where we were joined by our three maternal aunts. Girls were *strolling*, their long black hair *trailing* down their backs, their Ao dai dresses *fluttering* in the fresh breeze. *Giggling*, they played with their cone-shaped hats, whirling them in the air. Old men read newspapers on the benches. Children ran across the lawns. Young men played badminton. And vendors sold grilled peanuts and a *delicious* snack of sticky rice steamed with yellow beans and topped with fried onions, all wrapped in a banana leaf. (Vuong-Riddick 2007, 66; c'est nous qui soulignons les seuls termes « subjectifs » du passage)

D'entrée, Vuong-Riddick indique la mission identitaire qui a fait naître son projet de mémoires : « I needed to come back to the country where I was born to understand who I am » (Vuong-Riddick 2007, 6). Suit une métaphore filée assez banale, celle du travail souterrain et sismique de la formation de la personnalité dont le paradoxe est qu'il n'aboutit en définitive à rien qu'à d'autres mouvances « evergreen » — jamais finies, exigeant une perpétuelle mise à jour — comme l'est un « evergreen paper » dans le domaine des écrits administratifs : un document à caractère évolutif, en évolution constante ou même, tout simplement, un document vivant[4].

Une ou deux comparaisons dans le roman se conforment au schéma que nous espérions retrouver chez une écrivaine de la diaspora, du genre de celles qui avaient été occultées chez l'auteure de langue maternelle vietnamienne dont j'ai parlé en introduction. Elles consistent à décrire la réalité vietnamienne *indirectement*. Vuong-Riddick évoque l'image un peu clichée, elle aussi, des *deux paniers d'un fléau* portés par une marchande ambulante auxquels elle compare l'église catholique Saint-Antoine et la pagode qui se trouvaient l'une en face de l'autre au bout de la rue de Hanoi où vivait sa famille : « These two symbols of faith were like two baskets bending a yoke across the shoulders of the country » (Vuong-Riddick 2007, 15).

Comme son père importait des produits de France pour les vendre aux Français, produits que la famille ne goûtait pas, Vuong-Riddick voit dans leur conservation dans de grands contenants en verre le symbole des « deux solitudes » :

My father imported all his merchandise from France, so I grew up surrounded by Gruyere cheese, soap from Marseilles, Pastis wine, toilet water, and perfumes from Paris. We never tried the foods or used any of the other products ourselves;

their use was foreign to us, but they were piled one on top of the other in huge glass containers. I remember thinking we were two worlds facing each other: Chinese and Vietnamese facing our clients, who were mostly French. Nothing could bridge the divide. (Vuong-Riddick 2007, 16-17)

Bien que Vuong-Riddick fasse le lien entre les contenants en verre et les deux mondes, il faut bien constater qu'elle n'ose pas, ne s'est pas suffisamment affranchie du joug colonial, pour que les objets prennent d'eux-mêmes, dans le contexte d'une écriture plus libre, un sens second que les lecteurs détermineraient tout seuls. Son choix même du genre — les mémoires — est plus soumis et vaincu que le choix plus assuré de l'autofiction de *L'Amant* effectué sans vergogne par une Marguerite Duras, fut-elle issue d'une famille de pauvres blancs établie au Vietnam alors que Vuong-Riddick vient d'une famille chinoise prospère et bourgeoise.

Certaines images non seulement ne nous transportent strictement nulle part ailleurs mais nous confinent à nous-mêmes et à notre for intérieur. Dans le désarroi de l'immigration où l'écrivaine adulte ne se sent plus libre de faire des rapprochements et des comparaisons, il ne reste qu'un *double* niveau de représentation, une « différance » derridéenne dans laquelle la réalité passée *reste* irréelle et imaginaire, et ce, même quand elle est ressaisie pendant un voyage de retour au pays d'origine : « We travelled first by bus, then the long crossing by boat *felt like a dream landscape*, with the fog rising and other boatloads of pilgrims greeting us as we passed, and the lime rocks standing *like lines in Chinese paintings* » (Vuong-Riddick 2007, 194; c'est nous qui soulignons). Vuong-Riddick, on le voit, affiche une grande réticence à faire le moindre lien métaphorique ou comparatif entre les éléments du présent canadien et ceux de sa jeunesse indochinoise. En revanche, il lui arrive de faire des liens interculturels sur un ton légèrement didactique. Ainsi, elle explique une particularité du système d'appellation asiatique, celui qu'elle a connu au sein de sa famille même, dans laquelle elle appelait sa propre mère « An Chiêm » qui signifie « ma tante ». Apparemment, dans les familles riches et traditionnelles, afin d'instaurer une plus grande distance respectueuse entre enfants et parents, les enfants appelaient leurs parents « oncle » et « tante ». Comme le précise Vuong-Riddick, anticipant des regards critiques : « we see the same phenomemenon in French bourgeois families, who use the formal *vous* instead of *tu* to address their parents » (Vuong-Riddick 2007, 28). D'autres rapprochements interculturels sont établis entre des épisodes historiques, comme lorsque les Vietnamiens ont chassé les Chinois du pays ou les ont forcés à aller dans des camps de rééducation, « like Japanese Canadians who were interned or deported during World War II » (Vuong-Riddick 2007, 169) ou lorsque les Vietnamiens cherchent à rééduquer les populations montagnardes, comme les Canadiens envoyaient de force les enfants autochtones dans des pensionnats.

En citant son journal de jeunesse, Vuong-Riddick se plaint des difficultés que présente la traduction du vietnamien, en particulier certains termes d'appellation. Elle décrit le sentiment d'aliénation que ressent un Vietnamien quand il parle une autre langue, lui qui a l'habitude de faire référence à lui-même à la troisième personne et en terme de relation familiale au mieux, de relation féodale au pire, mais dans une langue où l'autre fait littéralement corps avec soi dans une unité reflétée par le terme vietnamien « chúng mình »[5], qui veut dire « nous », mais qui signifie littéralement « corps » :

> How does one translate the language of a people who, most of the time, speak of themselves in the third person and designate themselves according to their relation with the speaker, using appellations like son or daughter, nephew, uncle or aunt; rarely, so rarely, by the neutral "I"? For this person the emergence of individuality is especially difficult. [...] When a Vietnamese uses another language he or she feels at once exiled, depersonalized. The most usual term like "Chung minh," when translated to "we," loses its intimacy because neither English nor French has the term "minh," which means "body"; it shows that the person who says chung minh is so close to the others that he or she considers the others like a part of his or her body. (Vuong-Riddick 2007, 137-38)

Et de conclure, dans une des rares effusions nostalgiques lui échappant :

> The act of translation loses so much. From the warm syllables of simple Vietnamese words, I inhale a familiar perfume.

Here, in this country, love stories are lived in understatement, with inhibition, through secret thoughts and intuitions, beneath hints, which hold absolutely no significance for a European but are saturated with meaning for a Vietnamese or a Chinese. (Vuong-Riddick 2007, 138)

Sa propre écriture, justement, ne serait-elle pas remplie d'euphémismes, « saturée de sens » — plutôt que terne et dépouillée comme elle le paraît au début et en première analyse, ou « non sophistiquée et d'un ton sincère et simple » comme elle l'a affirmé.

Dans la façon retenue avec laquelle elle évoque son enfance et sa jeunesse, la rareté des métaphores et des comparaisons, la subtilité des émotions exprimées, ne conserve-t-elle pas, en définitive, mais *en anglais*, la tradition vietnamienne en voie de disparition de réserve et d'euphémisme? Pour emprunter une très belle image à Patrice Desbiens (cité par François Paré), Vuong-Riddick n'est-elle pas de ceux et celles d'entre nous qui parlent — je le cite — « doucement, en italiques » (Paré 56)?

Kim Thúy, Ru

Ru est le premier roman de Kim Thúy, membre d'une famille de *boat people* vietnamienne ayant abouti à Montréal lorsque l'auteure avait dix ans. Il a obtenu le Prix littéraire du gouverneur général en 2010. Dès ses premiers mots, dès le titre, Thúy semble être le contraire de Vuong-Riddick. Tout signifiant a une multitude de signifiés, rien n'est seulement ce qu'il dit être, comme en vietnamien, d'ailleurs, ou chaque *ton* change le sens du mot. Dès le titre, *Ru*, il y a polysémie. Prononcé [-ry] en français, un ru est un petit ruisseau au sens propre, et écoulement de larmes, de sang ou d'argent au sens figuré. Prononcé [-ru] en vietnamien, « ru » signifie berceuse. L'ouvrage n'est pas à proprement parler un roman, ni même une autofiction, mais une série de tableaux relatant la douleur de l'exil et de l'immigration des *boat people*, l'écoulement de ses larmes et de son sang, de manière poétique.

Dès la deuxième page, il y a explication des accents du vietnamien, langue à huit tons dont les différences subtiles effraient les Européens :

Je m'appelle Nguyễn An Tịnh et ma mère, Nguyễn An Tĩnh. Mon nom est une simple variation du sien puisque seul un point sous le *i* me différencie d'elle, me distingue d'elle, me dissocie d'elle. J'étais une extension d'elle, même dans le sens de mon nom. En vietnamien, le sien veut dire « environnement paisible » et le mien, « intérieur paisible ». Par ces noms presque interchangeables, ma mère confirmait que j'étais une suite d'elle, que je continuerais son histoire.

L'Histoire du Vietnam, celle avec un grand H, a déjoué les plans de ma mère. Elle a jeté les accents de nos noms à l'eau quand elle nous a fait traverser le golfe du Siam, il y a trente ans. Elle a aussi dépouillé nos noms de leur sens, les réduisant à des sons à la fois étrangers et étranges dans la langue française. (Thúy 12)

De temps en temps, Thúy tient même un discours métalinguistique, par exemple quand elle parle des différents verbes « aimer » en vietnamien : « Dans le cas du vietnamien, il est possible de classifier, de quantifier le geste d'aimer par des mots spécifiques : aimer par goût (*thích*), aimer sans être amoureux (*thương*), aimer amoureusement (*yêu*), aimer avec ivresse (*mê*), aimer aveuglément (*mù quáng*), aimer par gratitude (*tình nghĩa*) » (Thúy 104). Il y a des clichés — le paradis et l'enfer — mais moins frappants que chez Vuong-Riddick, car perdus dans la polysémie, au lieu de ressortir, comme chez cette dernière, dans une écriture de documentariste. On trouve des comparaisons qui nous rappellent que le « je » fictif est né et a été élevé au Québec où se trouvent ses nouvelles références. Ainsi, il arrive que deux comparaisons soient offertes au lecteur, l'une provenant de sa culture asiatique transmise par ses parents, et l'autre de sa vie québécoise. Les mouches du camp de réfugiés « s'agrippaient aux branches d'un arbre mort, [...] se plaçaient l'une contre l'autre autour des branches *comme les baies d'une grappe de poivrier*, ou *comme des raisins de Corinthe* » (Thúy 35; c'est nous qui soulignons).

Il y a d'insolites comparaisons d'inspiration chrétienne, par exemple, toujours au camp des réfugiés, lorsque des milliers de vers sortent de la fosse septique « comme s'ils avaient été appelés par un messie » (Thúy 37). Le débarquement en Malaisie des *boat people* est rapproché cruellement de l'image de Bo Derek, la pin-up de *Playboy* : « nous avons tous sauté dans l'eau comme lors du déploiement d'une armée. [...] Je me souviens de cette image avec la même précision et la même clarté que celle de Bo Derek sortant de l'eau en courant dans son maillot couleur chair » (Thúy 106). Lorsque le bateau se désagrège sous l'effet d'un ouragan, c'est un spectacle à l'américaine :

> Notre bateau a été totalement détruit par les vagues d'une simple pluie, qui est tombée tout de suite après notre débarquement. Nous étions plus de deux cents à regarder ce spectacle en silence, les yeux embués par la pluie et la stupeur. Les planches de bois sautillaient l'une après l'autre sur la crête des vagues, comme dans un numéro de nage synchronisée. (Thúy 107)

Mentionnons enfin une description et mise en abyme de l'étang à lotus en banlieue de Hanoi « où il y avait toujours deux ou trois femmes au dos arqué, aux mains tremblantes, qui, assises dans le fond d'une barque ronde, se déplaçaient sur l'eau à l'aide d'une perche pour placer des feuilles de thé à l'intérieur des fleurs de lotus ouvertes. Elles y retournaient le jour suivant pour les recueillir, une à une, avant que les pétales se fanent, après que les feuilles emprisonnées avaient absorbé le parfum des pistils pendant la nuit. Elles me disaient que chaque feuille de thé conservait ainsi l'âme de ces fleurs éphémères » (Thúy 49).

Comme les femmes sur l'étang, l'auteure place chaque anecdote qui lui est contée dans la fleur de lotus de ses vignettes pour les conserver tout en leur conférant un caractère unique.

Conclusions

Avons-nous répondu aux questions que nous avions posées au départ? Comment les auteures issues du Vietnam rendent-elles la complexité des systèmes d'appellation caractéristique de leur langue d'origine où le seul moyen de faire référence à une personne en dehors de la hiérarchie patriarchale et du sexisme est de transformer les personnes en lieux? Nous transportent-elles dans leur pays d'origine au risque de nous y

perdre par leurs comparaisons ou leurs métaphores, ou font-elles du
« sur place » ?

Toutes deux problématisent la difficulté de traduire, en français ou en
anglais, le système d'appellation et les tons du vietnamien, dans lesquels
sont distillées les subtilités de la culture.

Kim Thúy se lance d'emblée dans le genre européanisé de
l'autofiction dans laquelle elle fait une toute petite place à certains accents
vietnamiens — son nom de famille, Thúy, et celui qui distingue son nom
de celui de sa mère, au début — et les intègre même à la graphie de son
roman. Vuong-Riddick ne fait aucune place à la graphie vietnamienne.
Souvent, Thúy fait des comparaisons par lesquelles elle fait se confronter
ses deux expériences si différentes. Grandir au Canada de *boat people*
vietnamiens représente un choc culturel dont on ne contrôle pas les
éléments marquants. Ainsi, le parfum auquel Thúy associe le Canada
a quelque chose de saugrenu et d'insolite : le Canada, c'est l'odeur de
l'assouplissant *Bounce* qu'elle sent dans les vêtements de son mari (Thúy
117).

Dans l'échec et l'absence de métaphores reliant deux lieux ou plus,
Vuong-Riddick semble créer un genre de hors-lieu : l' « espace global »
entre « deux rives indéterminées » où la situe le critique Dan Duffy
dans l'analyse qu'il fait de son recueil de poèmes antérieur, *Two Shores /
Deux rives* (Duffy 327, 335). Dans *The Evergreen Country* s'effectue
une nouvelle fois la « reterritorialisation linguistique et culturelle »
caractérisée par une étonnante intertextualité que Kathleen Kellett-Betsos
avait déjà repérée dans les poèmes bilingues de l'auteure (106). Vuong-
Riddick rend la subtilité et la retenue de ses cultures d'origine par une
écriture pratiquement dénuée de fioritures mais qui exprime *en anglais*,
et par *le non-dit*, la profondeur du sentiment qu'il faut deviner. Elle aussi
tient un discours métalinguistique occasionnel — sur la distanciation
respectueuse de la mère qu'on appelle « tante » et sur la difficulté de
la traduction des appellations hiérarchisées — mais finit par poser
tranquillement les jalons d'une *nouvelle* forme d'expression, analogue
dans son ton « en italiques » à celle d'origine, quoique différente
dans sa langue. Elle crée un pays d'imagination purement littéraire

— l' « evergreen country » du titre — toujours à retoucher et à fignoler, fuyant la réification.

Bref, on trouve chez Vuong-Riddick comme chez Thúy les phénomènes que Rocío G. Davis identifie comme représentant les contributions les plus importantes de la littérature canadienne asiatique des « Short-story cycles » : la subversion des formes traditionnelles — roman, nouvelles, mémoires — et le travail de la forme, lesquels sont simultanément au service de la recherche d'identité personnelle et communautaire typique de cette littérature et *ultime métaphore* et « textual enactment » (Davis 20) de la fragmentation et de la perte de ces identités. Ce caractère diégétique avant-garde exige à son tour l'engagement de lecteurs avertis et désireux d'interagir avec un texte différent de ceux auxquels ils sont habitués. Pour fermer le triangle *auteur-lecteur-contexte institutionnel* de la communication littéraire, nous estimons avec Davis que « l'usage plus libre du langage et du genre » que l'on constate chez les écrivains américano et canado-asiatiques, est le produit « d'une appréciation accrue de la part des Américains et des Canadiens d'origine asiatique de la diversité culturelle des sociétés nord-américaines contemporaines et de la conscience qu'ils ont une place dans la littérature nationale »[6] (Davis 9; c'est nous qui traduisons).

NOTES

1. Communication présentée au colloque « Le roman en Asie et ses traductions » qui s'est tenu à l'Université de Provence les 15 et 16 octobre 2009 et intitulée « Pour la localisation des métaphores et des comparaisons dans la traduction des romans vietnamiens : Illustration de cette démarche au travers de quelques extraits d'*Itinéraire d'enfance* de Duong Thu Huong ». Duong Thu Huong est une écrivaine vietnamienne née en 1947, auteure à présent d'une dizaine de romans. Pendant la guerre du Viêtnam, de 1967 à 1977, elle est chef d'une brigade de la jeunesse communiste, troupe d'animation artistique. Elle finit par être désillusionnée par une guerre dont les ennemis sont des compatriotes ainsi que par le régime communiste qu'elle critique ouvertement, et elle commence à écrire en 1980. Notons en particulier le roman *Les paradis aveugles*, paru en 1988, traduit en français en 1991 et qui lui valut le prix Femina ainsi que le prix littéraire de l'UNESCO.

2. C'est le premier roman de Duong Thu Huong, datant de 1985.

3. « Đây peut être interprété soit spatialement comme 'place-ci', soit temporellement comme 'maintenant'. Mais il est patent que đây est aussi susceptible d'un emploi de

pronom personnel et dans ce cas, l'une de ses valeurs sera 'je/moi'. Ainsi dây à lui seul réunit sous la même morphologie les trois valeurs de la triade énonciative, [...] le moi/ici/maintenant ou, sous une forme généralisante, personne/espace/temps » (Nguyễn 163).

4. Voir le site de la terminologie du Bureau de la traduction du gouvernement fédéral TERMIUM sous « evergreen document » les traductions proposées.

5. Chúng mình ne comporte pas d'accents dans le texte.

6. « an expression of a new confidence demonstrated in a freer use of language and genre that stems from the Asian American and Asian Canadian's increased appreciation of cultural diversity in contemporary North American societies and the awareness that they have that they have a place in the canons. »

BIBLIOGRAPHIE

Davis, Rocío G. *Transcultural Reinventions: Asian American and Asian Canadian Short-Story Cycles*. Toronto: TSAR Publications, 2001.

Duffy, Dan. « Beyond the National Tradition: Thuong Vuong-Riddick's *Two Shores / Deux rives* ». *American Babel: Literatures of the United States from Abnaki to Zuni*. Dir. Marc Shell. Cambridge, MA: Harvard University Press, 2002. 322-42.

Duras, Marguerite. *L'Amant*. Paris: Les éditions de Minuit, 1984.

Dương, Thu Hương. *Hành Trình Ngày Thơ Ấu*. 1985. *Itinéraire d'enfance*. Trad. Phuong Dang Tran. Paris: Sabine Wespieser Éditeur, 2007.

———. *Những thiên đường mù*. Hanoi: The Women's Publishing House, 1988. *Les Paradis Aveugles*. Trad. Des Femmes. Paris: Éditions Des Femmes, 1991. *Paradise of the Blind*. Trans. Phan Huy Duong and Nina McPherson. New York: William Morrow and Company, 1993.

Kellett-Betsos, Kathleen. « *Two Shores / Deux rives* de Thuong Vuong-Riddick : Errance et ironie ». *Littérature et culture francophones de Colombie-Britannique: Espaces culturels francophones I*. Dir. Guy Poirier, Jacqueline Viswanathan et Grazia Merler. Ottawa: Les Éditions David, 2004. 85-106.

Nguyễn, Phú Phong. *Questions de linguistique vietnamienne : Les classificateurs et les déictiques*. Paris: Presses de l'École française d'Extrême-Orient, 1995.

Paré, François. *Les Littératures de l'exiguïté*. Hearst: Les Éditions du Nordir, 1992.

Thúy, Kim. *Ru*. Longueuil: Les Éditions Libre Expression, 2009.

Vuong-Riddick, Thuong. *The Evergreen Country: A Memoir of Vietnam*. Regina: Hagios Press, 2007.

———. *Two Shores / Deux rives: Poems/Poèmes*. Vancouver: Ronsdale Press, 1995.

STANDING ON A RAINBOW

Reading in Place, Position, and Time

Margaret Mackey

Readers are material beings, placed in time and space, history and geography, and the material conditions of each reader have an inevitable impact on the reading experience. In this chapter, I address questions of how our understanding of literature may shift when we consider the materiality of the audience as well as of the text and of those responsible for its production. To increase awareness of the specificity of that material audience—in contrast to the widely studied concept of the mass audience—I focus here on two singular readers of one particular book. I seek to balance what I can ascertain about the readers against what I have been able to learn about the author, and against my assessment of at least some aspects of the text under consideration, *Stand on a Rainbow* by Mary Quayle Innis. I then assess the conceptual implications of this tiny case study for how we may develop a principled literary map.

As readers, we each have some sense of our own position in time and space, often almost by default. As students and scholars, we are sometimes invited to consider the importance of an author's position in time and space. As contemporary lay readers (rather than scholars), we may also be encouraged to pay heed to the author's persona as developed in websites, Twitter accounts, reading tours, and the like. None of these readerly stances is particularly rare; yet it is unusual to develop an awareness of a reading experience that takes account of the placement of both author and readers. One reason for the scarcity of such an approach, of course, is that readers are multiple and largely unknowable in that very plurality. A book, simply by the fact of its existence, is designed on the broadcast model of one-to-many; to consider it in terms of one-to-one is to alter the exploration of its address in radical ways.

My aim here is to explore how we understand a reading experience if we balance an assessment of the text and a study of the author with an equivalent focus on readers. Already, my articles are betraying my argument. In my small case study, the text and the author can be designated through the definitive article "the," but my specimen readers must more accurately be labelled in the singular as "a" reader—in this case two particular readers, one of whom influenced the other. "The" reader does not exist, except as a generic category almost too abstract to be useful at all—an audience member whose experience is represented in an aggregate description or even a set of statistics. Very often a reference to "the" reader camouflages a self-referential assumption that all readers behave just like the person making the reference. Unpacking this careless generalization is one of the challenges of this study of the readerly experience.

Here are the units of my study. In 1943, an author named Mary Quayle Innis published a book entitled *Stand on a Rainbow*. It tells the story of Leslie, a housewife and mother of three children, two sons and a daughter. In the 1950s, my own mother regularly borrowed this book from the public library and read it over and over again; she described it as her favourite novel. Curious about what it was that inspired her so greatly, I also read this book more than once—initially as a child of ten or eleven and later as an adult, purposefully looking back on my childhood reading experiences. At this later date, I came full circle in some ways by locating comments on Mary Quayle Innis by her own daughter. I also made a discovery that recontextualized the author for me and altered my own reading relationship with her text.

Conventional studies of literature "place" fiction in time and space (with associated cultural and ideological implications) and often do the same for an author. My project entails an equivalent "placement" effort of two readers. Obviously not every reader of a book can be located in such a singular way, but I hope at least to reveal a standard omission in the conventional scholarly account of literature and to show how that absence can lead to an imbalance in our literary understanding that is so normalized as to be almost invisible.

The Story of the Characters

Stand on a Rainbow recounts a year in the life of Leslie Everett, and the book is told almost entirely through her perspective. Her husband, Arthur, is barely a character in this domestic novel, but her three children have sharply defined personalities. Leslie herself lacks confidence in her own judgement and defers frequently to her decisive fourteen-year-old son, John. The other children are Sheila, aged ten, and Miles, aged eight.

Stand on a Rainbow is a book about places, seasons, relationships, and emotional atmospheres. Not a lot actually happens in this novel. Events are summed up fairly explicitly by Leslie's reverie as she waits for Sheila to play her piece in the piano recital: "Leslie began to knit at an over-sized sock, thinking how her year was parcelled out like the year of a department store with its August—furniture, January—white sales. After the summer holidays her schedule ran, October–November–December, getting ready for Christmas; January–February, colds and at least one contagious disease; March–April, letting down her daughter's dresses and taking up her own; May–June, annual meetings and recitals" (Innis 219).

Leslie's is a pedestrian enough life for most of the year, punctuated by blissful summers at the cottage, which are described as a poem compared to "the long prose of the year" (Innis 11). There are times when Leslie seems to wallow in the drudgery of her existence, even in the face of seasonal changes that explicitly offer opportunities for more lyrical reflection:

On the Saturday before his birthday they set out. It was a radiant autumn day; looking out at breakfast time Leslie had thought not of orange maples, bronze oaks and the low-burning fire of scarlet sumac but of the fact that it would be a perfect day on which to wash the last of the blankets. She wanted to wash blankets, to make pear jam, to finish Sheila's new jumper dress. (95)

To want to get on with one's work is an honourable enough impulse, but as a reader I find this paragraph depressing.

Leslie is not impervious to the glories of the northern seasons, however. There is an ecstatic mid-book chapter in which she manages to get out into the heart of an ice storm. All three children are ill and she has been housebound for many days, but Arthur (who "had not come home on purpose to let her go out since Miles was a baby" [Innis 155]) actually leaves the office early, ostensibly to allow her to go to a tea organized by a friend. Instead, Leslie surreptitiously wanders through the glittering urban landscape: "She had not come out a moment too soon....Shadows fell long and sharp, painting blue images of crystal trees upon the porcelain earth....Houses had become mere scaffolding to hold draperies of diamond vine and trellis, flounces of crystal fringe....She had collected ice storms all her life and never a lovelier one than this" (156–57).

At another particularly cold stage in the long winter of this book, Leslie mulls over what she knows and imagines about a family who, in 1825, lived where her house now stands, and whose story she found in a pamphlet from the library. She thinks of them as "the other people" (177):

The children of the other people had waked crying at night and there had been no more blankets to give them. In the morning the loaf had to be sawn like a block of wood and Ruthie, running to the ox-stable, had frozen her cheeks and ears. Leslie pictured the ox-stable as standing where her garage stood and on each side of the bleak white street she saw the gray fence of forest drawn mena-cingly together. In that clearing during her first winter, one of the women had recorded her wish that the summer heat and winter cold, both so violent, could be carded through one another to make a proper climate. How many women on this ground had wished that? (178)

Such inner musing is the main focus of this book. Twenty-first-century readers may be frustrated with Arthur's overblown sense of male entitlement, but it does not seem to occur to Leslie to do anything but take it for granted. Her frustration lies largely with herself. She does not read the ambitious books she borrows from the library; she does not practise the piano; she does not discipline her children sufficiently. The quotidian episodes march forward quietly, with some joy, some irritation, some delight in the children, some unspoken annoyance at the headlong way they pursue life while their mother picks up the pieces behind them, with almost no mention of the absent Arthur.

Innis published forty-five short stories between 1938 and 1947, most in *Saturday Night*, and, according to the note in the Mary Quayle Innis fonds held at the University of Waterloo Library, "Several of these were rewritten for inclusion in *Stand on a Rainbow* (1943), an autobiographical 'novel.'" Yet Leslie never does anything intellectually independent such as publish short stories; the autobiographical links fall short of a complete match-up. From a contemporary perspective, Leslie's life seems to consist of an enormous quotient of drudgery.

The novel's title comes from a brief episode in the book. Leslie indulges in one of the superstitions of her childhood: she stamps one hand into the other on seeing a white horse. Her sons and daughter roll their eyes and she perceives in their dismissal of her quaint ways a new world that is deficient in the old magic. It soon becomes apparent, however, that the three have their own childish rituals. Sheila suddenly stands still, and then accounts for her conduct in these terms: "'I was wishing,' she explained. 'You stand on a rainbow and wish.' She pointed to an iridescent oil stain on the pavement" (196). Leslie is encouraged to discover that superstition still triumphs occasionally, even if in more modern guise, and seems to see it as a victory for romance.

The Story of the First Reader

Elizabeth McCurdy, my mother, has advanced Alzheimer's. Additionally, in 2007 she suffered a small but specific stroke that more or less destroyed her capacity to speak coherent sentences. From time to time, however, some important sentiment that can be expressed in a very short sentence will defeat the language scrambler in her brain. Not long after her debilitating stroke, I found *Stand on a Rainbow* on her bookshelf and asked if I could borrow it. She agreed and managed one of her rare short remarks: "I love that book."

My mother's copy is a library discard, but it does not indicate the name of the library. Inside the book I found a bookmark from Munro's Bookstore, which indicates that she continued to read this story after she and my father moved to Victoria in 1994 when she was seventy-one. If that is the case, her encounters with this novel spanned the best part of forty years and maybe more.

Stand on a Rainbow was published in 1943, the year my mother married my father. I do not know when she first read it. The parallels between the events of the book and her personal life are many. Although the geography of the autobiographical narrative is not specified, Mary Quayle Innis and her husband lived and worked in the Toronto region. The book begins and ends in cottage country, and the case for a southern Ontario setting is reasonably strong.

My mother grew up in Halifax in the 1920s and 1930s. At one point, her family was affluent enough to hire a single maid-of-all-work to help my grandmother. At another stage, during the Depression, times were so hard that there were days when the six children ate porridge for breakfast and porridge again for supper because their parents could afford only one proper meal a day (and that one heavy on potatoes). But during at least two summers, they rented a cottage in Merigomish, Nova Scotia, and my mother knew the intense pleasures of the summer escape that are described vividly in this book. Leslie is devoted to the charms of berry picking (making jam is her favourite domestic activity). My mother also liked to pick berries but she was even more attracted to the delights of wild flowers, and was knowledgeable about their names and habitats.

Leslie's choice is more domestic and productive; my mother's preference led to nothing but pleasure. I strongly suspect that the lyrical sections of the book, limning the joys of summer in the country or an ice storm in the city, spoke to her in important ways. Contemporary readers often value "relatability," a neologism that perhaps arises directly out of current reading practices; while I am certain my mother "related" to *Stand on a Rainbow*, I believe she also relished the delights of the kind of lyrical description that featured more prominently in an earlier age of vernacular reading than in today's relatable novels. Readers belong to their time as well as to their place.

Family financial restrictions prevented my mother from going to university. She took commercial classes after high school and earned her living as a secretary. She married young and was a stay-at-home mother like Leslie, eventually with five children. In 1950, our family moved to Newfoundland from Nova Scotia, and she set about making a new home.

In a perfect world, I would have had the opportunity to interview my mother about her affection for this book. In reality, the insidious destruction of dementia was well underway long before I had the idea of revisiting my own childhood literacy. I am very, very reluctant to put words into her mouth, or even to speculate too impertinently about the hold of this book on her imagination. The parallels are vivid: Halifax has the long winter and inadequate spring of *Stand on a Rainbow*; local history is important in Nova Scotia and, in her youth, my mother might well have had some sense of "the other people," one of the more evocative ingredients of Innis's novel. She certainly regretted never having had the chance for an education, so I am sure Leslie's frustrations resonated very deeply with her. On the more positive side, she enjoyed the evocation of summer recreations and childhood memories. She could read herself into this story in many deep and real ways, vivify it through the experience of her own felt life. There were, of course, few Canadian novels that treated the more or less contemporary world of a housewife and mother, so it is perhaps not surprising that my mother loved this one so fiercely.

The lifelong love affair between a reader and a particular book is a complex topic, and not one that necessarily receives the attention it deserves. To what extent did this book support and confirm my mother's life decisions? To what extent may it have consoled her for decisions she regretted? What it did do, I am certain, was provide her with some assurance that her own experiences were seen, recorded, shaped, and expressed in the form of a novel she could hold, borrow, read, and eventually own. She could stand outside these experiences and revisit them, re-savour the felt life in a newly framed perspective, feel the force of its limitations as perceived by another, sympathetic point of view—and perhaps play with its possibilities and alternatives.

It is very possible that she also read the book in more aesthetic and/or resistant ways, but I do not know. My very strong sense has always been that this book offered my mother a reading of validation. I cannot definitively account for all the sources of appeal in this book, but I can testify to her reiterated statements of its power in her life.

The Story of the Author

In 2007, the name Mary Quayle Innis meant little to me beyond her authorship of *Stand on a Rainbow*. When I began to seek out information about her, I made one of those discoveries that takes previous insights and gives them a vigorous shaking-out.

The Innis who gave Mary Quayle her married surname was Harold Innis, well-known Canadian communications scholar and a major influence on Marshall McLuhan. In addition to her novel, Mary Quayle Innis wrote *An Economic History of Canada*, which became a standard university textbook in its revised edition (also published in 1943). After Harold Innis died, she served as dean of women at University College in Toronto for nine years, and was a Canadian delegate to the Commonwealth Conference on Education in Oxford in 1959. She edited her husband's work, and communications scholar J. David Black has devoted an extensive article to teasing out ways in which her own scholarly interests and background may have fed into Harold Innis's widely known theories of communication.

Mary Quayle Innis herself, says Black, "thought her life and her writing inseparable" (435). According to Innis's daughter Anne, *Stand on a*

Rainbow is highly autobiographical: "The novel is an account of a year in the life of a middle-class family, and according to Anne Innis Dagg, is drawn almost entirely from incidents in Mary's domestic life" (Black 437). Mary Quayle Innis, according to her daughter, was frustrated at being taken only as an academic wife, not as an academic in her own right (Black 437). The frustration certainly made its way into the novel but her autonomous academic achievements did not.

There is no reason, of course, why a novel, even an autobiographical novel, need represent every facet of an author's life. Mary Quayle Innis may well have been interested in the constraints on the life of an "average" suburban mother. Be that as it may, she certainly made an authorial choice to reduce Leslie's options and to restrict both her outer and inner life to intensely domestic concerns.

No doubt some of the constrictions are linked to the time and space of the era. Here is a scene in which Leslie and the two younger children are late coming home: "Arthur stood at the window, John waited in the hall, both of them with the restless and expectant air of hungry men in a house where the kitchen is empty" (Innis 170). Even when Arthur later apologizes, his sense of responsibility is highly limited: "I should have put the kettle on but I brought some work home and I had started on it" (172). My own father was never so useless. Yet that sense of always being responsible for both the drudgery and the satisfactions of domestic order must nevertheless have dogged my mother's days.

The Story of the Second Reader

ADOLESCENT READING

I remember reading *Stand on a Rainbow* more than once at the age of ten or eleven, just because I knew my mother loved it, and I wanted to see what she admired so much. The book did an adequate job of transporting me to another world, but I did not find it gripping. I lacked some of my mother's immediate hooks into the story: I had no experience of spending a full summer in a cottage away from home (at most we made day trips to visit friends in cabins not far from town). I had no sense of any "other people" in my city, which for centuries was a temporary summer shelter for European fishermen rather than a permanent settlement. Most crucially, perhaps, I had not lived a housewife's life.

I did, of course, recognize the family dynamics that pulse through the book. But the picture of adulthood the novel painted was not one that appealed to me, though I certainly recognized it from my own life and from other reading material that surrounded me.

With books where I was more closely aligned with the implied reader, I could import my own experiences into my interpretation. With adult materials, it was more complicated. In many ways, because I was "reading up," looking outside my own experience to sample adult life, I had to "place" myself within the intertext of other adult materials. My own childish experience could offer only limited grounding to my reading of Innis's novel. And of course the available intertextual references were also "placed"—temporally, spatially, and ideologically.

Much of what Innis's book might have told me about my mother's life in the early 1960s was a message I did not want to hear. I was just beginning to understand that I would not be a girl forever, that someday I would become a woman. For all the considerable familiarity of its terms of reference, *Stand on a Rainbow* did not show me a world to which I aspired.

Overall, my best recollection (articulated in terms I could not have used at the time) is that, far from participating in a reading of validation as my mother did, my own encounters with this book involved a kind of reading as closing-down, a restriction of possibilities, a reading of disappointment.

ADULT RE-READING

I do not have enough information to know whether my mother changed her attitude in relation to *Stand on a Rainbow* over the course of her reading life. I suspect not, given her comment to me in her old age, but I have no way of confirming my suspicion. I, however, changed from a child reader to a highly educated and "professional" adult reader in the decades between my first and later readings of this book.

In 2007, as I began to consider the possibilities of a project involving the re-assembling of as many materials as possible from the textual universe within which I became literate, I knew that my mother's books would be important to my collection. My first re-reading of this title in 2007 left me simply dispirited. The source of this book's appeal to my mother was even more baffling to me as an adult. I could not ask her, and the only part of the book that evoked any positive response for me in 2007 was the notion of "the other people"—and that chiefly as a cause for regret, that my education in local history had been so wanting that my imagination had never been charged with any curiosity about the past of my own city. While I could appreciate the felt detail in Innis's account of a domestic life, I could not make myself want to read myself "into" its restrictions and limitations. I put the book aside.

In the summer of 2011, I thought the time had come to return to the book and took the standard scholarly step of seeing what I could learn about the author. The biographical reference to Harold Innis caught me completely by surprise. Mary Quayle Innis's own scholarly, literary, and public record was another shock. When I re-read the book yet again, I was attending to absences as well as presences. Leslie's diffidence about herself, compounded by the book's lack of any description of a single independent achievement on her part, took a different shape in my mind when outlined against the other biographical components of Innis's life, the experiences that were not translated into this fiction.

Mary Quayle Innis was writing for adults. She was not writing material for little girls to cut their developmental teeth on—and not writing for some academic woman of the future, either. As a pre-adolescent in the early 1960s, I was beginning to think about finding my place as a grown-up. The place offered in this book was discouraging, and made almost no room for an adult female life outside the yoke of domestic labour. I find it hard to set aside my contemporary self, angered on behalf of my child self, to look dispassionately at what Innis did achieve in this novel. In part this anger arises from the supporting cast of so many other female authors in the 1960s telling the same destructive story; Innis at least supplies the wistfulness and uncertainty that was the shadow of this apparently "fulfilled" woman's life.

What was Mary Quayle Innis doing as she excised her own intellectual interests in developing her autobiographically based story of Leslie? She certainly succeeded in presenting a particular set of choices. In some ways, Leslie embodies the issue that was later highlighted by Betty Friedan in *The Feminine Mystique* as "the problem that has no name" (15)—the depression that leads to a kind of housewifely anomie in the face of stifled talents and foreclosed opportunities. In her restricted portrait of Leslie, Innis presents one logical outcome of being the kind of woman society claimed to want and need.

As an adult looking back on my childhood reading, would I have been so sharply troubled by *Stand on a Rainbow* if it had been written by Mrs. George (or John or Joe) Innis (let alone Ms. Georgina Innis)? Was it only the discrepancy between Innis's life and her autobiographical novel that irritated me? I think I have been a resistant reader of Innis's book from my earliest encounters with her story, and being given a righteous finger to wag at its hypocritical lacunae was initially very satisfying. I now realize that Innis's total life experiences must have been rather closer to my own than Leslie's could ever be. Innis, too, was an academic woman who took time out to raise children. She chose to write her novel about the domestic world rather than the academy, a choice to which she is as entitled as any other writer.

Once I learned these basic biographical facts, however, I could not "unread" them out of my response to the novel. My 2011 reading differed from my 2007 encounter with the book because I read the protagonist's life against the backdrop of the author's more varied biography. As a reader, I am uneasy about Leslie's lack of self-confidence and willingness to be a drudge to the unworthy and ungrateful Arthur. I know women did behave this way in the 1940s, but Mary Quayle Innis did not, and she deliberately chose to omit other sources of satisfaction from her heroine's life. How much of the achievement of this novel lies in its creation of an interior life experienced within the confines of an inexorable and utterly accepted domesticity? Is it simultaneously a novel of protest? Leslie certainly does not question the conditions of her life; she seems only to question herself. In what ways is such a novel "readable" today? Does this book lend itself to resistant reading only in anachronistic ways? How difficult would it be for a contemporary young woman to read this novel compliantly?

In spite of the ways in which her own accomplishments meant that Mary Quayle Innis was living a life somewhat less constricted than her protagonist's, she created an "autobiographical" narrative of frustration, even while acknowledging the joys of being alive in a prosperous and comfortable society. To what extent was she simply recording a problem, even as she inadvertently extended her story's reach by showing little girls (never her chosen implied readers) that the future really might be dreary?

The iniquities for women of the postwar retreat to home and the suburbs have been well rehearsed. Innis's book suggests that the problem goes back further in time, but otherwise it describes a familiar issue. I am unlikely to add significantly to this debate by contributing my own childish grievances from that era. Nor do I want to put words into the mouth of my silenced mother. In fact, an ideological discussion of the historical role of women is not my main interest in this chapter. Instead, I am intrigued by the implications of such ideology for the study of reader reception.

Divergent Readers

My first reading position as a child interloper, outside the implied address of this novel, highlights questions about the place of readers in our literary landscape. Once this orange-and-pink hardback was let loose on the world, Innis and her publishers lost control of the readership. In practical terms, that is certainly a basic truth about publishing and, in a way, marks the end of the story, so to speak. In theoretical terms, however, I think we need to make more room for the counterweight to the author that is created by the engagement of many individual readers, even if specific details necessarily remain wanting.

As a white, middle-class female adult, I was not so far from the implied reader inscribed in this story; as a child, I was radically outside some of the terms of its address. My example is a very small case of the ways in which actual readers can distort the singular direction of the notional communicative "arrow" from writer to recipient. This account of me and my mother as two divergent readers is historically not very important, but theoretically I think it provides a significant reminder. Moreover, my own experience is bifurcated; I was by no means the same reader in 1961 as I was in 2007, and I was operating from a different knowledge base again in 2011.

Readers are notoriously hard to pin down and impossible to render stable. My mother's unchanging ardour for this book possibly reflects her delight at her identification with the implied reader; for Canadian readers at that time, this was a relatively unusual experience, one she clearly cherished. But my own reading relationship with this book was highly mutable and always resistant. My mother and I were two closely connected readers but we never made the same link to this story—nor could we.

An approach that takes account of the force supplied by readers in many ways localizes a text through the individual connections its various readers make to its fictional structures. Yet in many real ways, that local life is the only existence a novel can have. It changes the nature of the scholarly relationship to that text if, in addition to attending to the prism, we also acknowledge all the rainbows on the wall. But making room for individual readers in our schema of literature is an important step to consider.

Grounded Reading

My mother and I occupied the same space and time as we read *Stand on a Rainbow* in the early 1960s in St. John's, Newfoundland. But how we related our reading to our situation in time and space was different in a variety of vital ways.

Even a case study of two opens the door to a more plural approach to this or any novel. If we confine our study of this novel to the limits of Mary Quayle Innis's own trajectories, decisions, and life patterns, we distort the picture of a work of literature's own movement through time and space. I have attempted to define two examples of the book's trajectory after it left Innis's hands through the actions and imaginings of two different, though related readers. The point about any novel, however, is that it is always in motion through time and space when it is being read, savoured, analyzed, and written about—"carded through" the lives of its readers. The significance of a reader's placement in time and space is conventionally elided in much scholarly study, but that evaporation of the reader into some kind of impersonal analysis is itself a fiction. Even as we may have to create an empty set to represent the plurality of potential readers in time and space, we need also to make allowance for the located and specific nature of the scholar who presents "a" reading. No reader is disembodied; no reader exists outside of time and space. Acknowledging the force of that locatedness on the part of readers allows us to attend properly to the dynamics of reading that make literature what it is. Within the larger context of this scholarly collection, for example, this chapter is unusually autobiographical; but I bring the same history and experience to all my reading, no matter how neutrally and academically I write about a book.

Any mapping of a novel that tries to include its total readership would be utterly illegible, an irony of the one-to-many schema. Yet the novel comes to life only in the minds of individual readers and it should be possible to register the weight of that fact in some way. What would happen to our scholarship if the plenitude of digital space allowed us to consider a database category along the lines of "known readers of this novel," for example? How would such a change affect the balance of power that has for so many years privileged the author and rendered interpreters bodiless and placeless—a neutered stance that belies important elements of the accomplishment of any work of fiction that successfully reaches others?

By "known readers of this novel," I do not mean simple sales or borrowing figures—although, despite inherent limitations, such data would be of considerable interest if rendered specific. (How well did *Stand on a Rainbow* sell? Where did it sell well? How many libraries bought how many copies? In which branches were these copies placed? How many people borrowed them and from where?) In historical terms, these are not questions we may readily answer (although digital point-of-sale information and radio frequency identification technology used in libraries may well enable us to gather more substantial statistics in the future). But even acknowledging the importance of such questions alters an invisibly skewed balance of power between authors, critics, and readers. Adding responses from specific readers (lay and professional alike) to a database built to describe a literary culture also has the potential to enhance our understanding of literature and its influence on readers. Placing authors and readers on the same map, however conceptually or notionally, changes and enriches the literary landscape and alters how we think about the relationship between them.

The material audience is part of the world of literature. As critic Danielle Fuller suggests, we need to attend to "the importance of developing nuanced analyses of non-academic reading practices and theories capable of explaining the pleasures, politics, and social relations that reading practices both shape and resist" (31). One way of highlighting the importance of such readers and reading practices is simply to map them.

With our massive digital affordances, we are in a position to consider ways in which we might mark the activities and achievements of a book's readers located in time and space. Without belabouring the metaphor too heavily, current book history is indeed standing on a rainbow of varied and individual private responses to the materials whose details we otherwise record carefully—and if we simply stamp on it, the rainbow will dissolve into an oil slick of indecipherable and apparently insignificant uniformity. How can we acknowledge and make space for the variegated and transient power of that rainbow in our scholarly record keeping? Is it not time to take up that challenge?

WORKS CITED

Black, J. David. "'Both of Us Can Move Mountains': Mary Quayle Innis and Her Relationship to Harold Innis' Legacy." *Canadian Journal of Communication* 28 (2003): 433–47.

Friedan, Betty. *The Feminine Mystique*. New York: Dell, 1963.

Fuller, Danielle. "Listening to the Readers of 'Canada Reads.'" *Canadian Literature* 193 (Summer 2007): 11–34.

Innis, Mary Quayle. Mary Quayle Innis fonds. GA 127. Special Collections, University of Waterloo Library. https://uwaterloo.ca/library/special-collections-archives/collections/innis-mary-quayle-fonds

———. *Stand on a Rainbow*. Toronto: William Collins, 1943.

Contributors / Collaborateurs

Jeffery Antoniuk is a senior programmer and analyst with the Canadian Writing Research Collaboratory at the University of Alberta. In 2002, he started playing a supporting role in the Orlando Project and the online publication of *Orlando: Women's Writing in the British Isles from the Beginnings to the Present* by Cambridge University Press in 2006. He holds an MSC in computing science.

Susan Brown is professor of English at the University of Guelph and visiting professor at the University of Alberta. She researches Victorian literature, women's writing, and digital humanities. All of these interests inform *Orlando: Women's Writing in the British Isles from the Beginnings to the Present*, an ongoing experiment in digital literary history published online since 2006 by Cambridge University Press, which she directs and co-edits with Patricia Clements and Isobel Grundy. She leads development of the Canadian Writing Research Collaboratory, an online repository and research environment for literary studies in and about Canada.

Constance Crompton is assistant professor of digital humanities at the University of British Columbia's Okanagan campus. A digital humanist with research interests in queer history, Victorian popular and visual culture, and scholarly editing, she co-directs the Lesbian and Gay Liberation in Canada project. Her work has been published in the *Victorian Review*, *Nineteenth-Century Gender Studies*, and the UBC *Law Review*.

Ravit H. David manages the e-book service for all Ontario universities at Scholars Portal, University of Toronto. She holds a PHD in English modernism and an MLS in library and information studies. She specializes in digital publishing, and in her research she focuses on increasing the discoverability of digital collections, metadata, and e-books. She is also the primary contributor to CWRC's pilot project, Division of Space: Contextualizing Advertisements in Canadian Modernist Periodicals.

Patricia Demers, Distinguished University Professor of English and Comparative Literature at the University of Alberta, teaches and researches in the field of women's writing, with specific emphasis on early modern and contemporary Canadian works. With Marie Carrière she has co-edited a volume of essays from the first CWRC conference, *Regenerations: Canadian Women's Writing / Régénérations: Écriture des femmes au Canada* (University of Alberta Press, 2014).

Shawn DeSouza-Coelho is an MA candidate at the University of Waterloo (English, Experimental Digital Media) focusing on models and methodologies of game design as they pertain to adaptation and creation. His book, *Metamagic: An Introduction* (2013), explores the art of magic as a medium for discourse. A research associate with the University of Waterloo, he is currently investigating the relationships between traditional theatre practice and modern technology.

Cecily Devereux is professor in the Department of English and Film Studies at the University of Alberta. Her current research in the representation and circulation of women as erotic dancers in late nineteenth- and early twentieth-century North America arises from research on English-Canadian women writers of the same period, most of whom were not erotic dancers, and from the complicated relationships of mobile, pseud-onymous, and often extra-national or nationally ambiguous women to histories of settler subjectivity in literary and other discourse. She teaches courses in chick lit, gender and sexuality, popular fiction, and hysteria's cultural representation, as well as in Canadian literature.

Teresa M. Dobson is associate professor of Language and Literacy Education at the University of British Columbia. Her primary areas of research are digital humanities, literary education, and digital liter-acy. She is a member of several funded international teams researching in these areas and has published widely in humanities and education journals.

Sandra Gabriele is associate professor in the Department of Design at York University and has been practising and teaching graphic design for over thirty years. Her research interests are in the area of typography and information design, with a focus on legibility. Projects include the digital representation of large text collections and patient safety initiatives involv-ing graphic design.

Isobel Grundy is professor emeritus in the Department of English and Film Studies at the University of Alberta. With Susan Brown and Patricia Clements, she established the groundbreaking Orlando Project, the first full, collaborative scholarly history of women's writing in the British Isles, and produced *Orlando: Women's Writing in the British Isles from the Beginnings to the Present*, published online since 2006 by Cambridge University Press. She is the author of *Lady Mary Wortley Montagu: Comet of the Enlightenment* (1999), and co-author with Virginia Blain and Patricia Clements of *The Feminist Companion to Literature in English: Women Writers from the Middle Ages to the Present* (1990).

Andrea Hasenbank is a PHD candidate at the University of Alberta, where she is a Killam Memorial Scholar and a past doctoral fellow of Editing Modernism in Canada, as well as project co-ordinator for the Proletarian Literature & Arts project. Her research is grounded in the area of print history with a focus on the intersections between print, politics, and propaganda. As part of EMiC, she is editing a volume of Canadian manifesto print, while her dissertation, "Proletarian Publics: Leftist and Labour Print in Canada, 1930–1939," examines radical pamphlets circulating in western Canada during the Depression years.

Paul Hjartarson, professor emeritus in English and Film Studies, leads the Editing Modernism in Canada research group at the University of Alberta (EMiC UA). His scholarly work is on life writing, Canadian literature, modernism, print culture, and the digital humanities. In 2014, with Shirley Neuman, he published *The Thinking Heart: The Literary Archive of Wilfred Watson*, the catalogue of an exhibition the authors curated in Bruce Peel Special Collections. With Gregory Betts and Kristine Smitka, he is co-editing *Counterblasting Canada: Into the Social and Intellectual Vortex of Wyndham Lewis, Marshall McLuhan, Sheila Watson, and Wilfred Watson*, a collection of essays that assesses the importance of McLuhan's media theories for Canadian writers and artists, particularly the Watsons.

Kathleen Kellett est professeure agrégée au département des langues, littératures et cultures de l'Université Ryerson. Elle est titulaire d'un doctorat de l'Université de Toronto, et spécialiste en littérature québécoise. Ses travaux de recherche actuels portent sur la littérature franco-canadienne minoritaire, surtout en Ontario français, ainsi que la littérature migrante au Canada. Elle a publié, entre autres, des articles sur Anne Hébert, Antonine Maillet, Daniel Poliquin, et Thuong Vuong-Riddick.

Sasha Kovacs is a PHD candidate at the University of Toronto, Department of Drama, Theatre, and Performance Studies. She currently is completing her dissertation on the performances of E. Pauline Johnson

Tekahionwake. She teaches courses in Canadian theatre history at Ryerson Theatre School and acting at the University of Toronto. Most recently, she guest co-edited the Winter 2015 issue of *Canadian Theatre Review* on Performance and Human Rights in the Americas. Sasha is also a founding member of the Toronto-based theatre company Ars Mechanica.

Vanessa Lent holds a PHD in Canadian literature. Her work focused on late modernism in Canadian literature. In particular, her dissertation, "'I am not I': Late Modernism and Metafiction in Canadian Prose," traces a number of collaborative networks between writers and artists in mid-twentieth-century Canada. She currently lives and teaches in Halifax, Nova Scotia.

Margaret Mackey is professor in the School of Library and Information Studies at the University of Alberta. She teaches and researches in the area of reading and multimodal literacy. Her most recent book is *Narrative Pleasures in Young Adult Novels, Films, and Video Games* (Palgrave Macmillan, 2011). Her current research project entails an in-depth study of all the materials with which she herself became literate in Newfoundland in the 1950s: children's and adult literature, school textbooks, newspapers and magazines, Sunday school materials, Brownie handbooks, recipes, knitting patterns, radio and television programs, movies, museum exhibits, and much more.

Breanna Mroczek worked on the Orlando Project from 2011 to 2012 as a research assistant and geomapping tester. She holds an MA in English from the University of Alberta (2012) and a BA (Honours) in English from the University of Calgary (2011). Her research projects and interests include digital humanities, postmodern literature, and violence and trauma theory. She is currently the editor of *Where Calgary* magazine and assistant editor of *Glass Buffalo* magazine.

Bethany Nowviskie is director of Digital Research and Scholarship at the University of Virginia Library, special advisor to the UVa Provost, and sitting past president of the Association for Computers and the Humanities. Nowviskie holds a PHD in English from the University of Virginia, and her research interests lie in the intersection of algorithmic or procedural method with traditional humanities interpretation. Among her recent projects at the University of Virginia Scholars' Lab (which she also directs) is Neatline, a digital tool for handcrafted, interactive spatial, and temporal storytelling.

Ruth Panofsky is professor of English at Ryerson University. She organized the second CWRC conference, "Space / Place / Play," held at Ryerson University in October 2011. Under the aegis of Editing Modernism in Canada, she completed the first critical edition (with digital apparatus) of the collected poetry of Miriam Waddington (University of Ottawa Press, 2014). She is also the author of *The Literary Legacy of the Macmillan Company of Canada: Making Books and Mapping Culture* (University of Toronto Press, 2012).

Mariana Paredes-Olea joined the Orlando Project in January 2009 as textbase manager. She holds an MA in humanities computing from the University of Alberta (2009) and an MA in Spanish from the University of Toronto (2006). Her research interests include the politics of print and the role of electronic publishing in the history of text. She also is interested in representations of science and technology in literature and popular culture. In 2010, she joined the Canadian Writing Research Collaboratory as metadata co-ordinator, where she contributes to the process of modelling digital objects with a focus on interoperability across repositories and different types of digital media.

Harvey Quamen is associate professor of English and humanities computing at the University of Alberta, where he teaches courses on digital humanities, cyberculture, posthumanism, and database development. He also teaches an annual database course at the Digital Humanities

Summer Institute at the University of Victoria. His research interests include "big data" humanities, including text mining, social network analysis, and data visualizations. Recent publications include "The Limits of Modelling: Database Culture and the Humanities" in *Scholarly and Research Communication* and (as co-author) "Before the Beginning: The Formation of Humanities Computing as a Discipline in Canada" in *Digital Studies.*

Jennifer Roberts-Smith is associate professor of drama at the University of Waterloo, where she directs departmental productions and teaches acting and theatre history. She is principal investigator for the SSRHC-funded Simulated Environment for Theatre project and associate co-editor, performance for *Queen's Men Editions.* In 2014, she won an Ontario Early Researcher award for her ongoing work on games and other digital pedagogical tools with the Stratford Festival. She publishes on early English theatre, Shakespeare's language, and theatre and technology.

Omar Rodriguez-Arenas is a computer analyst at the University of Alberta's Arts Resource Centre. He holds MSC (University of Alberta, 2010) and BSC (University of Sonora, 2004) degrees in computing science. As part of his research at the University of Alberta's Graphics Lab, he worked on simulations of non-Newtonian fluids. His current research interests include real-time 3D graphics, physically based animation, and humanities visualization.

Mary-Jo Romaniuk has held various roles in the Learning Services portfolio of University of Alberta Libraries as director and associate vice-provost, having overall responsibilities for budget and finance, fund development, communication and strategic planning across the portfolio units. She spent 2008 on secondment to the Office of the Provost. Immediately prior to her current appointment in 2009, she held the position of associate university librarian, Information and Financial Services.

Stan Ruecker is associate professor at the IIT Institute of Design in Chicago, with current research interests in the areas of humanities visualization, the future of reading, and information design. He holds a PHD, MDES, MA, BSC Hons, and BA. He has supervised graduate students and led seminars on experimental interface design, knowledge management and analysis, research methods, and interdisciplinary research project management. His work focuses on developing prototypes to support the hermeneutic or interpretive process.

Lori Saint-Martin is professor in the Department of Literary Studies at the University of Quebec in Montreal. She has published three collections of short stories, including *Mathématiques intimes* (2014), and a novel, *Les portes closes* (2013). In addition to critical editions of two major Quebec women writers, Anne Hébert and Germaine Guèvremont, she is the author of over a dozen scholarly works on women's writing in Quebec. Her latest non-fiction works are *Au-delà du Nom. La question du père dans la littérature québécoise actuelle* (2010) and *Postures viriles, ce que dit la presse masculine* (2011). With Paul Gagné, she has translated more than eighty Canadian works of fiction and non-fiction into French, winning the Governor General's Award in 2000 and 2007. She received the Career Award for Excellence in Research-Creation from the Université du Québec network of universities in 2010 and the Prix André-Laurendeau, a career award for the humanities granted by ACFAS (Association canadienne francophone pour le savoir), in 2013.

Michelle Schwartz is research associate in the Learning & Teaching Office at Ryerson University and a member of the Ryerson Centre for Digital Humanities. She holds a master's in library and information science, and is interested in exploring the ways that radical queer spaces intersect with libraries and archives. She is an editor and writer for *Shameless*, an independent feminist magazine for young women and trans youth, and co-directs the Lesbian and Gay Liberation in Canada project.

Stéfan Sinclair is associate professor of digital humanities at McGill University. His primary area of research is in the design, development, usage, and theorization of tools for the digital humanities, especially for text analysis and visualization. His co-authored book, *Visual Interface Design for Digital Cultural Heritage* (with Milena Radzikowska and Stan Ruecker), was released in 2011 by Ashgate Press.

Mireille Mai Truong est chargée de cours au département des langues, littératures et cultures de l'Université Ryerson. Ses recherches pluridisciplinaires portent, entre autres, sur les littératures coloniales et postcoloniales, en particulier celles issues de l'Indochine, ainsi que sur la philosophie cartésienne, la philosophie de Wittgenstein et l'esthétique.

Stéphanie Walsh Matthews est professeure agrégée au département des langues, littératures et cultures de l'Université Ryerson. Elle enseigne la linguistique, les études culturelles, la littérature canadienne française, la sémiotique et la communication. En plus de son travail sur le réalisme magique, elle effectue une recherche sur la sémiotique robotique.

Heather Zwicker is an English professor by training, a cultural studies practitioner by preference, and a feminist by conviction. Her research has brought postcolonial and feminist theories to bear on problems such as stereotypes, universities, classrooms, and cities. She co-edited *Not Drowning But Waving: Women, Feminism and the Liberal Arts* (University of Alberta Press, 2011) and edited *Edmonton on Location: River City Chronicles* (NeWest Press, 2005). Her essay is part of Edmonton Pipelines, an ongoing collaborative project that uses urban theory to produce digital maps to represent citizens' experience of Edmonton.

Index

The index to the French chapters appears on pages 307–310.
L'index des textes francophones se trouve aux pages 307–310.

Page numbers with "f" refer to illustrations.

Aboriginal people
  Edmonton settlements, 129–30, 135, 136
academy
  asymmetrical power relations, 27–28
  collaboration in, 25, 28, 30, 46
  individual vs. collaborative credit,
    43–44, 47
  mentoring in, 25, 34–35, 41
  trust and sharing, 33–34
  See also collaborative theory and
    practice
acoustic maps, 134, 138n7
advertisements
  in modernist periodicals, 97–99
  See also Canadian Bookman digital
    edition
AIDS crisis, 145
Al-Solaylee, Kamal, 54
Alberta
  Treaty 6 maps, 130
  See also Edmonton, Alberta
Allan, Maud
  archives, 168–69
  autobiography, 161
  costumes, 160, 166, 173, 177n8
  international tours, 161, 168, 169, 173–
    74, 176n3, 176n5, 177n10

life of, xiv, 161, 167, 169, 177n11
  nationality, 167, 177n9
  online record of, 167–69
  "pose" dancing, 169
  Salome postcards, xiv, 159–60, 167–74,
    177n10
  staging of female mobility, 166–67,
    172–76
  See also Salomania
alternative theatre, 53, 55–56, 83n2,
    83nn4–5
"Amiskwaciwâskahikan" (Edmonton
  Pipelines), 130–31
Andersen, Marguerite, xiv
Andrew Connington (Irwin), 183, 185,
    188–89
Antoniuk, Jeffery, 279
  on mapping literary history, 3–24
archives, digital. See digital humanities
  (DH)
Archives gaies du Québec, 144
archives of lesbian and gay liberation
  movement. See Canadian Lesbian
    and Gay Archives (CLGA); Lesbian
    and Gay Liberation in Canada
    (LGLC) project
archives of theatre performances. See
    Bluemouth Inc.; Simulated
    Environment for Theatre (SET)
Arias, Santa, 3–4, 5
Association for Social Knowledge, 144
AT&T Office Space, Toronto
  productions of What the Thunder Said
    at, 61, 62–64, 63f, 84n11

Atlas of Early Printing, 17

Ball, John Clement, 184
Barry, James, 149–50
Barton, Bruce, 57, 60, 63–64, 79
Beck, Kent, 31–32, 39
Benson, Eugene, 83n2
Bentley, Toni, 162, 165
Berque, Augustin, 137
Betts, Gregory, 28
Biber, Douglas, 67
bilingualism. *See* languages
biomapping, 134
Black, J. David, 270
Blackbridge, Persimmon, 152–53
Blackwell, Christopher, 100–01
Blais, Marie-Claire, 142
Blakey, Rebecca, 28, 39–40
Bloor Street Viaduct, Toronto
    in literary history, 84n13
    set design in *White Biting Dog*, 58, 69f,
        75–76, 78f, 80f
    suicide barrier on, 58, 68, 73–76,
        74f–76f
Bluemouth Inc.
    archives of *What the Thunder Said*, 61f,
        62–64, 63f, 70
    integration of audience with
        performance, 84n11
The Body Politic (*TBP*), 145–46, 154
Bol, Peter K., 4
book identifiers
    digital rights management, 92, 93
    e-publishing industry and, 93–96
    international identifier systems, 91–92
    See also digital identifiers; International
        Standard Text Code (*ISTC*); ISBN
        (international standard book
        numbers)
Borgman, Christine, 100
Bouchard, Matt, 28–29, 49
Bretz, Andrew, 26
Brontë, Charlotte, Emily, and Anne,
    223–24
Brown, Susan, xii, 26–27, 279
    on mapping literary history, 3–24

Brunswick Four, 149, 151–52

cabinet cards, 172
calling cards, 172, 174
Canada Foundation for Innovation, viii
Canadian Bookman digital edition
    advertisements in, 97–99
    copyright issues, 99, 100
    CWRC project, 90, 97, 99–100
    digital edition, 89, 97, 99
    ISTC coding, 97, 99–100, 103
    versions of, 99–100
Canadian Bookseller and Library Journal, 97
Canadian Institute for Research
    Computing in Arts (CIRCA), xiii, 129
Canadian Lesbian and Gay Archives (CLGA)
    location of archives, 146–47
    McLeod's research, 142–44, 152
    name change of, 146–47
    National Portrait Collection, 141–42,
        147–48, 153
    overview, 144–45, 148
    use by LGLC project, 143
    women's materials, 148
Canadian Theatre Review, 55
Canadian Women's Movement Archives,
    144
Canadian Writing Research Collaboratory/
    Collaboratoire scientifique des
    écrits du Canada (CWRC/CSÉC)
    collaborations, viii–x
    collaboratory as term, 28
    conference (2011), vii, xi, 126n1
    EMiC partnership, viii, 41
    international identifier systems, 91–92
    lesbian and gay liberation history
        project, 142
    overview, vii–ix, xi
    partnerships, viii, ix, 41
    projects, 5, 14–16, 90, 142
    TEI markup language, 142
    women's writing, viii, 5–6, 142
    See also *Canadian Bookman* digital
        edition; Orlando Project and
        mapping

Canadian Writing Research Collaboratory/
Collaboratoire scientifique des
écrits du Canada (CWRC/CSÉC) and
mapping
ambiguity in visualizations, 22
automated services, 9
dynamic data, 16–17
EMiC projects, 5
filters on data, 17
mapping of literary data, 4–5
maps as interpretative tools, 16–17, 108
misleading data, 18–22
overview, 4–5
political boundaries, 18
projects, 5, 14–16
single vs. collaboratory projects, 16
WatsonWalk app, 5
See also digital maps; Orlando Project
and mapping
Casey, Edward S., 137
Catholic Church
orders for women, 10
See also Ward, Mary
censorship
of LGBT publications, 145–46, 154
Chalmers Award for Best New Canadian
Play, 56, 83n3
charter for collaboration. See Editing
Modernism in Canada University of
Alberta (EMiC UA), project charter
CHAT (Community Homophile Association
of Toronto), 151–52
Cherniavsky, Felix, 161, 163, 168, 176n3,
176nn5–6, 177n7
Cherniavsky Trio, 168
Chow, Rey, 41–42
cigarette cards, 172, 177n10
CIRCA (Canadian Institute for Research
Computing in Arts), xiii, 129
city/cities
female participation in, 182
openness of, 181–82
overview, 130–33
as a place and space, 130–31
polarizations in, 138n3, 181
power relations in, 182

Raymond Williams on, 181
regional theatres in, 83n4
renaming of, 218
transnational urbanism, 182
typicality of, 132–33
ubiquity of digital maps, 131–32
urban games, 133–34, 137, 138n6
See also Edmonton, Alberta; Toronto,
Ontario; urban studies
Clark, Christopher Saint George, 182–83
classics and digital humanities, 110–11
Clay, Jenny Strauss, 110–11
Clean Code (Martin), 37–39
Clements, Patricia, 5
Cleveland, Ohio, digital maps, 134
CLGA. See Canadian Lesbian and Gay
Archives (CLGA)
Coleman, Daniel, 35
collaborative theory and practice
acceptance of responsibility, 32–33
asymmetrical power relations, 27–28
collaboratory, as term, 28
collective vs. individual ownership,
32–33
communication, 40–43, 48
credit and recognition, 35–36, 40, 47
dialogue model, 31
documentation, 37–40, 47
funding, 26
interdisciplinary dialogue, 30, 34–35,
41–43
interface of the digital-humanities
divide, 26–27, 38–39
project charters, 33, 35, 46
right to refuse to continue, 33, 46
XP principles and, 31–33
See also Canadian Writing Research
Collaboratory/Collaboratoire
scientifique des écrits du Canada
(CWRC/CSÉC); Editing Modernism
in Canada University of Alberta
(EMiC UA), project charter
Community Homophile Association of
Toronto (CHAT), 151–52
Compensation (Irwin), 185, 193–94
Conolly, L.W., 83n2

contact zones, 27, 49n1
Contend with Horses (Irwin), 183, 185, 189–90
"A Convenience of Marriage" (Hutcheon and Hutcheon), 42
Corrigan, John, 16–17
Crane, Gregory, 101
Crompton, Constance, xiii, 280
on Canadian queer authorship, 141–56
csÉc. *See* Canadian Writing Research Collaboratory/Collaboratoire scientifique des écrits du Canada (cwrc/csÉc)
Cultural Mapping and the Digital Sphere (Panofsky and Kellett, eds.), ix–x
cultural materialism
materialist-semiotic approach to theatre, 59–64, 68
Cushman, Robert, 54, 58, 73, 75
cwrc/csÉc. *See* Canadian Writing Research Collaboratory/ Collaboratoire scientifique des écrits du Canada (cwrc/csÉc)

Dagg, Anne Innis, 264, 270–71
dance, 19th and 20th c.
archives, 168–69
"pose" dancing, 169
representations of Salome in, 161–63
See also Salomania
Dance Collection Danse (dcd), 168–69, 173
Dance Marathon (Bluemouth), 84n11
"Dance of the Seven Veils," 161–63
A Daughter of To-Day (Duncan), 175
David, Ravit H., xiii, 280
on digital edition of *Canadian Bookman*, 89–106
Davies, Tony, 31
Dayman, Ron, 146–47
dcd (Dance Collection Danse), 168, 169, 173
de Certeau, Michel, 62
DeFehr, Wayne, 28
Demers, Patricia, xiv, 280
on Grace Irwin, 181–96
Derrida, Jacques, 38

Desert of the Heart (Rule), 141, 154
DeSouza-Coelho, Shawn, 280
on the theatrical canon and set, 51–88
Devereux, Cecily, xiv, 280–81
on Maud Allan and Salomania, 159–79
digital humanities (dh)
cartographic awareness, 111–13
change management in projects, 31
collaboration in projects, 26–29
as contact zone, 27
·data on readers, 277–78
documentation in projects, 37–40, 47
funding in, 26
impact of technologies on, 30–31
interdisciplinary collaboration, 26–27, 30–31, 34–35, 41–43
interface of the digital-humanities divide, 26–27, 38–39
interpretative possibilities, 16–17, 101, 112–14
mentoring in, 34–35
Neatline tool for storytelling, 16, 110, 124–25
new pedagogies, 27
precursors to digital culture, 160, 175–76
project charters, 33, 35
training in, 45, 46, 109–10
See also publishing and digital humanities
digital identifiers
associated services and, 91
copyright, 91, 92, 100
discoverability of objects, 92, 104n6
doi systems, 91–92
ideal digital library infrastructure, 101
illustrated works and, 95–96
interoperability across media, 92, 93–94
isbn system and, 93–96, 104n2
lgbt categories, 150–51, 155n1
overview, 89–93
Semantic Web and, 101, 104n6
standards for, 91
uniqueness of, 90–93, 100–02
various editions of texts, 99–101

version control, 92
works as objects, 104n5
See also International Standard
Text Code (ISTC); Text Encoding
Initiative (TEI)
digital maps
ambiguity in visualizations, 22, 112
assumptions of, 107–08
biomapping, 134
cartographic awareness, 111–13
dynamic data, 16–17
emotion maps, 134
GIS practices, 110–13
Hitotoki projects, 131, 134, 137n2
interpretive possibilities, 112–14, 119
literary data, 4–5
misleading data, 18–22
oral traditions and, 110–11
overview, 134–35
political boundaries, 18
potential uses, 12, 14–17, 20–22
real-world referents in, 108
sound maps, 134, 138n7
space vs. place, 130–31
uniformities of scale and symbology,
108
urban creativity and, 131–32
use in urban games, 133–34, 137, 138n6
See also Canadian Writing Research
Collaboratory/Collaboratoire
scientifique des écrits du Canada
(CWRC/CSÉC) and mapping;
Edmonton Pipelines; GIS
(geographic information systems)
and digital humanities; Orlando
Project and mapping
Digital Urbanism Collaboratory (CIRCA),
xiii, 129
Dobson, Teresa M., 281
on the theatrical canon and SET, 51–88
Document Type Definition (DTD)
Semantic Web and, 101, 104n6
documentation in digital humanities,
37–40, 47
documents, defined, 94–95
Dollimore, Jonathan, 70

domestic life
Salomania's invasion of, 165–66, 174,
176
in Stand on a Rainbow, 265–67, 268,
271, 274–75
women in postwar era, 273–75
drama, Canadian
canonization and anthologies, 82n1
canonization of text vs. performance,
51–52, 57–59, 63–64, 81–82
collectively created works, 55–56
Governor General's Literary Award-
winning plays, 51, 53–55, 56, 83n3
Massey Commission on, 55–56, 81,
83n4
See also Simulated Environment for
Theatre (SET); theatre, Canadian
Drucker, Johanna, 22, 113
Duncan, Isadora, 160–61
Duncan, Sara Jeannette, 175
Durrant, Ulla Maude, 177n11
See also Allan, Maud

Editing Modernism in Canada/Édition
du modernisme au Canada (EMiC/
EMAC)
collaboration in, 26
credit and recognition, 40, 45, 47
funding, 40, 47
overview, 26
partnerships, 41, 45
training in digital production, 45
Editing Modernism in Canada University
of Alberta (EMiC UA)
communication, 40–43, 48
credit and recognition, 35–36, 40,
43–44, 45, 47
funding, xii, 45, 46
horizontal administrative structure,
40–41, 46
overview, 28–29, 45
partnerships, 41
project website, 36, 47
smart phone apps, 5
training, 45, 46

Wilfred and Sheila Watson projects, 5, 29–30, 36, 39–41
Editing Modernism in Canada University of Alberta (EMiC UA), project
  charter
  collaboration, 32, 45–46, 49
  collaborators and collaboratory, defined, 46
  collective *vs.* individual ownership, 32–33
  communication, 32, 43–44, 48
  credit and recognition, 35–36, 40, 43–44, 47
  documentation, 37–40, 47
  mentorship principles, 34–35
  ongoing revision of, 43, 45
  overview, xii, 28–29, 33, 49
  peer feedback, 32
  "play nice" cluster, 29, 45, 47
  purpose of, 35, 43, 45
  questions of interest, 43–44
  right to refuse to continue, 33, 46
  sharing of documentation, 40, 47
  "trust" cluster, 29, 33–34, 43, 45
  values in, 32
  XP principles as basis for, 31–33, 43
Editing Wilfred Watson Archive Project (EMiC UA), 29
Edmonton, Alberta
  Aboriginal settlements, 129–30, 135, 136
  conflicts in values, 136
  overview, 132
  Ribbon of Green parks, 136
  Rossdale, 135–37
  as understoried, 132
  urban games, 133–34, 137, 138n6
Edmonton Pipelines
  city as place *vs.* space, 130–31, 133–34
  digital maps, 134–35
  HyperCities platform, 130, 136
  overview, xiii, 129–30, 133–34
  research questions, 130, 133, 136–37
  theoretical assumptions, 130–32
education
  geographical pedagogy (19th c.), 115–19, 121, 123

  in *In Little Place*, 192–93
Education and Research Archive (ERA), ix
Elizabeth, Heather Beyer (now Lamar Van Dyke), 142, 149, 152
Ell, Paul, 113
Eltinge, Julian, 163
EMiC/EMaC. *See* Editing Modernism in Canada/Édition du modernisme au Canada (EMiC/EMaC)
EMiC UA. *See* Editing Modernism in Canada University of Alberta (EMiC UA)
emotion maps, 134
England
  Brontë sisters, 223–24
  history of postcards, 170–72
  history of women's writing (Orlando Project), 5–6
  Society of Friends travels (17th c.), 17f, 18–19, 19f
  sound maps, 134
  Stockport emotion map, 134
  Mary Ward's travel, 10, 12–16, 12f–13f, 18–19
  See also London, England
erotic culture, 19th and 20th c.
  postcards, 159–60, 174–76
  Salome as "viral" culture, xiv, 160, 162–65, 175–76
  staging of white femininity, 174–76
  See also Salomania
ethnicity. *See* race and ethnicity
Europe
  Salomania, 169–70
  Society of Friends travels (17th c.), 17f, 18–19, 19f
  Mary Ward's travel, 10, 12–16, 12f–13f, 18–19
Exhibit 2.0 (mapping tool), 10, 12
Extensible Markup Language (XML), 101, 104n6
Extreme Programming (XP), 31–33

Factory Theatre, Toronto, 56, 83n2, 83n5
Fast, Kristin, 28, 49

females
 city life and, 182
 education (19th c.), 115–19, 121, 123
 photographs on postcards, 172
 postwar domestic life, 273–75
 Wikipedia editors and entries, 153–54,
  155n2
 See also Salomania
"Une femme, seule" (Saint-Martin), 223
Filewod, Alan, 55, 81, 83n4
Flaunting It! (Jackson and Persky, eds.),
 143–44
Foucault, Michel, 21
"Four Fruits/Quatre fruits" (Saint-Martin),
 225–28, 229
francophones. *See* languages; Saint-
 Martin, Lori
Fraser, James, 143–44
Fremstad, Olive, 163
Frogner, Raymond, 28–29
Fronteras Americanas (Verdecchia)
 awards, 51, 56
 canonical status, 54–55
 productions of, 53, 82n1, 84n6, 84n8
 publication of, 84n8
 Verdecchia as actor and director, 57,
  84n9
Fronteras Americanas (Verdecchia),
 Tarragon production (1993)
 overview, 56–57, 84nn8–9
 performance technologies, 57–58
Fronteras Americanas (Verdecchia),
 Soulpepper revival (2011)
 overview, 51–52, 56–58, 84n9
 performance technologies, 57–59
 reception of, 54–55, 73
 set design, 58–59
Fuller, Danielle, 278
Fuller, Loïe, 161–62
Fyfe, Paul, 104n5

Gabriele, Sandra, 281
 on the theatrical canon and SET, 51–88
Gagné, Paul, 221–22
Gall, Brendan, 84n8
games, urban, 133–34, 137, 138n6

Garden, Mary, 163
Garelick, Rhonda, 161
gay and lesbian liberation project. *See*
 Lesbian and Gay Liberation in
 Canada (LGLC) project
gender
 Wikipedia editors and entries, 153–54,
  155n2
 See also females
geocaching, 133–34, 137
geography
 pedagogy for female students (19th c.),
  115–19, 123
 as social construction, 3–4, 19
 See also digital maps; maps
Geography Made Easy (Morse), 116, 118, 121,
 123
GeoPy geo-referencing tool, 9
German language, 218
Gilbert, Pamela, 185
Gillen, Julia, 171
GIS (geographic information systems) and
 digital humanities
 cartographic awareness, 111–13
 interpretive possibilities and, 112–14,
  119, 124–25
 need for humanities versions of tools,
  124–25
 overview, 110–13, 124–25
 reluctance to use, 111–13
 training in, 109–10
 ubiquity of GIS, 109, 131–32
 usefulness of tools, 112, 119
 See also digital maps
Glassco, Bill, 56
Google searches
 customized results, 151–52
 LGBT cultural history and, 151–54
Goyette, Linda, 132
Grace Irwin Award, 184
Grand Theatre, 82n1
graphic novels and book identifiers, 95–96
Greece, ancient, 110–11
Gregory, Ian, 7, 113
Grundy, Isobel, 5, 281
 on mapping literary history, 3–24

Guinand, Louise, 57

Hagen, Darrin, 132
Halbertstam, J. Jack, 150
Hall, Nigel, 171
Hammill, Faye, 5
Hasan-Rokem, Galit, 173
Hasenbank, Andrea, xii, 282
  on modelling collaboration, 25–50
Haworth, England, 223–24
Hébert, Anne, xv
Henshaw, Frances
  geography book by, 114–19, 120f, 121,
    122f, 123
  life of, 108, 114
  online availability of maps, 119, 121
Hindle, Annie, 149
Hislop, George, 151
Historical GIS (Gregory and Ell), 113
Hitotoki projects, 131, 134, 137n2
Hjartarson, Paul, xii, 282
  on modelling collaboration, 25–50
Hjørland, Birger, 94
Hockey, Susan, 6
Hoffmann, Gertrude, 163, 177n7
Hoile, Christopher, 54
Holt, Tonie and Valmai, 171, 172
Homer, 110–11
housewives. See domestic life
How to Lie with Maps (Monmonier), 107
humanities
  collaboration in, 30
  interdisciplinary collaboration, 26–27,
    30, 34–35, 41–43
  interface of the digital-humanities
    divide, 26–27, 38–39
  mentoring in, 25, 34–35, 41
  See also digital humanities (DH)
Hutcheon, Linda and Michael, 31, 42, 176n5
HyperCities
  Edmonton Pipelines project, 130, 136
  mapping features, 10, 14

identifiers, book. See book identifiers
identifiers, digital. See digital identifiers
If We Were Birds (Shields), 84n8

illustrated works and digital identifiers,
  95–96
Imperial Eyes (Pratt), 27, 49n1
Implementing New Knowledge
  Environments (INKE) project
  charter, 28, 33
In Little Place (Irwin), 185, 191–93
Innis, Harold, 270, 273
Innis, Mary Quayle
  archives, 267
  career, 267, 271, 273–74
  daughter's comments on, 264, 270–71
  domestic life of, 267, 268–69, 270–71,
    274
  An Economic History of Canada, 270
  See also Stand on a Rainbow (Innis)
international identifier systems, 91–92
international standard book numbers
  (ISBN), 93–96, 104n2
International Standard Text Code (ISTC)
  derivation field, 96, 97, 100, 103
  digital editions, 101–02
  example of use of, 96–97
  illustrated works, 95–96
  ONIX-based schema, 96–97, 103
  overview, 90–91, 95–97, 101–02
Internet
  Google custom searches, 151–52
  LGBT cultural history on, 151–54
  spatial information on, 4
  See also Wikipedia
Internet Archive website, 99
Irwin, Grace
  life of, 183–85, 191, 193
Irwin, Grace, works
  Andrew Connington, 183, 185, 188–89
  Compensation, 185, 193–94
  Contend with Horses, 183, 185, 189–90
  Least of All Saints, 183, 186–88
  In Little Place, 191–93
  overview, xiv, 182–83, 185
  Servant of Slaves, 184
  The Seventh Earl, 184–85
  translations of, 183, 184, 191
  See also Toronto, Ontario, as place in
    Irwin's works

Isadora software, 62
ISBN (international standard book numbers), 93–96, 104n2
ISTC. *See* International Standard Text Code (ISTC)

Jared D. Sessions House, Toronto, 147
Jenstad, Janelle, 21
Jessop, Martyn, 111–13, 124
Juxta (textual collation tool), 119

Kamboureli, Smaro, 35
Kareda, Urjo, 84n10
Kirschenbaum, Matthew G., 92
Kiss and Tell (art collective), 153
Kitchener, Herbert, 1st Earl, 218
Kitchener, Ontario, 218
Knowles, Ric, views
  bias of transhistoricism, 77
  instability of meanings, 78–79
  materialist-semiotic approach, 59–65, 68
  performance text, 59–60, 65
  production conditions, 59–60, 65, 70, 72–73
  reception conditions, 59–60, 65, 73, 75–77
  revival movement, 51–52, 58
  theatre canon, 82n1, 85
Kovacs, Sasha, xii–xiii, 282–83
  on the theatrical canon and SET, 51–88
Kultermann, Udo, 162–63

Lam, Shyong, 153, 155n2
LaMarsh, Judy, 142
Langerfeld, Edith, 163
languages
  bilingualism, 217
  naming of cities, 218
  otherness and sameness, 221–22
  self-translation, 225–28, 229
  simultaneous interpretation, 219–21
  as spaces, 216, 222, 228
  translation, 221–22
  See also Saint-Martin, Lori

Lasting Change (Bretz, Brown, and Mcgregor), 26
Least of All Saints (Irwin), 183, 185, 186–88
Lent, Vanessa, xii, 283
  on modelling collaboration, 25–50
LePage, Sue
  set for *White Biting Dog*, 57–58, 69f–70f, 77–78, 78f, 80f
Lesbian and Gay Liberation in Canada: A Selected Annotated Chronology, 1964–1975 (McLeod), 141–45, 152
Lesbian and Gay Liberation in Canada (LGLC) project
  identity debates, 149–50
  online availability, 145
  overview, xiii–xiv, 141–43
  TEI coding, 145, 149–51, 152
  use of CLGA archives, 143
  women's materials, 148, 151–54
lesbian and gay liberation movement
  activism, 144–46
  censorship of publications, 145–46, 154
  identity debates, 149–50
  McLeod's history of, 141–45, 152
  newspapers, 145–46, 154
  novels, 141, 154
  online information about, 141–42, 151–54
  publishers, 145–46
  trans community, 149–50
  See also Toronto, Ontario, lesbian and gay community
Lesbian Images (Rule), 154
LGBT Life with Full Text, 145
LGBT movement. *See* lesbian and gay liberation movement
LGLC project. *See* Lesbian and Gay Liberation in Canada (LGLC) project
libraries
  digital identifiers, 89–90
  ideal digital library infrastructure, 101
  works, texts, and documents, 94–95
  See also University of Alberta Libraries; University of Toronto Libraries
Loiselle, André, 82n1
London, England

as mapping example, 6, 8, 9, 12, 14, 15f
Salomania in, 160–61, 163, 165, 166,
    177nn7–8
sound maps of, 134
The Luminous Veil (Bloor Street Viaduct),
    75f
Luscombe, George, 83n2

Mackey, Margaret
    career, 272–73, 274, 283
    early life, 271–72, 276
    on reading in place, position, and time,
        263–78
Mackey, Margaret, case study on reader
    reception
    adolescent readings of *Stand on a
        Rainbow*, 264, 271–72, 276
    adult readings of *Stand on a Rainbow*,
        264, 272–75, 276
    divergent readers, 275–76
    grounded reading, 276–78
    implied readers, 272, 273, 275–76
    mother's reading of *Stand on a
        Rainbow*, 264, 268, 271
    overview, xv, 263–65
    readers as material beings, 263–64,
        276–78
    resistant readers, 274, 276
    See also McCurdy, Elizabeth (Margaret
        Mackey's mother)
MacKinnon, Joseph, 28, 39–40
MacLeod, Angus, 168, 177n10
Manhunt (urban game), 133–34, 137
Manthorne, Jackie, 142
maps
    assumptions in, 107–08
    drawing as a way of knowing, 113, 118
    Foucault's heterotopias, 21
    geographical pedagogy in 19th c.,
        115–19, 123
    interpretive possibilities and, 16–17,
        108, 112–14, 119, 134–35
    places that cannot be mapped, 21
    playfulness and lies in, 107–08, 113–14,
        125
    real-world referents in, 108, 116

subjective mapmaking, 117–18, 123
uniformities of scale and symbology,
    108
See also digital maps; Henshaw,
    Frances
Martha Ostenso Project (EMiC UA), 29
Martin, Robert C., 37–39
Massey, Doreen, 184
Massey Commission, 55–56, 81, 83n4
Mata Hari, 161–62, 176n6
materialist-semiotic approach to theatre,
    59–64, 68
McCarty, Willard, on collaboration, 25
McCurdy, Elizabeth (Margaret Mackey's
    mother)
    ill health, 268, 269, 273
    life of, 268–69, 271, 272, 276
    life parallels with *Stand on a Rainbow*,
        268–70, 272
    love for *Stand on a Rainbow*, 264, 268–
        70, 271, 276
McDearmon, Lacy, 162
McGann, Jerome, 98
McGregor, Hannah, 26, 28–29, 49
McKinnon, Joseph, 49
McLeod, Donald, 141–45, 152
Mead, Margaret, 171
mentorship and collaboration, 25, 28,
    34–35, 41
Michael Young Theatre, 70–71, 71f, 82n1
    See also Soulpepper Theatre Company
Middlebury Female Academy, Vermont,
    114, 115, 116
Milne, Esther, 170, 173–74
mobile digital devices
    maps on smart phones, 5, 12
    urban maps and creativity, 131–32
Modern Canadian Plays (Wasserman, ed.),
    82n1
modernism and modernist studies
    periodical advertising, 97–99
    See also *Canadian Bookman* digital
        edition; Editing Modernism in
        Canada/Édition du modernisme au
        Canada (EMiC/EMaC)
"Mon père, la nuit" (Saint-Martin), 223

Monmonier, Mark, 107
Montreal
    as bilingual city, 217
    sound maps of, 138n7
Morra, Linda, 28
Morse, Jedidiah, 116, 118, 121, 123
Moruzi, Kristine, 5
Mroczek, Breanna, 283
    on mapping literary history, 3–24
Ms. Mentor (Emily Toth), 25, 34
Murphy, Pat, 142, 149, 151–52
music and sound
    sound maps, 134, 138n7
My Life and Dancing (Allan), 161

Nancy, Jean-Luc, 170, 174
narrative
    digital storytelling using Neatline, 16,
        110, 124–25
    Hitotoki projects, 131, 134, 137n2
    urban spaces and, 133–34
National Gay Rights Coalition/Coalition
    national pour les droits des
    homosexuels, 144, 145
National Portrait Collection (NPC) of CLGA,
    141–42, 147–48, 152, 153
The Nature of "A Work" (Smiraglia), 94–95
Neatby, Hilda, 193
Neatline project, 16, 110, 124–25
Nestruck, J. Kelly, 54–55, 60, 64
Neuman, Shirley, 28–29
New York City
    gay and lesbian archives, 144
    Salomania in, 164–65
    sound maps of, 138n7
    See also Salomania
newspapers and magazines
    advertisements in, 97–99
    CWRC projects, 5, 97
    LGBT newspapers, 145–46, 154
    modernism and mass production,
        97–99
    See also Canadian Bookman digital
        edition
Nobles, Charlotte, 49
Nold, Christian, 134

novels
    graphic novels and book identifiers,
        95–96
    LGBT novels, 141, 154
    See also Irwin, Grace, works; Stand on a
        Rainbow (Innis)
Nowviskie, Bethany, xiii, 284
    on playing with maps, 107–27
NPC (National Portrait Collection) of CLGA,
    141–42, 147–48, 153

Of Toronto the Good (Clark), 182–83
ONIX (ONline Information eXchange)-
    based schema, 96–97, 103
Ontario. See Kitchener, Ontario; Toronto,
    Ontario
oral tradition and digital humanities, 110–11
Orlando Project and mapping
    ambiguity in visualizations, 22
    contextualization of data, 9
    CWRC collaboration, ix, 5, 7, 8, 14–17
    dynamic data, 16–17
    filtering of data, 17
    geo-referencing place names, 9–10
    granularity of spatial data, 15–18, 20–22
    "London" as example, 6, 8, 9, 12, 14, 15f
    mapping tools, 10
    markup languages, 6
    methodology to create maps, 8–10
    misleading data, 18–22
    overview, 5–8
    potential uses, 12, 14–17, 20–22
    Quaker travels, 17f, 18–19, 19f
    semantic tags, 7–8
    spatial information, 6–9, 15–16
    TEI markup language, 6–8
    temporal information, 7, 9, 11f, 14, 15f,
        16
    Mary Ward's travel, 10, 12–16, 12f–13f,
        18–19
    See also Text Encoding Initiative (TEI)
Ostenso, Martha, 29

Palace of the End (Thompson), 84n10
Palace Theatre, London, 161, 176n4, 177n7
Palk, Nancy, 57, 58

Panofsky, Ruth, 284
Paredes-Olea, Mariana, 284
    on mapping literary history, 3–24
parkour (urban game), 133–34, 137
Paskin, Norman, 90–91
"Past Futures" (Edmonton Pipelines), 130
penmanship, 19th c.
    geography books, 114
    See also Henshaw, Frances
performance simulation systems
    theatrical text in, 79
    See also Simulated Environment for
        Theatre (SET)
periodicals. *See* newspapers and
    magazines
photography and postcards, 172
The Picture Postcard and Its Origins
    (Staff), 171
Picture Postcard Magazine, 172
Pink Triangle Press, 145–46
Pipelines, Edmonton. *See* Edmonton
    Pipelines
place and space
    city/cities as, 130–31, 133–34
    digital humanities and, 3–4
    geography and, 3–4, 5
    languages as spaces, 216, 222, 228
    place *vs.* space, 130–31
    places that cannot be mapped, 21
    readers as material beings, 263–64,
        276–78
    Ricoeur on time and, 189–90, 195
    space as social construction, 3–4, 19
    time and, 3, 4, 117, 189–90
Poddubiuk, Christina
    design for *White Biting Dog*, 57–58, 69f,
        77, 78f
poetry
    self-translation, 225–28, 229
Pollard, Percival, 171
popular culture. *See* Salomania
Les portes closes (Saint-Martin), 222
postcards
    ambiguity of, 174
    as commodities, 172–73
    female mobility and, 172–75

history of, 170–72
overview, 159–60, 170
photography and, 172
precursors to digital culture, 175–76
Salome postcards, 167–70
Potts, Adrienne, 149
Pratt, Mary Louise, 27, 49n1
Prickman, Gregory, 17
project charter for collaboration. *See*
    Editing Modernism in Canada
    University of Alberta (EMiC UA),
    project charter
publishing and digital humanities
    advertisements in modernist
        periodicals, 97–99
    data on readers, 277–78
    digital distribution of works, 89–90
    ISBN system, 93–96, 104n2
    ISTC system, 95–97
    life cycle of a work, 94, 104n5
    text, documents, and works, 94–95
    See also digital identifiers

Quakers
    travels (17th c.), 17f, 18–19, 19f
Quamen, Harvey, xii, 284–85
    on modelling collaboration, 25–50
queer identity coding, 151
    See also lesbian and gay liberation
        movement

race and ethnicity
    Aboriginal early settlements, 129–30,
        135, 136
Radzikowska, Milena, 28, 33
Rae, Kyle, 147
readers
    data on, 277–78
    divergent readers, 275–76
    implied readers, 272, 273, 275–76
    as material beings, 263–64, 276–78
    relatability to text, 269
    resistant readers, 274, 276
    See also Mackey, Margaret, case study
        on reader reception
Reeves, Sabrina, 63f

religion. *See* Catholic Church; Quakers
Retooling the Humanities (Coleman
and Kamboureli, eds.), 34–35
Ricoeur, Paul, 189–90, 195
Roach, Joseph, 60, 63
Roberts-Smith, Jennifer, 285
on the theatrical canon and SET, 51–88
Rodriguez-Arenas, Omar, 285
on the theatrical canon and SET, 51–88
Roman Catholic Church. *See* Catholic
Church
Romaniuk, Mary-Jo, 285
Ross, Mike, 72f
Rossdale, Edmonton, 135–37
See also Edmonton, Alberta
Roy, Gabrielle, 217
Rubin, Don, 55
Ruecker, Stan, 28, 33, 286
on the theatrical canon and SET, 51–88
Rule, Jane, 141, 154
Rumsey, David, 114, 121

Saint-Martin, Lori
author, 217, 222–23, 225–28
on the Brontë sisters, 223–24
English language use, 216–17, 219–21,
225–28
French language use, 216–17, 219–21,
223, 225–28
life and career, xiv–v, 216–22, 286
literary translation, 221–22
self-translation, 225–28, 229
simultaneous interpretation, 219–21
Spanish language use, 216, 221, 228
Saint-Martin, Lori, works
"Une femme, seule," 223
"Four Fruits/Quatre fruits," 225–28,
229
"Mon père, la nuit," 223
Les portes closes, 222
Salomania
dinner dances for women, 160–61, 164,
166, 173
as disease, 159–60, 163–66, 174–76
domestic invasion by, 165–66, 174, 176
female impersonators, 163

female mobility, 166–67, 172–76
imitation of Maud Allan, 166–67
media representations of, 162–66
as moral corruption, 164, 165
overview, xiv, 159–62
postcards, 167–70
staging of white femininity, 174–76
as "viral" culture, xiv, 160, 162–65,
175–76
"The Vision of Salome" dance, 159–62,
166–67, 169, 173, 176n3, 176nn5–6,
177n7
See also Allan, Maud
Salome (Strauss), 161–62, 163
Salome (Wilde), 161–62, 167, 176n2, 176n5
Salter, Denis, 55, 81
San Francisco, emotion map, 134
Sassen, Saskia, 138n3, 182
Schagerl, Jessica, 34–35, 41
Schechner, Richard, 60
Scholar's Lab. *See* University of Virginia,
Scholar's Lab
Schreibman, Susan, 95
Schulten, Susan, 116–17
Schwartz, Michelle, xiii, 286
on Canadian queer authorship, 141–56
Scotland, literary maps, 20–21, 20f
Sedgwick, Eve Kosofsky, 150
Semantic Web and XML, 101, 104n6
Servant of Slaves (Irwin), 184
SET. *See* Simulated Environment for
Theatre (SET)
The Seventh Earl (Irwin), 184–85
sexuality. *See* lesbian and gay liberation
movement
SGML (Standard Generalized Markup
Language), 6
Shields, Erin, 84n8
Sigel, Lisa Z., 170
SIMILE project (MIT), 10
Simulated Environment for Theatre (SET)
annotations, 65f–66f, 67, 72f–73f, 73,
76–77, 79–80, 80f
archival tool, 52–53, 81–82
archive of *White Biting Dog*, 64–68,
65f–66f, 69f–72f, 70–73

avatars, 65, 65f–66f, 67, 72–73
Character View, 65, 65f–66f
conditions of production, 70–73,
    71f–72f
conditions of reception, 73–77, 73f–76f
export as print archive, 67, 78
limitations of, 79
materialist-semiotic approach, 64–65,
    68
overview, 52–53, 64–65, 79–82
potential uses of, 52, 67–68, 77–81,
    84n12
production histories, 52–53
Reading View (includes Text View), 65,
    65f, 79–81, 80f
Stage View, 65, 65f, 67–68, 80–81, 80f
user control of, 65, 65f, 67, 77–79
See also *White Biting Dog* (Thompson),
    Tarragon production (1984); *White
    Biting Dog* (Thompson), Soulpepper
    revival (2011)
Sinclair, Stéfan, 287
    on the theatrical canon and SET, 51–88
Sinfield, Alan, 70
smart phone apps, 5
Smiraglia, Richard P., 94–95
Smith, Michael Peter, 182, 185
So Little for the Mind (Neatby), 193
Social Sciences and Humanities Research
    Council (SSHRC), xii, 34–35, 45
Society of Friends
    travels (17th c.), 17f, 18–19, 19f
Soulpepper Theatre Company
    conditions of production, 70–73, 71f
    history of, 53–55, 83n3
    materialist-semiotic approach to
        revivals by, 59–64, 68
    productions of award-winning plays, 51,
        53–55, 56, 83n3
    revivals, 51–52, 56–60
    See also *Fronteras Americanas*
        (Verdecchia), Soulpepper
        revival (2011); *White Biting Dog*
        (Thompson), Soulpepper revival
        (2011)
sound maps, 134, 138n7

space. *See* place and space
spatial technologies
    ubiquity of, 4, 109–10, 131–32
    See also digital maps; GIS (geographic
        information systems) and digital
        humanities
SSHRC. *See* Social Sciences and
    Humanities Research Council
    (SSHRC)
Staff, Frank, 171
Stand on a Rainbow (Innis)
    as autobiographical novel, 267, 269,
        271, 274–75
    domestic life in, 265–67, 268, 271,
        274–75
    inner musings in, 265–67
    local history in, 266–67, 269, 273
    overview, 264–67
    See also Mackey, Margaret, case study
        on reader reception
Standard Generalized Markup Language
    (SGML), 6
Steiner, George, 226
Stockport emotion maps, 134
Strauss, Richard, 161–62, 163
La Sylphe (dancer), 163

Tarragon Theatre
    alternative theatre movement, 56, 83n2,
        83nn4–5
    conditions of production, 70–71
    playwrights in residence, 84n7
    premieres of new plays, 56
    productions of Thompson's plays, 82n1,
        84n10
    stage and backstage architecture,
        70–71, 70f
    See also *Fronteras Americanas*
        (Verdecchia), Tarragon production
        (1993); *White Biting Dog*
        (Thompson), Tarragon production
        (1984)
Taylor, Diana, 60, 62, 78
TBP (*The Body Politic*), 145–46, 154
Text Encoding Initiative (TEI)

connections of events, places, and people, 152
example, 6
LGBT identity categories, 150–51, 155n1
overlapping hierarchies, 121
Semantic Web and, 101, 104n6
use in LGLC project, 142, 145, 149–51, 155n1
use in Orlando Project, 6–7
texts, defined, 94–95
theatre, Canadian
  alternative theatre movement, 53, 55–56, 83n2, 83nn4–5
  canon as process, 60, 81–82
  canonization of text *vs.* performance, 51–52, 57, 58–59, 63–64
  conditions of production, 70–73, 70f–71f
  Massey Commission on, 55–56, 81, 83n4
  materialist-semiotic approach to canonization, 59–64, 68
  performance simulation systems, 79
  production histories, 52–53
  regional theatres, 83n4
  revival movement, 51–52, 58–60
  universalism, 58–59
  See also drama, Canadian; Simulated Environment for Theatre (SET)
Theatre Aquarius, 82n1
Theatre Passe Muraille (TPM), 83n2, 83n4
Thompson, Judith, 71, 84n10
  See also *White Biting Dog* (Thompson)
Tiessen, Paul, 29
Tipton, Billy, 149–50
Toronto, Ontario
  francophone culture, xiv
  history (19th c.), 182–83
  sound maps of, 138n7
  See also Bloor Street Viaduct, Toronto
Toronto, Ontario, as place in Irwin's works
  Andrew Connington, 188–89
  and change, 190, 193–95
  city and country contrasts, 192–94
  clerical vocation and churches, 183–84, 186–90, 194

Compensation, 193–94
Contend with Horses, 189–90
  education, 192–93
  lawyers, 190–91
  Least of All Saints, 183, 186–88
  In Little Place, 185, 191–93
  missing landmarks, 194–95
  overview, xiv, 182–86
  television broadcasts, 192–93
  topographic realism, 185
  walking itineraries, 186, 189, 192
Toronto, Ontario, lesbian and gay community
  archives of, 146–48
  bookstores, 152
  Brunswick Four, 149, 151–52
  censorship of, 145–46, 154
  history of organizations, 151–52
  lesbian histories, 149
  newspapers, 145–46, 154
  online presence, 151–52
  publishers, 145–46
  trans histories, 149–50
Toronto Warehouse, 61, 62, 84n11
Toronto Women's Bookstore, 152
Toronto Workshop Productions (TWP), 83n2, 83n4
The Torontonians (Young), 194–95
Toth, Emily, 25, 34
transexual community
  identity categories, 149–50, 155n1
  See also lesbian and gay liberation movement
translation. *See* languages
travel
  mapping of Society of Friends travels (17th c.), 17f, 18–19, 19f
  mapping of Mary Ward's travel, 10, 12–16, 12f–13f, 18–19
Treaty 6 maps, 130
Trent University, training in DH, 45
Troy Female Seminary, New York, 115

United Kingdom
  history of women's writing (Orlando Project), 5–6

literary maps of Scotland, 20–21, 20f
See also England
United States
Salomania in, 164–65
See also New York City
University of Alberta, EMiC. *See* Editing
Modernism in Canada University of
Alberta (EMiC UA)
University of Alberta, Orlando Project. *See*
Orlando Project and mapping
University of Alberta, Pipelines. *See*
Edmonton Pipelines
University of Alberta Libraries
CWRC collaboration, ix–x
digital scholarship, ix–x
Education and Research Archive, ix
EMiC partnership, 41
University of Alberta Press
CWRC collaboration, ix–x
University of British Columbia
gay and lesbian archives, 144
University of California at Los Angeles
(UCLA)
Maud Allan archives, 168, 169
University of Toronto
in Irwin's Connington trilogy, 186–89
University of Toronto Libraries
archives of *Canadian Bookman*, 99
EMiC partnership, 41
research respository, 145
University of Victoria, 45
University of Virginia, Scholar's Lab
digital humanities programs, 108–11
Neatline project, 16, 110, 124–25
textual collation tool (Juxta), 119
urban games, 133–34, 137, 138n6
urban studies
city as place *vs.* space, 130–31, 133–34
globalization theory, 182
Hitotoki projects, 131, 134, 137n2
pace of urbanization, 131
research questions, 133
ubiquity of data and, 131
See also city/cities; Edmonton Pipelines

Van Dyke, Lamar (formerly Heather Beyer
Elizabeth), 142, 149, 152
van Orden, Nick, 28, 39–40
Verdecchia, Guillermo, 56–58, 84n9
See also *Fronteras Americanas*
(Verdecchia)
Vertical Suburbia (Edmonton Pipelines),
130
"Victories and Defeats" (Fraser), 143–44
"viral" culture, xiv, 160, 164–65, 175–76
"The Vision of Salome" dance, 159–62
See also Salomania
visualization of theatre text. *See* Simulated
Environment for Theatre (SET)

Walkowitz, Judith, 166–67, 169, 173, 175
Ward, Mary
travel and influence, 10, 12–16, 12f–13f,
18–19
Warf, Barney, 3–4, 5
Warren, Jim, 56, 57–58
Washburn, Michaela, 72f
Wasserman, Jerry, 82n1
Watching the Script project, 52
Watson, Wilfred and Sheila
EMiC UA projects on, 5, 29–30, 36,
39–41
Webster, Noah, 116
Wells, Sue, 149
What the Thunder Said (play), 61–64, 61f,
63f, 84n11
White Biting Dog (Thompson)
awards, 51, 54
Bloor Street Viaduct, 58, 68, 73, 74f–76f
canonical status, 54–55
"dog spoke" event, 68, 69f, 72f, 80f
productions of, 53, 84n8
publication of, 84n1, 84n8
"suicide" event, 58, 68, 73–76, 74f–76f
versions of, 68
White Biting Dog (Thompson), Tarragon
production (1984)
archive using SET, 69f–70f, 78f, 80f
"dog spoke" event, 68, 69f, 80f
overview, 56–58
premiere of, 58, 84n10

reception of, 57, 73, 74f–76f, 75–77
set design, 58, 69f–70f, 70–71, 78f, 80f
"suicide" event, 58, 68, 73–76, 74f–76f
   See also Simulated Environment for
   Theatre (SET)
White Biting Dog (Thompson), Soulpepper
   revival (2011)
   archive using SET, 52–53, 64–68,
      65f–66f, 69f, 71f–72f, 76f, 78f, 80f
   "dog spoke" event, 68, 69f, 72f, 80f
   overview, 51–52, 57–58
   reception of, 54–55, 57, 58, 73, 74f–76f,
      75–77
   set design, 58, 69f, 70–71, 71f, 78f, 80f
   "suicide" event, 58, 68, 73–76, 74f–76f
   See also Simulated Environment for
      Theatre (SET)
Wide Awake (Gall), 84n8
Wikipedia
   gender imbalance, 153–54, 155n2
   LGBT cultural history, 141–43, 151,
      152–54
Wilde, Oscar, 161–62, 167, 176n2, 176n5
Wilfred and Sheila Watson projects
      (EMiC UA), 5, 29–30, 36, 39–41
Willard, Emma, 115–18, 123
Williams, Raymond, 181
Willson, Marcius, 117–18
Wilson, Elizabeth, 184
women. *See* females; gender
A Women's Place, Toronto, 152
works, defined, 94–95

XML (Extensible Markup Language), 101,
   104n6
XP (Extreme Programming), 31–33

Young, Phyllis Brett, 194–95
Young Centre for the Performing Arts,
   70–71, 71f, 82n1
   See also Soulpepper Theatre Company

Zaiontz, Keren, 84n11
Ziegler, Joseph, 57
Zwicker, Heather, xiii, 287
   on Edmonton Pipelines, 129–39

Index

L'index des textes anglophones se trouve aux pages 289-305.
The index to the English chapters appears on pages 289-305.

Addis-Abeba, et M. Andersen, 205
Andersen, Marguerite
  biographie, 197-98, 199
  écriture littéraire à Paris, 199, 206
  écrivaine et francophones à Toronto,
    199, 206-09
  enfance et origine à Berlin, 197, 198,
    199-202, 210, 211
  fils et petits-enfants, 203, 204-05
  immigrante et professeure à Montréal,
    198-99, 204-05
  libération et réconciliation avec le
    passé, 211-12
  dans la littérature, 198
  maris et mariages, 202-03, 204-05
  mère, 199-200
  noms des protagonistes, 198
  parenté, 200-01, 209
  passé de l'auteure, 198, 211-12
  pauvreté et mariage à Tunis, 198,
    202-03
  père, 198, 199-201, 207, 208, 212n2
  et régime nazi, 197, 199-202, 209
  rôle du figuier, 210-11
  ville multiculturelle, 209-12
  Voir aussi chacune de ses œuvres
antisémitisme en Allemagne, 200-01
appellation (système), en vietnamien,
  250-51, 254-55, 258-59

Association des auteures et des auteurs de
  l'Ontario français, 199, 208
autofiction
  M. Andersen, 197, 198, 199-202, 209,
    212
  K. Thúy, 259

Bakhtine, Mikhail, et ambivalence, 240
banalisation, effet de, 237-38
Berlin, et M. Andersen, 197, 198, 199-202,
  210, 211
Bishop, Neil, 243
Bleu sur blanc (Andersen), 198, 202
Bohner, Theodor Werner, 198, 199-201,
  207, 208, 212n2
Bourassa, André, 233

Chanady, Amaryll Beatrice, 234-35
Coleman, Daniel, 209
comparaisons
  chez Thúy, 257-58, 259
  en traduction, 249-50
  chez Vuong-Riddick, 253-54, 259
culture d'origine, et traduction, 251, 258-59

Davis, Rocío G., 260
De mémoire de femme (Andersen)
  écriture, 206, 207
  enfance, 199-200
  mariage et pauvreté, 202-03
  Montréal, 204-05
  protagoniste, 198
Duffy, Dan, 259
Duong, Thu Huong, 249-50

effacement, en traduction, 250, 251
effet de banalisation, 237-38
Einstein, Albert, 200-01
Les enfants du sabbat (Hébert)
  et ambivalence, 240, 244
  codes antinomiques, 237-38, 242
  et contexte social, 236-37, 239-40, 244
  et critique sociale, 241-42
  effet de banalisation, 237
  et libération, 242, 243, 244
  parution, 236-37
  réalisme magique, 232-33, 236, 237-38, 239, 243-44
  religion, 232-33, 236, 238-39
  résumé, 232-33
  et sorcellerie, 239
  subversion sociale, 237, 242-43, 244
  et surnaturel, 237
  viol par le père, 238
The Evergreen Country: A Memoir of Vietnam (Vuong-Riddick), 251-56, 259
  écriture et style, 252-53

fantastique, genre littéraire, 235
figuier, chez M. Andersen, 210-11
Le figuier sur le toit (Andersen)
  mariage et pauvreté, 202-03
  origine des immigrants, 197
  père et famille, 208
  prix, 198
  protagoniste, 198
  rôle du figuier, 210-11
  silence et passé, 212
  Toronto, 206, 208, 210
  vie sous le régime nazi, 200-01, 209
  ville multiculturelle, 209-10
Fonteneau, Anne, 244

Gaulin, André, 243

Harel, Simon, 204
Hébert, Anne, réalisme magique, 232-33
  Voir aussi *Enfants du sabbat*

immigrants
  et nationalisme, 204
  origine, 197, 209-10
interpellation (système), en vietnamien, 250-51, 254-55, 258-59
Itinéraire d'enfance (Huong), 249-50

Kellett, Kathleen, 282
  autofiction de Marguerite Andersen, 197-212
Kellett-Betsos, Kathleen, 259
Kwaterko, Jozef, 236-37

langue vietnamienne. *Voir* vietnamien
Lemieux, Marie-Hélène, 236
Das Licht und sein Schatten (La lumière et son ombre) (Bohner), 199
liens interculturels, chez Vuong-Riddick, 254-55
lieu et personne, en vietnamien, 251
littérature québécoise
  et contexte social, 236-37
  éléments du réel, 233-34
  réalisme magique, 232-34, 237

Magical Realism and the Fantastic: Resolved Versus Unresolved Antinomy (Chanady), 234-35
Márquez, Gabriel García, effet de banalisation, 238
métaphores
  écriture de la diaspora, 254
  en traduction, 249-50
  chez Vuong-Riddick, 259
Montréal, et M. Andersen, 198-99, 204-05
multiculturalisme, et ville, 209-12
Munley, Ellen W., 242

nationalisme, au Québec, 204
Nepveu, Pierre, 236
Nguyễn Phú Phong, 250-51

Parallèles (Andersen)
  lieu de naissance, 199
  Montréal et immigration, 204, 205
  protagoniste, 198

Toronto et francophones, 206, 207-08
vie sous le régime nazi, 201-02
Paré, François, 207
Paris, et M. Andersen, 199, 206
Paterson, Janet, 240
personne et lieu en vietnamien, 251
pronoms personnels, en vietnamien,
   250-51, 255

réalisme magique
   et ambivalence, 240
   et contexte socioculturel, 234-36,
      239-40
   et critique sociale, 241
   description et définition, 231-32, 234,
      235-36, 239
   effet de banalisation, 237-38
   Les enfants du sabbat (Hébert), 232-33,
      236, 237-38, 239, 243-44
   et libération, 242
   littérature québécoise, 232-34, 237
   et magie, 238
   et paradoxes, 231, 234-35, 240-41
   et subversion, 243-44
régime nazi, et M. Andersen, 197, 199-202,
   209
religion
   Les enfants du sabbat (Hébert), 232-33,
      236, 238-39
   au Québec, 204, 207
respect, en vietnamien, 250-51
révolte, idéologie, 236
Révolution tranquille, 236
Robin, Régine, 212n1
roman mémoriel, 212n1
Ru (Thúy), 256-58

Scheel, Charles, 235
Seeberg, Reinhold, 200, 209
Seeberg-Adresse, 200
Société des écrivain(e)s de Toronto, 199
sorcellerie, et contexte social, 239-40
surnaturel, 233-34, 237

Tennier, Julie, 206
Thúy, Kim
   autofiction, 259
   comparaisons, 257-58, 259
   écriture et style, 260
   langue d'expression, 249, 251
   langue vietnamienne, 256-57
   Ru, 256-58
Todorov, Tzvetan, 235
Toronto
   francophones et écriture, 207-08
   et M. Andersen, 199, 206-09
   ville multiculturelle et tolérante,
      209-10
traduction
   comparaisons, 249-50
   et culture d'origine, 251, 258-59
   problèmes, 249-51, 255, 259
Truong, Mireille Mai, 287
   lieu et personne chez Vuong-Riddick et
      Thúy, 249-61
Tunis, et M. Andersen, 198, 202-03
Two Shores / Deux rives (Vuong-Riddick),
   252, 259

La vie devant elles (Andersen), 198, 205,
   211-12
vietnamien
   accents et tons, 256-57, 259
   graphie, 259
   lieu et personne, 251
   problèmes de traduction, 249-50, 255
   pronoms personnels, 250-51, 255
   système d'appellation, 250-51, 254-55,
      258-59
Virages, 208
Vuong-Riddick, Thuong
   comparaisons et métaphores, 253-54,
      259
   écriture anglaise et style, 252-53, 255,
      259-60
   langue d'expression, 249, 251
   liens interculturels et intertextualité,
      254-55, 259
   mémoire et identité, 253

nom et biographie, 251-52
et traduction, 255-56
Voir aussi *Evergreen Country*

Walsh Matthews, Stéphanie, 287
Les enfants du sabbat d'Anne Hébert,
231-45

OTHER TITLES FROM THE UNIVERSITY OF ALBERTA PRESS

REGENERATIONS / RÉGÉNÉRATIONS
Canadian Women's Writing / Écriture des
femmes au Canada
Marie Carrière & Patricia Demers, Editors
328 pages | Foreword, 1 image, bibliography,
afterword, notes, index
978-0-88864-627-9 | $39.95 (T) paper
978-1-77212-026-4 | $31.99 (T) EPUB
978-1-77212-027-1 | $31.99 (T) Kindle
978-1-77212-028-8 | $31.99 (T) PDF
Literary Studies | Cultural Studies | Humanities Computing

NOT DROWNING BUT WAVING
Women, Feminism and the Liberal Arts
Susan Brown, Jeanne Perreault, Jo-Ann Wallace &
Heather Zwicker, Editors
496 pages x 5 B&W photographs, introduction,
notes, bibliography, index
978-0-88864-550-0 | $39.95 (T) paper
978-0-88864-613-2 | $31.99 (T) EPUB
978-0-88864-669-9 | $31.99 (T) Kindle
978-0-88864-614-9 | $31.99 (T) PDF
Feminism | Humanities | Women's Studies

RETOOLING THE HUMANITIES
The Culture of Research in Canadian Universities
Daniel Coleman & Smaro Kamboureli, Editors
336 pages | Notes, bibliography, index
978-0-88864-541-8 | $49.95 (T) paper
978-0-88864-678-1 | $39.99 (T) PDF
University Administration | Economics | Humanities